The Undefendable Trial II

Volume One

By

James Coghill

© Copyright 2018 All Rights Reserved

I know you're out there...I can feel you now. I know that you're afraid. You're afraid of us, you're afraid of change...I don't know the future...I didn't come here to tell you how this is going to end, I came here to tell you how this is going to begin. Now, I'm going to hang up this phone, and I'm going to show these people what you don't want them to see. I'm going to show them a world without you...a world without rules and controls, without borders or boundaries. A world where anything is possible. (Neo from The Matrix)

Table of Contents

Preface 4
Day One 6
Day Two 201
About The Author 406

Preface

By now you should understand what you're reading so I won't waste your time with an explanation. I will only say once again that the references to page numbers refers to the page numbers of this book.

Day One

```
        IN THE SUPERIOR COURT OF THE STATE OF ARIZONA
                    IN THE COUNTY OF PIMA


STATE OF ARIZONA,           )
                            )
        PLAINTIFF,          )
                            )
vs.                         )    CR-2004 2573
                            )
                            )    2-CA-CR 2009-2047
JAMES PRENTISS COGHILL,     )
                            )
        DEFENDANT.          )
_____)



BEFORE:   THE HONORABLE TERESA GODOY
          JUDGE OF THE SUPERIOR COURT



                                        FEB 23 '18 PDA PM 4:26


              JURY TRIAL - DAY ONE
                 MARCH 17, 2009
                 TUCSON, ARIZONA


                                        COPY
REPORTED BY:

        BONITA ROBERTSON, RMR
        CERTIFIED REPORTER #50454
```

APPEARANCES:

        SHAWN JENSVOLD, ESQ.,
        DEPUTY COUNTY ATTORNEY,
        APPEARING ON BEHALF OF THE STATE.

        DAVID EUCHNER & PAUL SKITZKI, ESQS.,
        APPEARING ON BEHALF OF THE DEFENDANT.

PIMA COUNTY SUPERIOR COURT

	INDEX	
		PAGE
	JURY VOIR DIRE	13
	MOTIONS IN LIMINE	58
	JURY VOIR DIRE	79
	JURY SELECTED	150
	INDICTMENT READ	151
	PRELIMINARY INSTRUCTIONS	157
	STATE'S OPENING STATEMENT	165
	DEFENSE OPENING STATEMENT	179

PIMA COUNTY SUPERIOR COURT

                    P-R-O-C-E-E-D-I-N-G-S

    THE COURT: State of Arizona versus James Coghill, 2004-2573.

    MR. JENSVOLD: Shawn Jensvold for the State.

    MR. EUCHNER: David Euchner and Paul Skitzki on behalf of Mr. Coghill; present, out of custody.

    THE COURT: So, a couple of housekeeping matters.

    Is there any reason that we will need to decide the motions in limine before we complete jury selection? Obviously, we'll do it before you all open, but --

    MR. EUCHNER: I don't see why we couldn't do it prior to the lunch break; have the jurors go out to lunch and we could talk about it.

    THE COURT: Okay. How many days do you all think this trial is going to last; with the knowledge that on Friday, I'm not in in the morning, so I was going to have us start at about 12:30 that day.

    MR. EUCHNER: Okay. Well, with that knowledge, is there any possibility of a 9:00 or 10:00 start tomorrow or Thursday?

    THE COURT: No, because I have no dark day anymore.

    MR. EUCHNER: Well, our case should be able to finish, that's -- that gives us four-and-a-half hours minus the breaks. We hope we can finish our case in that amount of

1 time then. And given the interview we did with our forensic
2 computer expert prior to trial, it doesn't seem like she'll be
3 on the stand for several hours, but we do want to give this
4 case to the jury by Friday, 5:00.
5   THE COURT: Okay.
6   MR. JENSVOLD: I'm not so sure that's going to be
7 possible, but --
8   MR. EUCHNER: Yeah, without, without the Friday
9 morning, with that knowledge it makes it a little bit less
10 possible, and then we have to tell the, I think we have to
11 tell the jury qualifying Monday through Tuesday.
12   MR. JENSVOLD: So you're not able to do Monday,
13 right?
14   THE COURT: No, Monday is all Drug Court, so we
15 wouldn't be able to do closing arguments or anything on that
16 day. We could certainly come back Tuesday.
17   MR. JENSVOLD: Well, qualify them through Wednesday
18 in case the deliberations go over.
19   MR. SKITZKI: Judge, could you, later in the week
20 when we see where we're at, maybe you could call Division 16
21 and let Judge Hantman know that perhaps maybe we could start
22 later on Tuesday? I have a trial in front of him on Tuesday.
23   THE COURT: Okay.
24   MR. EUCHNER: Our problem is we have two witnesses
25 scheduled for Friday, who are both currently traveling and are

                set to come in on Friday in the morning. So we can obviously
                bump them a couple of hours. But, I mean, we can easily get
                them finished, but closings might take a little longer. Could
                we stay later on Friday to get the closings done, like past
                5:00 to 5:30?

                I know we generally don't like to do that, but --

                THE COURT: Yeah, let me -- let's play it by ear. I
                can start, I can't start any later -- or any earlier than
                12:15. I have to come all the way from the eastside. This is
                something that's be set forever, when Friday was my dark day.
                And, yeah, and what I was going to do, I know I told the State
                that we wouldn't get any witnesses on today, but what I was
                hoping, if you're telling me it can't be done, it can't be
                done. But if we get through jury selection and openings, and
                we're sitting around at 3:00 or 3:30 looking at each other, I
                may ask you just over the lunch hour to see if you have
                someone who could come down.

                MR. JENSVOLD: I could. The only difficulty with us
                is the two witnesses, Alan Kreitl and Detective Englander
                really aren't available until Thursday, so I may run out of
                witnesses tomorrow, then, if we start this afternoon, because
                most of my witnesses tomorrow except for Mr. Franks are going
                to be fairly short.

                MR. EUCHNER: And, Judge, I don't really even think
                that that's the problem now. I think the problem is, I think

Mr. Jensvold's case was going to be finished by Thursday, whether we put witnesses -- the two witnesses we're talking about having available today, maybe, they're short ones. They weren't going to eat up a lot of time tomorrow morning.

The problem then becomes do we have enough time to put on our case plus closing. And I think if we make any record that needs to be made, we stay late on Thursday, we finish jury, finalizing jury instructions, we make whatever record, Rule 20 record needs to be made, and all we do on, we, Friday, get, you know, get right into motion and we close it out, I think we can do it. But that's the concern is that we don't, we're losing out on that time on Friday that we needed.

THE COURT: Okay. All right. So let's just play it by ear right now, but I'll voir dire the jury through Wednesday in an abundance of caution.

The witnesses that I have listed that I was going to tell the jury about, include, I have Alan Kreitl, Jeff Englander, Jace Judd, William Knuth.

MR. JENSVOLD: I think that's right.

THE COURT: Brian McGraw, Gerard Moretz.

MR. JENSVOLD: Moretz.

THE COURT: Moretz, I'm sorry, a little dyslexic or something. Brenda Schupbach.

MR. JENSVOLD: Schupbach, I think.

THE COURT: Schupbach, Jacob Franks, Kathleen

1 Bright-Birnbaum, and Tami Loehrs.
2   MR. JENSVOLD: We're not going to call
3 Ms. Bright-Birnbaum. I think we have stipulation to the
4 fingerprints.
5   MR. EUCHNER: I think that's McGraw as well as the
6 technician that checked the fingerprints.
7   MR. JENSVOLD: I think McGraw, I'm going to call
8 McGraw briefly, I think, but --
9   THE COURT: Does the defense have any witnesses
10 besides Ms. Loehrs?
11   MR. EUCHNER: It's pronounced Loehrs, and we have
12 William Hoppe, H-O-P-P-E.
13   THE COURT: Okay.
14   MR. JENSVOLD: And you said Englander, correct?
15   THE COURT: I did.
16   MR. JENSVOLD: Okay.
17   THE COURT: And what does he do now?
18   MR. JENSVOLD: He's a private forensic examiner,
19 computer forensic examiner with Lighthouse Solutions, I think
20 is the name.
21   THE COURT: All right.
22   Anything else we can take up before we bring in the
23 jury?
24   MR. EUCHNER: I think that's good for now. We can
25 do the rest at the lunch break.

PIMA COUNTY SUPERIOR COURT

1	THE COURT: Okay. Oh, I know what I wanted to ask
2	you both. In terms of doing the voir dire, I want to tell the
3	jury, I want to be able to tell the jury that they in no way
4	are we going to have to view, review, see any images
5	whatsoever.
6	I think that if they're under the impression that
7	they may ultimately have to view, we're going to lose our
8	entire panel. Maybe not, maybe that's an exaggeration. But I
9	want to be able to tell them that they are not going to be
10	expected to view any images, any videos, anything related to
11	this case; that both counsel have entered a stipulation about
12	what is on those particular items that are at issue. Any
13	problem with that?
14	MR. JENSVOLD: No, that's fine.
15	MR. EUCHNER: And in addition, Your Honor, in my
16	experience of reading lots of transcripts, it seems to be most
17	efficient if the jury knows what the case is about first
18	before we start getting into who has a travel plan. In these
19	kinds of cases they seem to drop like flies really early.
20	THE COURT: Generally I do the hardship thing first.
21	Since we are going through Wednesday, I mean, I think that
22	we're going to lose folks that way. So, I think it's six of
23	one and half a dozen of the other. So --
24	MR. EUCHNER: And, Judge, we have this stipulation.
25	It actually stipulates to two different things.

PIMA COUNTY SUPERIOR COURT

1   THE COURT: Okay. Great.
2   MR. JENSVOLD: David, I have the redacted KaZaA logs
3 marked over there.
4   MR. EUCHNER: Okay. I have some unredacted ones, so
5 we can look at those, because we want to --
6   MR. JENSVOLD: It's 12-C. I have redacted 12-D as
7 well, the registry report.
8   THE COURT: Did you guys need this on the record?
9   MR. EUCHNER: No, it's something that we can talk
10 about later.
11   THE COURT: All right.
12   MR. EUCHNER: Your Honor, we're going to be
13 introduced to the jury as Public Defenders.
14   THE COURT: You what?
15   MR. EUCHNER: We'll be introduced to the jury as
16 Public Defenders.
17   THE COURT: Okay.
18   MR. JENSVOLD: Your Honor, there must have been a
19 miscommunication between myself and your -- there's actually
20 supposed to be a "Y" after the A symbol on all these files.
21   MR. EUCHNER: I noticed that briefly, but I wasn't
22 sure on one of them. But I wasn't sure.
23   MR. JENSVOLD: I think what happened is the original
24 document there was an A. It should have been an "at" symbol,
25 but the "Y" should be there.

PIMA COUNTY SUPERIOR COURT

                THE COURT: Would you mind writing it in mine and I
will give it to Christina and we'll fix it.
                Thanks, Shawn.
                MR. EUCHNER: Is there any of them that don't have
the "A" sign?
                (11:00 a.m. Prospective Jurors enter the
courtroom.)
                THE COURT: Sorry about the tight quarters, folks,
we asked for 70, and they sent us 90, so there may be a few
that are going to be standing for a bit. If there is somebody
that can't stand, we may be able to find you a chair or swap
you a seat with a juror with a chair who doesn't mind standing
for a period of time.
                Is that closet clean? I am a little embarrassed if
it's not.
                Could counsel approach, please, off the record -- or
on the record.
                (Whereupon the Court and counsel confer at the
bench, out of the hearing of the prospective jurors, as
follows:)
                THE COURT: Do you guys think 90 is going to be too
many? I can maybe send 15 back downstairs. I hate to keep
them standing. But it's up to y'all.
                MR. EUCHNER: I don't think we're going to need 90.
                THE COURT: So do you have any objection if the last

1 15 names on the list, I call out their names and send them
2 back down?
3   MR. JENSVOLD: No.
4   (Whereupon proceedings continued in open court, on
5 the record, as follows:)
6   THE COURT: Before we get started, folks. I didn't
7 know they were going to send me 90 of you. I am going to call
8 the names of 15 people. If your name is called, what I need
9 you to do is go back down to the first floor and check in with
10 the Jury Commissioner. Okay.
11   Kelli Gaither-Banchoff. Wow, I even got someone who
12 didn't have a seat. Tannis Gibson.
13   THE CLERK: I need to know the numbers. 76 --
14   THE COURT: 76 through 90 I am going to release.
15   (Whereupon the Court calls the names of prospective
16 jurors 76 through 90, and excuses them to return to the Jury
17 Commissioner's Office on the first floor.)
18   THE COURT: For the record, we excused 76 through 90
19 by stipulation of counsel.
20   All right.
21   Counsel, you can have a seat.
22   Thank you so much.
23   Thank you, Mr. Coghill.
24   All right. This is the time set for the trial in
25 criminal cause number CR-2004 2573, State versus James

1   Coghill.
2   Is the State ready to proceed?
3   MR. JENSVOLD: Yes, Your Honor.
4   THE COURT: Is the defense ready to proceed?
5   MR. EUCHNER: Yes, Your Honor.
6   THE COURT: All right. Folks, what we need you all
7   to do, for those of you who have a seat, if you wouldn't mind,
8   we are going to administer the oath that you take to be
9   potential jurors.
10   (Whereupon the prospective jurors were duly sworn on
11   voir dire.)
12   THE COURT: You can all take a seat, thank you; if
13   you can. I'm sorry for those of you who can't.
14   What we are going to do now is the clerk is going to
15   call the names of the first 26 people that are seated up here.
16   When she calls your name, say, "here", and raise your hand so
17   we can make sure we have you in the right seat.
18   THE CLERK: Farshad Shirazi? Did I say that right?
19   PROSPECTIVE JUROR SHIRAZI: Yeah.
20   THE CLERK: Rosalie Tucker. Joel Madlambayan.
21   Brenda Syverson.
22   PROSPECTIVE JUROR SYVERSON: Syverson.
23   THE CLERK: Syverson.
24   THE CLERK: Angelica Walters. Eleanor Horton.
25   Rosemary Lozoya.

```
 1            PROSPECTIVE JUROR LOZOYA:  Right here.
 2            THE CLERK:  Susan Ouimette.  Bess Lanes.  Darrell
 3   Dains.
 4            PROSPECTIVE JUROR DAINS:  Dains.
 5            THE CLERK:  Dains.
 6            PROSPECTIVE JUROR DAINS:  Here.
 7            THE CLERK:  Karen Yoho.
 8            PROSPECTIVE JUROR YOHO:  Here.
 9            THE CLERK:  Mike Kinsella.
10            PROSPECTIVE JUROR KINSELLA:  Here.
11            THE CLERK:  Alan Ravitz.
12            PROSPECTIVE JUROR RAVITZ:  Ravitz.  Here.
13            THE CLERK:  William Buntin.
14            PROSPECTIVE JUROR BUNTIN:  Here.
15            THE CLERK:  Lindsay Bly.
16            PROSPECTIVE JUROR BLY:  Here.
17            THE CLERK:  Jose Flores.
18            PROSPECTIVE JUROR FLORES:  Here.
19            THE CLERK:  Amanda Arbogast.
20            PROSPECTIVE JUROR ARBOGAST:  Arbogast.
21            THE CLERK:  Nina Graves.
22            PROSPECTIVE JUROR GRAVES:  It's Nina.
23            THE CLERK:  Nina.  Laura Weinstein.
24            PROSPECTIVE JUROR WEINSTEIN:  Here.
25            THE CLERK:  Rebecca Kauk.
```

PIMA COUNTY SUPERIOR COURT

```
 1            PROSPECTIVE JUROR KAUK:  Kauk.
 2            THE CLERK:  Kauk.  Charles Winkenwerder.
 3            PROSPECTIVE JUROR WINKENWERDER:  Winkenwerder.
 4   Here.
 5            THE CLERK:  David Ruelas.
 6            PROSPECTIVE JUROR RUELAS:  Here.
 7            THE CLERK:  Paul Leschak.
 8            PROSPECTIVE JUROR LESCHAK:  Yup.
 9            THE CLERK:  Elizabeth Machado.  Dawn
10   Crawford-Rogers.
11            PROSPECTIVE JUROR CRAWFORD-ROGERS:  Yes.
12            THE CLERK:  And Melissa Schwager.
13            PROSPECTIVE JUROR SCHWAGER:  Uh-huh.
14            THE COURT:  All right.
15            This is the time set for voir dire.  And what's
16   going to happen over the course of the next, I don't know,
17   it's hard to predict, but at least the next couple of hours,
18   is that we are going to ask you a series of questions about
19   yourselves.
20            It's certainly our hope that these questions don't
21   unnecessarily pry into your lives and your personal affairs.
22   They're certainly not designed to do that.  However, some of
23   the questions may seem a little bit more personal in nature.
24   And our goal in doing this, is that it is necessary for us to
25   find out if you have any knowledge about this particular case,
```

if you have any preconceived opinions or ideas about this case, or about the parties in this case, that you might find difficult to set aside.

We also need to find out if any of you, maybe family members or close friends, have any, have ever had any personal experiences that might cause you to identify maybe with one side or the other in this case. In other words, we need to ask you these questions to assure that the jurors that are actually picked to hear this case can give both sides a fair trial.

So, when we ask the questions, please don't withhold information in order to be seated on the jury. It's not a test. There is no right or wrong answer to any question that we ask. It's just simply the truth of whatever it is that we're asking about at that particular time.

The questions are designed that if you have a "no" answer, you don't need to do anything. You just sit tight. If your answer to a question is "yes," raise your hand, and then we'll identify who the people are that have "yes" answers, and then we'll go through and get your answers to each of the questions.

If there is ever a time that we ask a question that you would prefer to discuss privately up here at the bench with myself and the lawyers, just ask if you can approach the bench, and we'll have you come on up and talk up here at the bench.

For you folks in the back whose names have not been called, you don't need to raise your hands if you have "yes" answers at this point. I think we have given you something to write with and some paper. If you do have a "yes" answer, make a note of it on the paper. And if your name is called to substitute in for one of the folks up here who may be excused, I'll ask you if you have any "yes" answers, and then you can let us know what your "yes" answers are at that time.

I'm going to go ahead and start by introducing the parties in this case.

The State is represented by Shawn Jensvold. Mr. Jensvold is a Deputy County Attorney at the Pima County Attorney's Office. Barbara LaWall is the County Attorney.

Do any of you think you know Mr. Jensvold, or know anybody that is employed at the County Attorney's Office in whatever capacity.

You can have a seat.

Thanks, Mr. Jensvold.

Ms. Walters -- I'm sorry, Ms. Horton, who do you know, ma'am?

PROSPECTIVE JUROR HORTON: I'm good friends with David and Judy Berkman, who is a Criminal Deputy.

THE COURT: Do you socialize with the Berkmans?

PROSPECTIVE JUROR HORTON: Yes.

PIMA COUNTY SUPERIOR COURT

```
 1            THE COURT:  All right.  Is there anything about your
 2   friendship with Mr. Berkman and his wife that would make it
 3   difficult for you to be fair to both sides in this case?
 4            PROSPECTIVE JUROR HORTON:  I don't think so.
 5            THE COURT:  Does Mr. Berkman ever discuss his work
 6   with you?
 7            PROSPECTIVE JUROR HORTON:  No.
 8            THE COURT:  Okay.  All right.
 9            Does anybody else know Mr. Jensvold or anybody at
10   the County Attorney's Office?
11            Yes, Ms. Tucker.
12            PROSPECTIVE JUROR TUCKER:  Kathy Mayer.
13            THE COURT:  How do you know Ms. Mayer?
14            PROSPECTIVE JUROR TUCKER:  Just very casually.
15            THE COURT:  Do you ever socialize with Ms. Mayer?
16            PROSPECTIVE JUROR TUCKER:  Maybe once a year.
17            THE COURT:  Does she ever discuss her work with you?
18            PROSPECTIVE JUROR TUCKER:  Oh, no.
19            THE COURT:  Is there anything about your seeing
20   Ms. Mayer once a year that would make it difficult for you to
21   give both sides a fair trial in this case?
22            PROSPECTIVE JUROR TUCKER:  No.
23            THE COURT:  All right. Any other "yes" answers to
24   that question?
25            (No response.)
```

PIMA COUNTY SUPERIOR COURT

1   THE COURT: All right.
2   The defendant in this case is represented by David
3 Euchner and Paul Skitzki. They are both lawyers at the Pima
4 County Public Defender's Office. Robert Hirsh is the head of
5 that office. He's the Public Defender.
6   Do any of you think you know Mr. Skitzki,
7 Mr. Euchner, or anybody who works at the Public Defender's
8 Office.
9   All right. Mr. Shirazi, Ms. Tucker, and
10 Ms. Weinstein. All right. And Mr. Dains.
11   Counsel, you can have a seat.
12   Thank you.
13   Mr. Shirazi.
14   PROSPECTIVE JUROR SHIRAZI: Robert Hirsh was my
15 attorney.
16   THE COURT: Mr. Hirsh was your attorney?
17   PROSPECTIVE JUROR SHIRAZI: Yeah.
18   THE COURT: All right. For what sort of matter?
19   PROSPECTIVE JUROR SHIRAZI: Divorce.
20   THE COURT: How long ago was that?
21   PROSPECTIVE JUROR SHIRAZI: A year-and-a-half.
22   THE COURT: A year-and-a-half? If I could get you
23 to speak up, you're in the worst seat for folks to hear you,
24 and I apologize for that. You said a year-and-a-half ago?
25 Yes?

PIMA COUNTY SUPERIOR COURT

1   PROSPECTIVE JUROR SHIRAZI: Yes.
2   THE COURT: All right. Is there anything about the
3   fact that Mr. Hirsh represented you about a year-and-a-half
4   ago that would make it difficult for you to give both sides a
5   fair trial in this case?
6   PROSPECTIVE JUROR SHIRAZI: No.
7   THE COURT: Other than that representation, was, do
8   you socialize with him, or do you have a friendship
9   independent of that?
10   PROSPECTIVE JUROR SHIRAZI: No.
11   THE COURT: Okay.
12   Mr. Dains.
13   PROSPECTIVE JUROR DAINS: I can't remember -- Mike,
14   I can't remember his last name, but he works in the Public
15   Defender's Office. He was my attorney.
16   THE COURT: All right. And what sort of matter was
17   that for?
18   PROSPECTIVE JUROR DAINS: A class six undesignated
19   felony.
20   THE COURT: Okay. How long ago was that?
21   PROSPECTIVE JUROR DAINS: Over two years.
22   THE COURT: Is there anything about the fact that a
23   lawyer that works in the Public Defender's Office represented
24   you that would make it difficult for you to give both sides a
25   fair trial in this case?

PIMA COUNTY SUPERIOR COURT

                    PROSPECTIVE JUROR DAINS: Not really.
                    THE COURT: Did you have a friendship with him
beyond the representation?
                    PROSPECTIVE JUROR DAINS: No.
                    THE COURT: Okay.
                    Ms. Weinstein.
                    PROSPECTIVE JUROR WEINSTEIN: Jeff Weinstein is my
ex-husband.
                    THE COURT: Okay. Anything about that relationship
that would make it difficult for you to sit fairly in this
case?
                    PROSPECTIVE JUROR WEINSTEIN: No.
                    THE COURT: Did he ever discuss his work with you?
                    PROSPECTIVE JUROR WEINSTEIN: No.
                    THE COURT: And, Ms. Tucker, did you have your hand
up as well?
                    PROSPECTIVE JUROR TUCKER: Yes.
                    Did I miss you? I apologize. Who do you know?
                    PROSPECTIVE JUROR TUCKER: Alex Heveri.
                    THE COURT: How do you know Ms. Heveri?
                    PROSPECTIVE JUROR TUCKER: From Landmark Education.
                    THE COURT: Do you, do you socialize with her
outside of your knowledge of her through Landmark Education?
                    PROSPECTIVE JUROR TUCKER: Occasionally we show up
at the same gathering together.

PIMA COUNTY SUPERIOR COURT

1 THE COURT: Anything about knowing Ms. Heveri that
2 would make it difficult for you to be fair to both sides in
3 this case?
4 PROSPECTIVE JUROR TUCKER: No.
5 THE COURT: Anybody else have a "yes" answer to the
6 last question?
7 (No response.)
8 THE COURT: And would you introduce Mr. Coghill for
9 us, Counsel.
10 MR. SKITZKI: Ladies and gentlemen, this is James
11 Coghill, our client.
12 THE COURT: Do any of you think that you know
13 Mr. Coghill, or any member of his family?
14 All right. I see no hands.
15 Thank you, Mr. Coghill.
16 Thank you, Counsel.
17 I'm now going to read to you a list of witnesses
18 whose name may be either mentioned during this trial or who
19 actually could be called to testify during this trial. If you
20 know any of these names, or recognize these names, raise your
21 hand and we'll talk to you about how.
22 A gentleman by the name of Alan Kreitl. He works
23 with the Department Of Public Safety as a Criminalist. Jeff
24 Englander. Deputy Jace Judd, who is with the Pima County
25 Sheriff's Department. Deputy William Knuth, who is also with

the Sheriff's Department. Brian McGraw, who works in the Identification Section at the Sheriff's Department. Deputy Gerard Moretz, who is with the Sheriff's Department. I'm sorry, he's a detective. Deputy Brenda Schupbach, with the Sheriff's Department. Jacob Franks. Tami Loehrs, and William Hoppe.

All right. I see no hands.

So, folks, all of us in the courtroom today recognize that jury selection, and jury service, can be inconvenient to everyone and to one extent or another. And I'm sure you also recognize how important it is that we have folks like yourselves that are willing to serve so that we can actually carry out criminal trials.

Let me tell you what the schedule for this trial is going to be like. We're going to start each day at about 10:30 in the morning. We'll break at noon for lunch. We'll start up again at 1:00 or 1:30. And then we'll break every day at a little bit before five, because I like to get people the opportunity who took the bus to make the bus, or get a little jump on traffic. That will be our schedule today, Wednesday and Thursday. Friday, we won't start until 12:15, and we will end at 5:00 on Friday. There is a chance this trial will go into next week, including deliberations.

We want you to know you could be here through Wednesday of next week. With the exception of Friday, every day you'd be here at 10:30 in the morning until, essentially, 5:00 at night. During the afternoon time what we do is when we come back from lunch, we'll break in the afternoon about 3:00, give you a stretch break, give you a chance to get something to drink, something to eat if you need that, and then start up again about 15, 20 minutes later.

Now, I understand that there is going to be folks that may not be able to serve on this jury, but I need to let you know legally how it is that I am able to excuse a juror from service.

The law says that I can excuse you from service only if your absence from work would tend materially and adversely to affect the public safety, health, welfare, or interest, or if jury service would impose an undue hardship on you.

Based on the length of trial that I've described and the schedule that I've told you that this trial will occur, are any of you asking to be excused for a hardship reason or because maybe you've got, you know, some other reason that you think may qualify?

All right. I'm going to go ahead and get your names. I have Mr. Shirazi.

Anyone else in the back row? Mr. Dains. All right.

In the middle row I have Mr. Ravitz. Anybody else in the middle row and in the front row?

Mr. Ruelas.

PIMA COUNTY SUPERIOR COURT

```
 1              THE COURT:  Mr. Ruelas.  Oh, I'm sorry,
 2   Ms. Schwager.
 3              PROSPECTIVE JUROR SCHWAGER:  Schwager.
 4              THE COURT:  I'm sorry.
 5              All right.  Mr. Shirazi, what's your situation, sir?
 6              PROSPECTIVE JUROR SHIRAZI:  I was actually a backup
 7   for a colleague of mine that got ill, and I'm actually working
 8   in the trauma section.  I'm a physician, so I was designated
 9   cover for the sick.  So that leaves them without a sick leave
10   doctor.
11              THE COURT:  Okay.  Any objection by the State?
12              MR. JENSVOLD:  No.
13              THE COURT:  Any by the defense?
14              MR. SKITZKI:  No.
15              THE COURT:  All right.  Thank you, Mr. Shirazi.  I'm
16   going to excuse you, but I have to send you back down to the
17   first floor.  They may have another trial that they send you
18   to, okay?  Go ahead and check in though.
19              (Whereupon the prospective juror was excused from
20   service and leaves the courtroom.)
21              THE COURT:  Mr. Dains, sir, what's your situation,
22   sir?
23              PROSPECTIVE JUROR DAINS:  Monday of next week, Your
24   Honor, I have a medical appointment at the Veterans Hospital
25   for my left foot.
```

PIMA COUNTY SUPERIOR COURT

1   THE COURT: Well, here's the good news. We're not
 2 going to be doing anything on Monday. Is there anything about
 3 the medical appointment that would incapacitate you on Tuesday
 4 or Wednesday of next week?
 5   PROSPECTIVE JUROR DAINS: Going over surgery.
 6   THE COURT: But nothing that's going to make it that
 7 you couldn't continue to serve on Tuesday and Wednesday if the
 8 trial goes that long?
 9   PROSPECTIVE JUROR DAINS: Not that I know of.
10   THE COURT: Okay. Great. Thank you, Mr. Dains.
11 Mr. Ravitz.
12   PROSPECTIVE JUROR RAVITZ: My wife is suffering from
13 a mold disease in her eyes, and this afternoon I'm supposed to
14 go with her to her doctor. Thursday she's got another
15 appointment with another doctor, and that's basically, we
16 were, she's been on medicines for almost three months.
17   THE COURT: That's quite incapacitating, isn't it?
18   PROSPECTIVE JUROR RAVITZ: It's terrible.
19   THE COURT: Any objection by the State?
20   MR. JENSVOLD: No, Your Honor.
21   THE COURT: By the defense?
22   MR. SKITZKI: No.
23   THE COURT: And, Mr. Ravitz, if you want to mention
24 to them that I ask that you be excused for the rest of the
25 day, given the fact that I don't think your wife can probably

PIMA COUNTY SUPERIOR COURT

take herself to the doctor and it sounds like she really has to go. All right. Thank you, sir.

Mr. Ruelas.

PROSPECTIVE JUROR RUELAS: I'm needed at work. We are short-staffed and there's people that need me. As well as next week I am scheduled to be out of town on Thursday.

THE COURT: Where do you work, sir?

PROSPECTIVE JUROR RUELAS: Wells Fargo.

THE COURT: Okay. And you're scheduled to leave out of town on Tuesday of next week you said?

PROSPECTIVE JUROR RUELAS: Yeah.

THE COURT: I take it this is something preplanned for a while, vacation, or otherwise?

PROSPECTIVE JUROR RUELAS: Family, yeah.

THE COURT: Any objection, Mr. Jensvold?

MR. JENSVOLD: No, Your Honor.

THE COURT: Mr. Skitzki?

MR. SKITZKI: No.

THE COURT: Thanks.

You're excused, sir. Go head and check in with them on the first floor. They might have another trial they will send you to. It's not punishment, we just recycle jurors.

(Whereupon the prospective juror was excused from service and leaves the courtroom.)

THE COURT: Ms. Schwager.

PIMA COUNTY SUPERIOR COURT

1   PROSPECTIVE JUROR SCHWAGER: I'm going out of town
2 Friday, and I'm a full-time student.
3   THE COURT: Do you want to go to school?
4   PROSPECTIVE JUROR SCHWAGER: Yeah.
5   THE COURT: All right.
6   Any objection, Mr. Jensvold?
7   MR. JENSVOLD: No.
8   THE COURT: Mr. Skitzki?
9   MR. SKITZKI: No.
10   THE COURT: You're excused, ma'am. Check back in
11 with the first floor. Okay.
12   (Whereupon the prospective juror was excused from
13 service and leaves the courtroom.)
14   THE COURT: Was there anyone else who had their hand
15 up asking to be excused that I missed?
16   (No response.)
17   THE COURT: All right. Let's call names to fill
18 seats, 1, 13, 22, and 26.
19   THE CLERK: Seat number 1, Morgan Beal.
20   THE COURT: Ms. Beal, good morning.
21   PROSPECTIVE JUROR BEAL: Good morning.
22   THE COURT: Did you have any "yes" answers so far?
23   PROSPECTIVE JUROR BEAL: I did.
24   THE COURT: Which one?
25   PROSPECTIVE JUROR BEAL: To the financial hardship.

PIMA COUNTY SUPERIOR COURT

1   THE COURT: Okay.
2   PROSPECTIVE JUROR BEAL: Also with work, I do see
3 patients on a regular basis for therapy. If they're missed,
4 they have to start all over again.
5   I am also the only parent that works in my
6 household, so I wouldn't be able to be out of work for that
7 long.
8   THE COURT: I take it you don't get paid when you're
9 not at work.
10   PROSPECTIVE JUROR BEAL: That's right.
11   THE COURT: Any objection, Mr. Jensvold?
12   MR. JENSVOLD: No, Your Honor.
13   THE COURT: Mr. Skitzki?
14   MR. SKITZKI: No.
15   THE COURT: Thank you, Ms. Beal. You're excused.
16 Report back down to the first floor.
17   (Whereupon the prospective juror was excused from
18 service and leaves the courtroom.)
19   THE COURT: Another juror for seat number one.
20   THE CLERK: Richard Foard.
21   THE COURT: Is that how we say your name?
22   PROSPECTIVE JUROR FOARD: Yes. Hardship of, my
23 girlfriend is bipolar. I am the only one that she's got if
24 she does go into a depression. We're also planning on moving
25 to Colorado early next week. So --

PIMA COUNTY SUPERIOR COURT

1	THE COURT: I don't think we want to hold you up.
2	PROSPECTIVE JUROR FOARD: I hope not.
3	THE COURT: Any objection, Mr. Jensvold?
4	MR. JENSVOLD: No.
5	THE COURT: Mr. Skitzki?
6	MR. SKITZKI: No.
7	THE COURT: All right. You're excused. Thank you,
8	sir. Check in with the first floor. They might send you
9	someplace else.
10	PROSPECTIVE JUROR FOARD: For a day I wouldn't mind.
11	THE COURT: Good luck with that.
12	(Whereupon the prospective juror was excused from
13	service and leaves the courtroom.)
14	THE CLERK: For seat number one, Robert Struse.
15	PROSPECTIVE JUROR STRUSE: Yes, Your Honor, the
16	schedule. I'm an attorney. And I'm one of the only people in
17	the State of Arizona that can sign for SBA loans. And this is
18	the week that loans have to go to L.A. So, all small business
19	loans, basically, come through me. And it would be, well, no
20	one else can sign them. I'm the authorized signatory.
21	THE COURT: Mr. Jensvold?
22	MR. JENSVOLD: No objection.
23	THE COURT: Mr. Skitzki?
24	MR. SKITZKI: No.
25	THE COURT: You're excused, sir. Head back down to

PIMA COUNTY SUPERIOR COURT

```
 1  the first floor.
 2          (Whereupon the prospective juror was excused from
 3  service and leaves the courtroom.)
 4          THE COURT: Seat number one is proving hard to fill.
 5          PROSPECTIVE JUROR: Nice chair.
 6          THE COURT: Ms. Tucker says it's a nice chair. Call
 7  another name for seat one.
 8          THE CLERK: Joe Korinko.
 9          THE COURT: Mr. Korinko, good morning.
10          PROSPECTIVE JUROR KORINKO: Here.
11          THE COURT: Did you have any "yes" answers, sir?
12          PROSPECTIVE JUROR KORINKO: No, I didn't.
13          THE COURT: Great. We have a really comfortable
14  chair for you.
15          Seat number 13.
16          THE CLERK: For seat number 13, James Burpee.
17          PROSPECTIVE JUROR BURPEE: Yes.
18          THE COURT: Did you have any "yes" answers, sir?
19          PROSPECTIVE JUROR BURPEE: No.
20          THE COURT: Great. Come on up and we'll show you to
21  your seat.
22          THE CLERK: For seat number 22, Ramon Guerrero.
23          THE COURT: Mr. Guerrero, did you have any "yes"
24  answers this morning, sir?
25          PROSPECTIVE JUROR GUERRERO: Yes. This morning I
```

PIMA COUNTY SUPERIOR COURT

1   got a phone call that the brother of my mother died in Mexico
2   City, so I have to attend the funeral.
3   THE COURT: Any objection by the State?
4   MR. JENSVOLD: No, Your Honor.
5   THE COURT: Mr. Skitzki?
6   MR. SKITZKI: No.
7   THE COURT: You're excused, sir. Head back down to
8   the first floor and check in. I'm very sorry.
9   (Whereupon the prospective juror was excused from
10 service and leaves the courtroom.)
11   THE CLERK: For seat number 22, Miriam Kogan.
12   THE COURT: Ms. Kogan, did you have any "yes"
13 answers this morning?
14   PROSPECTIVE JUROR KOGAN: No, I didn't.
15   THE COURT: Come on up and we'll show you to your
16 seat.
17   THE CLERK: For seat number 26, Jayne Knew.
18   THE COURT: Is that you, Ms. Knew? Did you have any
19 "yes" answers this morning?
20   PROSPECTIVE JUROR KNEW: Unfortunately, no.
21   THE COURT: All right. We have a not so comfortable
22 chair for you. I'm very sorry about that.
23   You folks that are still standing in the back, if
24 you'd care to take a seat we've got some open now.
25   Any other "yes" answers to the question of asking to

PIMA COUNTY SUPERIOR COURT

be excused for a hardship reason?

(No response.)

THE COURT: All right.

Now, I'm going to tell you what the charges are in this case. But before I do, I want to tell you a little bit about the indictment. The indictment in this case, the fact that the State has brought charges, is absolutely in no way any evidence at all against the defendant. The indictment is just merely a piece of paper that the State uses to put someone on notice of what they say they allege that they've done.

Mr. Coghill has pled not guilty to each of the counts in this indictment. Now, there are 15 counts in this indictment. Counts 1 through 14 charge sexual exploitation of a minor under 15, a dangerous crime against children. Again, counts 1 through 14 allege that on or about the 1st day of April, 2003, James Prentiss Coghill, knowingly committed sexual exploitation of a minor by possessing, receiving, or exchanging any visual depiction in which a minor under 15 years of age is engaged in exploitive exhibition or other sexual conduct.

Count 15 alleges that on or about the 1st day of April, 2003, James Prentiss Coghill knowingly committed sexual exploitation of a minor in the second degree by attempting to receive, exchange, or possess any visual depiction in which a minor under 15 years of age is engaged in exploitive exhibition or other sexual conduct.

Again, Mr. Coghill has pled not guilty to these charges.

What the lawyers have advised me, and what you can be sure of if you are a juror in this case, is you will not, I repeat, you will not have to watch or see any images, or view any of the videos or files that are at issue in this case. You're not going to have to watch or see any images in this case of the conduct that's described in the indictment. Okay.

Knowing what this charge is, what the case is about, I want to ask -- I know you have very limited information -- have any of you ever seen, heard, or read anything about this case, or maybe had someone express an opinion to you about this case?

All right. I see no hands.

Is there anything about the nature of this case that would make it difficult for you to sit as a fair and impartial juror?

All right. Keep your hands up.

Ms. Walters.

PROSPECTIVE JUROR WALTERS: Yes.

THE COURT: Mr. Dains.

All right. And Ms. --

PROSPECTIVE JUROR MACHADO: Machado.

```
 1          THE COURT:  Ms. Walters.
 2          PROSPECTIVE JUROR WALTERS:  I have a relative and I
 3  have a boy that age, and I just couldn't do it.
 4          THE COURT:  As you sit here right now, have you
 5  already just made up your mind?
 6          PROSPECTIVE JUROR WALTERS:  Yes.
 7          THE COURT:  Any objection, Mr. Jensvold?
 8          MR. JENSVOLD:  No.
 9          THE COURT:  Mr. Skitzki?
10          MR. SKITZKI:  No.
11          THE COURT:  Then you're excused, Ms. Walters.
12          Thank you for your honesty.  Head back down to the
13  first floor and check in with them, okay.
14          (Whereupon the prospective juror was excused from
15  service and leaves the courtroom.)
16          THE COURT:  Mr. Dains.
17          PROSPECTIVE JUROR DAINS:  I had a friend's daughter
18  who was --
19          THE COURT:  Why don't you come up and we'll talk at
20  the bench.  Thank you, sir.
21          (Whereupon the Court and counsel and prospective
22  juror confer at the bench, on the record, as follows:)
23          PROSPECTIVE JUROR DAINS:  I had a friend's daughter
24  who was raped, molested over and over again.  And it just, and
25  I wouldn't be -- I think he ought to be fried.
```

PIMA COUNTY SUPERIOR COURT

1	THE COURT: Have you already made up your mind?
2	PROSPECTIVE JUROR DAINS: Yes.
3	THE COURT: Mr. Jensvold, any objection?
4	MR. JENSVOLD: No.
5	THE COURT: Mr. Skitzki?
6	MR. SKITZKI: No.
7	THE COURT: You're excused.
8	You can go ahead, and -- let me give her a chance to
9	take off her equipment. We are going to go ahead and excuse
10	you, Mr. Dains. Go ahead and check in with them.
11	(Whereupon the prospective juror is excused from
12	service, and the Court and counsel confer at the bench, on the
13	record, as follows:)
14	MR. JENSVOLD: I don't know if you were going to do
15	this, but I'm wondering if people, when they hear -- while
16	some people might not say yes to this question, might say when
17	they hear the descriptions of the videos.
18	THE COURT: Essentially possessing or receiving
19	child pornography?
20	MR. JENSVOLD: Yeah. And I'm just, I guess I just
21	wonder whether, because they're going to eventually, they're
22	going to see the specific descriptions.
23	MR. SKITZKI: Yeah.
24	MR. JENSVOLD: That might cause more hands to be
25	raised, because it's a lot more graphic.

PIMA COUNTY SUPERIOR COURT

1 THE COURT: Do you want me to go ahead and read the
2 description?
3 MR. JENSVOLD: You may as well.
4 MR. SKITZKI: You might as well.
5 THE COURT: All right.
6 (Whereupon proceedings continued in open court, on
7 the record, as follows:)
8 THE COURT: What I'm going to do, folks, and
9 Ms. Machado, I'm going to get to you, I haven't forgotten you,
10 but I want to give you a little bit more of an idea about what
11 this case is about.
12 So I told you about count 1, sexual exploitation of
13 a minor. The images that the defendant is alleged to have
14 possessed or received or exchanged, include a video and/or a
15 movie showing an adult male, perhaps female, performing oral
16 sex on a prepubescent girl, and an adult male engaging in
17 penile/vaginal intercourse with a prepubescent female.
18 The image or video at issue in count 2 alleges that
19 it is a movie depicting a prepubescent female performing oral
20 sex on an adult male.
21 Count 3 alleges a video and/or movie depicting a
22 prepubescent girl masturbating and having a dildo inserted
23 into her anus.
24 Count 4 alleges a video and/or movie depicting an
25 adult male attempting to vaginally penetrate a prepubescent

PIMA COUNTY SUPERIOR COURT

```
 1  female.
 2          Count 5 alleges a video and/or movie depicting two
 3  prepubescent males masturbating each other, and an adult male.
 4          Count 6 alleges a video and/or movie depicting a
 5  prepubescent female performing oral sex on an adult male.
 6          Count 7 alleges a video/and or movie depicting an
 7  adult male ejaculating into the mouth of a prepubescent
 8  female.
 9          Count 8 alleges a video and/or movie depicting a
10  prepubescent female masturbating, then performing oral sex on
11  an adult male.
12          Count 9 alleges a video and/or movie depicting a
13  prepubescent female stripping, displaying her genitals, and
14  performing oral sex on an adult male.
15          Count 10 alleges a video and/or movie depicting an
16  adult male ejaculating into the mouth of a partially clothed
17  prepubescent female.
18          Count 11 alleges a video and/or movie depicting a
19  bound prepubescent female vaginally, anally, and digitally
20  penetrated by an adult male.
21          Count 12 alleges a video and/or movie depicting a
22  prepubescent female performing oral sex on an adult male.
23          Count 13 alleges a video and/or movie depicting a
24  prepubescent female performing oral sex on an adult male.
25          Count 14 alleges a video and/or movie depicting a
```

prepubescent female taking off her underwear, masturbating, and being vaginally penetrated by an adult male.

And Count 15 alleges a video and/or movie depicting multiple scenes of prepubescent males and females engaging in various sexual acts with each other.

Now again, folks, if you are part of the jury that actually is selected to pick this case -- or to try this case, to hear this case, you will not, you will not be required at all, as part of your service, to view any of these videos, to see any of these images. I think counsel, in fact, have reached a stipulation with regard to that.

But we needed to let you know what the nature of the counts were, so that I could ask the question again. And I'll get back to you, Ms. Machado; if there is anything about the nature of this case that would make it difficult for any of you all to serve? Did I have anymore "yes" answers to that question?

Okay. Mr. Burpee. All right. Ms. Lozoya.

Anybody else? Okay. I am sorry, Ms. Hogan. All right.

Ms. Machado.

PROSPECTIVE JUROR MACHADO: May I approach the bench, please?

THE COURT: Yes. Yes. Come on up.

(Whereupon the Court and counsel and prospective

PIMA COUNTY SUPERIOR COURT

juror confer at the bench, on the record, as follows:)

PROSPECTIVE JUROR MACHADO: I've worked for Kindercare for 17 years, in child care. I could not, I could not be impartial in this case, not at all.

THE COURT: Okay.

Mr. Jensvold?

MR. JENSVOLD: No objection.

THE COURT: Mr. Skitzki?

MR. SKITZKI: No objection.

PROSPECTIVE JUROR MACHADO: Am I excused?

THE COURT: Just one second.

(Whereupon proceedings continued in open court, on the record, as follows:)

THE COURT: Ms. Machado, you're excused. Please head down to the first floor and check in with them, okay.

PROSPECTIVE JUROR MACHADO: Yes, ma'am.

THE COURT: All right.

(Whereupon the prospective juror was excused from service and leaves the courtroom.)

THE COURT: Ms. Lozoya.

PROSPECTIVE JUROR LOZOYA: I just don't think I can be fair.

THE COURT: Is it just based on what I've read that the images contained? Does it make a difference that you will not at all be required to view them?

PIMA COUNTY SUPERIOR COURT

```
 1          PROSPECTIVE JUROR LOZOYA:  Just hearing it is
 2  disgusting.
 3          THE COURT:  Mr. Jensvold, any objection?
 4          MR. JENSVOLD:  No objection.
 5          THE COURT:  Mr. Skitzki?
 6          MR. SKITZKI:  No, Your Honor.
 7          THE COURT:  Thank you, Ms. Lozoya.  Please head back
 8  down to the first floor and check in with them.
 9          (Whereupon the prospective juror was excused from
10  service and leaves the courtroom.)
11          THE COURT:  Mr. Burpee.
12          PROSPECTIVE JUROR BURPEE:  You Honor, I have a
13  17-year-old daughter.  Just listening to that I can't, I can't
14  be fair.
15          THE COURT:  Mr. Jensvold?
16          MR. JENSVOLD:  No objection.
17          THE COURT:  Mr. Skitzki?
18          MR. SKITZKI:  No objection.
19          THE COURT:  Thanks, Mr. Burpee.  Please check in
20  with them on the first floor.  Thank you, sir.
21          (Whereupon the prospective juror was excused from
22  service and leaves the courtroom.)
23          THE COURT:  Ms. Hogan.
24          PROSPECTIVE JUROR HOGAN:  Just hearing it is making
25  me nauseous.  I couldn't listen to that for another hour.
```

PIMA COUNTY SUPERIOR COURT

```
 1        THE COURT:  Mr. Jensvold, any objection?
 2        MR. JENSVOLD:  No.
 3        THE COURT:  Mr. Skitzki?
 4        MR. SKITZKI:  No.
 5        THE COURT:  Thank you, Ms. Hogan.  Please check in
 6   with them on the first floor.
 7        Anybody that I missed?
 8        (No response.)
 9        THE COURT:  All right.
10        We'll call some names to fill the empty chairs.
11        THE CLERK:  Juror Number Five, seat number five,
12   Robert Hines.
13        THE COURT:  Hi, Mr. Hines.
14        PROSPECTIVE JUROR HINES:  Hi.
15        THE COURT:  Did you have any "yes" answers?
16        PROSPECTIVE JUROR HINES:  Yes, I did.
17        THE COURT:  What?
18        PROSPECTIVE JUROR HINES:  About the nature of the
19   trial.  Even just hearing it, I can't deal with it.
20        THE COURT:  Okay.
21        Mr. Jensvold, any objection?
22        MR. JENSVOLD:  No objection.
23        THE COURT:  Mr. Skitzki?
24        MR. SKITZKI:  No, Your Honor.
25        THE COURT:  Thank you, Mr. Hines.  Check back in
```

PIMA COUNTY SUPERIOR COURT

with them on the first floor. You're excused, sir.

(Whereupon the prospective juror was excused from service and leaves the courtroom.)

THE CLERK: For seat number five, Patricia Goldsmith.

THE COURT: Ms. Goldsmith, any "yes" answers?

PROSPECTIVE JUROR GOLDSMITH: Yes, to the first one. I am, I am faculty at the College Of Nursing. I'm here during the spring break. I have the week off. As of next week I'm back in and I supervise nursing students in the field. We're short of faculty this semester, and it will be difficult to replace me. So --

THE COURT: Was that your only "yes" answer so far?

PROSPECTIVE JUROR GOLDSMITH: Yes.

THE COURT: I'm going to have you go ahead and come on up and have a seat. But we'll keep that in mind, Ms. Goldsmith. Thank you.

THE CLERK: For seat number 10, Michal Ratliff.

THE COURT: Mr. Ratliff, hi. Did you have any "yes" answers this morning, sir?

PROSPECTIVE JUROR RATLIFF: No.

THE COURT: No? Good. Come on up, sir, we have a chair for you.

THE CLERK: For seat number 24, Sean Bennett.

THE BAILIFF: I don't remember which chair.

1 THE CLERK: Seat five --
2 THE BAILIFF: Where does Mr. Ratliff go?
3 THE COURT: He's going to go to seat 10.
4 THE CLERK: Seven will come later.
5 THE COURT: Mr. Bennett, any "yes" answers, sir?
6 PROSPECTIVE JUROR BENNETT: Yes, Your Honor. I am a
7 sole provider for my household. I'm a full-time student and
8 full-time employed. I couldn't afford to be out.
9 THE COURT: I take it you don't get paid while
10 you're --
11 PROSPECTIVE JUROR BENNETT: No.
12 THE COURT: And you're missing a decent amount of
13 school?
14 PROSPECTIVE JUROR BENNETT: Well, not for spring
15 break, but starting Monday.
16 THE COURT: All right.
17 Any objection, Mr. Jensvold?
18 MR. JENSVOLD: No, Your Honor.
19 THE COURT: Mr. Skitzki.
20 MR. SKITZKI: No.
21 THE COURT: Thanks, Mr. Bennett, you're excused.
22 Check back in with them on the first floor.
23 (Whereupon the prospective juror was excused from
24 service and leaves the courtroom.)
25 THE CLERK: Seat number 24, Lisa Walker.

PIMA COUNTY SUPERIOR COURT

1	THE COURT: Hi, Ms. Walker. Any "yes" answers?
2	PROSPECTIVE JUROR WALKER: Yes. I couldn't even
3	listen to the list of charges.
4	THE COURT: Mr. Jensvold, any objection?
5	MR. JENSVOLD: No, Your Honor.
6	THE COURT: Mr. Skitzki?
7	MR. SKITZKI: No.
8	THE COURT: You're excused, Ms. Walker. Please
9	check in with the first floor.
10	THE CLERK: For seat number 24, John Sarikas. How
11	do I say it?
12	THE COURT: How do we say your name?
13	PROSPECTIVE JUROR SARIKAS: Sarikas.
14	THE COURT: Any "yes" answer?
15	PROSPECTIVE JUROR SARIKAS: Yes, that I know some
16	attorneys.
17	THE COURT: Do they work at the Public Defender or
18	County Attorney's office?
19	PROSPECTIVE JUROR SARIKAS: Both. Robert Hirsh and
20	Rick Unklesbay.
21	THE COURT: Anything about your knowledge of either
22	of those gentlemen that would make it difficult for you to sit
23	fairly in this case?
24	PROSPECTIVE JUROR SARIKAS: No.
25	THE COURT: Great. We have a seat up front here for

PIMA COUNTY SUPERIOR COURT

```
 1  you, sir.
 2          THE CLERK:  For seat number seven, Brian Nez.
 3          THE COURT:  Hi, Mr. Nez.  Any "yes" answers?
 4          PROSPECTIVE JUROR NEZ:  Yes, I do.  I'm with the
 5  Department of Homeland Security.  Also assigned to the
 6  Department of Defense, and I'm leaving for the country of
 7  Uzbekistan this coming Thursday, so I don't know if I will be
 8  here.
 9          THE COURT:  I'm sorry.
10          PROSPECTIVE JUROR NEZ:  That's why I've got to go.
11          THE COURT:  You've got to go?
12          PROSPECTIVE JUROR NEZ:  (Nods.)
13          THE COURT:  I'll let you go then.  Please check in
14  with the first floor.
15          THE CLERK:  For seat number four, Donald Bagwell.
16          PROSPECTIVE JUROR BAGWELL:  Present.
17          THE COURT:  Hi, Mr. Bagwell.
18          Any "yes" answers, sir?
19          PROSPECTIVE JUROR BAGWELL:  No.
20          THE COURT:  Great.  Come up, sir.  We have a seat in
21  the back row for you, I think.
22          THE CLERK:  For seat number three, Nancy Gruhl.
23          THE COURT:  Hi, Ms. Gruhl.
24          PROSPECTIVE JUROR GRUHL:  Hi.
25          THE COURT:  Any "yes" answers?
```

PIMA COUNTY SUPERIOR COURT

PROSPECTIVE JUROR GRUHL: I'm not sure that I can. I'm a court appointed special advocate, and one of my cases has to do with sexual --

THE COURT: Charges similar, or --

PROSPECTIVE JUROR GRUHL: Well, yeah.

THE COURT: Mr. Jensvold, any objection?

MR. JENSVOLD: No objection.

THE COURT: Mr. Skitzki?

MR. SKITZKI: No.

THE COURT: Thank you, Ms. Gruhl. You're excused. Please check in with the first floor.

(Whereupon the prospective juror was excused from service and leaves the courtroom.)

THE CLERK: For seat number 13, Sierra Russell.

THE COURT: Hi, Ms. Russell. Any "yes" answers?

PROSPECTIVE JUROR RUSSELL: Yes, actually to both. The first being financial. I am really, I support myself and go to school, and I really can't afford to take even the next few days off.

THE COURT: You don't get paid when you're not at work?

PROSPECTIVE JUROR RUSSELL: I don't.

THE COURT: Any objection, Mr. Jensvold?

MR. JENSVOLD: No.

THE COURT: Mr. Skitzki?

PIMA COUNTY SUPERIOR COURT

                    MR. SKITZKI: No.

                    THE COURT: Thanks, Ms. Russell. You are excused.

                    (Whereupon the prospective juror was excused from service and leaves the courtroom.)

                    THE CLERK: For seat number 13, Clark Sawyer.

                    THE COURT: Hi, Mr. Sawyer.

                    PROSPECTIVE JUROR SAWYER: Hi.

                    THE COURT: Any "yes" answers?

                    PROSPECTIVE JUROR SAWYER: No.

                    THE COURT: Great. We have a seat for you, lucky number 13 I think.

                    PROSPECTIVE JUROR SAWYER: In the front row?

                    THE COURT: It's the easiest chair to get to, I think.

                    THE CLERK: For seat number 22, Stella Padilla.

                    THE COURT: Ms. Padilla, are you here?

                    PROSPECTIVE JUROR PADILLA: Yeah.

                    THE COURT: Hi.

                    PROSPECTIVE JUROR PADILLA: Hi.

                    THE COURT: Any "yes" answers, ma'am?

                    PROSPECTIVE JUROR PADILLA: Well, I work for Pima County Finance, and I do know some of the attorneys. But it wouldn't have any, I just know them through work.

                    THE COURT: Okay. Any other "yes" answers?

                    PROSPECTIVE JUROR PADILLA: No.

PIMA COUNTY SUPERIOR COURT

                THE COURT: Perfect. Come on up and you can take a seat in the front row, Ms. Padilla.
                Any other "yes" answers to the last question?
                (No response.)
                THE COURT: Okay. We'll let Ms. Padilla take a seat.
                What time did y'all get here this morning?
                PROSPECTIVE JUROR: 7:30.
                THE COURT: They let you sleep in a little bit, I see.
                Have any of you, any family members or close friends ever studied law? Okay. We have Ms. Goldsmith, Mr. Korinko, Mr. Bagwell, Ms. Horton, Ms. Ouimette.
                Middle row, I have Ms. Graves and Ms. Bly.
                PROSPECTIVE JUROR BLY: Yes.
                THE COURT: And Buntin?
                PROSPECTIVE JUROR BUNTIN: Yes.
                THE COURT: And in the front row, I have Mr. Winkenwerder and Mr. Sarikas.
                PROSPECTIVE JUROR SARIKAS: Yes.
                THE COURT: Mr. Sarikas, we'll start with you.
                PROSPECTIVE JUROR SARIKAS: I am a law school graduate. One of my brothers is also a lawyer.
                THE COURT: Anything about the fact that you went to law school or you know someone that practices law that would

1 make it difficult for you to sit fairly in this case?

2 PROSPECTIVE JUROR SARIKAS: No.

3 THE COURT: Now, one of the reasons we ask this
4 question is because some folks come before us and they have an
5 idea about what the law is, or they have an idea what the law
6 should be, or they just have ideas about what the law should
7 be. What we want are jurors that, regardless of what someone
8 has told them that the law is or maybe what they think the law
9 is, we want jurors that will be able to follow the law that I
10 give you.

11 Mr. Sarikas, do you think that you will be able to
12 follow whatever law it is that I give you and disregard any
13 notion that you may think the law is?

14 PROSPECTIVE JUROR SARIKAS: Yes. I was a tax
15 lawyer, so it's not much related to this.

16 THE COURT: All right. Great.

17 Let's see, Mr. Winkenwerder.

18 PROSPECTIVE JUROR WINKENWERDER: Yes.

19 THE COURT: Yes, sir. Who do you know?

20 PROSPECTIVE JUROR WINKENWERDER: I don't know
21 anyone. But in terms of studying the law, I used to be an
22 aviation safety inspector for the Federal Aviation
23 Administration working in their regulatory enforcement branch
24 for aviation matters.

25 THE COURT: Okay. So nothing criminal?

1	PROSPECTIVE JUROR WINKENWERDER: Nothing criminal.
2	THE COURT: And you'd able to follow the law,
3	whatever it is, that I give to you?
4	PROSPECTIVE JUROR WINKENWERDER: Absolutely.
5	THE COURT: Perfect.
6	Ms. Graves.
7	PROSPECTIVE JUROR GRAVES: I have a nephew who is an
8	attorney in San Francisco, California.
9	THE COURT: Does he practice any criminal law?
10	PROSPECTIVE JUROR GRAVES: No.
11	THE COURT: Any trouble following the law that I
12	give to you?
13	PROSPECTIVE JUROR GRAVES: No.
14	THE COURT: Okay. Ms. Bly.
15	PROSPECTIVE JUROR BLY: My uncle was a DUI judge.
16	I think he's retired.
17	THE COURT: Did he ever discuss the law with you?
18	PROSPECTIVE JUROR BLY: Unh-huh.
19	THE COURT: No?
20	PROSPECTIVE JUROR BLY: Not unless I had a question.
21	THE COURT: Any trouble, if I tell you what the law
22	is and maybe it was different than what he gave you, to follow
23	the law that I give you?
24	PROSPECTIVE JUROR BLY: No.
25	THE COURT: Mr. Buntin.

PIMA COUNTY SUPERIOR COURT

1 PROSPECTIVE JUROR BUNTIN: Took some classes at Pima
2 College 30 years ago.
3 THE COURT: Any criminal-type law?
4 PROSPECTIVE JUROR BUNTIN: Criminal justice, basic
5 entry law.
6 THE COURT: If I give you the law and it's different
7 from what you learned, will you follow the law that I give
8 you?
9 PROSPECTIVE JUROR BUNTIN: Yes, ma'am.
10 THE COURT: Okay. Mr. Sawyer?
11 PROSPECTIVE JUROR SAWYER: I'm good.
12 THE COURT: Okay. Don't want to admit you know
13 lawyers, hum? It's just smart.
14 Mr. Korinko.
15 PROSPECTIVE JUROR KORINKO: I have a nephew that is
16 insurance fraud. I don't know if that's criminal or what
17 that's considered. My niece also does family law. I'm sure
18 that doesn't apply.
19 THE COURT: Any issue following the law that I give
20 to you?
21 PROSPECTIVE JUROR KORINKO: No.
22 THE COURT: Okay. Ms. Goldsmith.
23 PROSPECTIVE JUROR GOLDSMITH: My husband is a
24 commercial litigator.
25 THE COURT: Did he ever at any time practice

PIMA COUNTY SUPERIOR COURT

1 criminal law?
2   PROSPECTIVE JUROR GOLDSMITH: No.
3   THE COURT: Any difficulty following the law that I
4 give you?
5   PROSPECTIVE JUROR GOLDSMITH: (Shakes head.)
6   THE COURT: Ms. Horton.
7   PROSPECTIVE JUROR HORTON: My dad is an attorney.
8 My uncle is a judge.
9   THE COURT: Did your father practice criminal law?
10   PROSPECTIVE JUROR HORTON: Some. He had his own
11 practice.
12   THE COURT: Any issue with following the law that I
13 give to you?
14   PROSPECTIVE JUROR HORTON: No.
15   THE COURT: Mr. Bagwell?
16   PROSPECTIVE JUROR BAGWELL: My uncle, now deceased,
17 was a lawyer.
18   THE COURT: Did he practice criminal law?
19   PROSPECTIVE JUROR BAGWELL: Early in his career, and
20 then he went into business.
21   THE COURT: Would you have any issue following the
22 law that I give to you?
23   PROSPECTIVE JUROR BAGWELL: No.
24   THE COURT: And Ms. Ouimette.
25   PROSPECTIVE JUROR OUIMETTE: Ouimette.

PIMA COUNTY SUPERIOR COURT

1   THE COURT: Ouimette.

2   PROSPECTIVE JUROR OUIMETTE: My brother is an
3   attorney, corporate litigation, nothing criminal.

4   THE COURT: All right. So you wouldn't have any
5   problem following the law that I give to you?

6   PROSPECTIVE JUROR OUIMETTE: No.

7   THE COURT: Would anybody have any problem
8   whatsoever following the law that I give to you, disregarding
9   any notions about what you think the law is or what you think
10   the law should be?

11   (No response.)

12   THE COURT: All right. Have any of you ever had any
13   specialized training or knowledge related to computers?

14   Okay. We have Mr. Korinko, Ms. Goldsmith,
15   Ms. Horton, Mr. Bagwell.

16   Anybody in the middle row? Oh, I'm sorry,
17   Ms. Tucker. We have Ms. Bly.

18   Anybody in the front row? Ms. Knew. Oh, I'm sorry,
19   Ms. Ouimette.

20   Ms. Knew, what kind of training do you have?

21   PROSPECTIVE JUROR KNEW: I put together and repair
22   computers.

23   THE COURT: All right.

24   Ms. Bly.

25   PROSPECTIVE JUROR BLY: I have a degree in graphic

PIMA COUNTY SUPERIOR COURT

1 design and work on a computer daily, creative and business.
2   THE COURT: Okay. Ms. Ouimette.
3   PROSPECTIVE JUROR OUIMETTE: I work at the
4 University of Arizona, and I am friends with the Director of
5 our Info Tech Department. So he has told me some stories
6 about secret service agents coming to follow-up on hacked U.S.
7 government web sites. Visits from, well, at the other
8 college, which is where I work, we have people, we have
9 someone who is working on something called Dark Web which
10 infiltrates terrorist web sites.
11   And also we're involved in Homeland Security grants
12 to study border issues. So, you know, I know that we have
13 secret service, U.S. Marshalls, in and out of the building,
14 F.B.I. And I use the computers other than that.
15   THE COURT: Okay. Mr. Bagwell.
16   PROSPECTIVE JUROR BAGWELL: 25 years with IBM.
17   THE COURT: That qualifies.
18   Ms. Horton.
19   PROSPECTIVE JUROR HORTON: Computer analyst for
20 Liberty Life Insurance.
21   THE COURT: Okay. And Ms. Goldsmith.
22   PROSPECTIVE JUROR GOLDSMITH: I teach a class,
23 researching via the internet.
24   THE COURT: And Mr. Korinko.
25   PROSPECTIVE JUROR KORINKO: Bachelor's degree in

PIMA COUNTY SUPERIOR COURT

electrical engineering. I specialize in computer design, within missiles.

THE COURT: Okay. How about anybody on the jury that has any specialized training or knowledge related to the internet? If you know how to get on it, that doesn't count. Any specialized training or knowledge on the internet.

Mr. Bagwell, is that through IBM as well?

PROSPECTIVE JUROR BAGWELL: Correct.

THE COURT: Ms. Goldsmith, what you've already discussed?

PROSPECTIVE JUROR GOLDSMITH: Um-hum.

THE COURT: Anybody else?

And Mr. Korinko.

PROSPECTIVE JUROR KORINKO: Master's degree in telecommunications software.

THE COURT: All right. Is there anybody here who has never gotten on the internet? Never.

(No response.)

THE COURT: Is there anybody here who has no idea how to use a computer?

I'm the only one. Okay.

Have any of you, any members -- well, you know what? Is it a good time to take a break, Counsel, give you an early jump on lunch? Because we're going to go into the afternoon, so I would just as soon get you out of here before the rest of

PIMA COUNTY SUPERIOR COURT

the jurors.

All right. So what we're going to do, is take our afternoon or our lunch recess. Be back out in the hallway at 1:15. That includes all of you folks back there.

PROSPECTIVE JUROR: I am sorry, what's that --

THE COURT: Be back out in the hallway where we brought you up before we called you into the courtroom at 1:15.

For you 26 people that we have up here in front of the bar, please remember where your seats are, because after lunch we're going to ask you to take those exact same seats.

While you're on your lunch hour, do not discuss with anybody, nobody at all, anything that's gone on in the courtroom. Don't discuss this case. Don't discuss anything, and don't let anybody talk to you about it. That's what we call the admonition.

Make sure you keep your juror badges on. If anybody talks about this case in your presence, make sure you let Christina know and we'll chat with you about that.

PROSPECTIVE JUROR: Are we allowed to go across the street to get a sandwich?

THE COURT: Absolutely. You can go anywhere you want as long as you're back by 1:15. You guys have a good lunch and we'll see you back at 1:15.

PROSPECTIVE JUROR: Your Honor, can we leave things

PIMA COUNTY SUPERIOR COURT

1 here?

2 THE COURT: If you want to leave things in the
3 courtroom, it will be locked over the lunch hour.

4 PROSPECTIVE JUROR: Okay.

5 (Whereupon Prospective Juror Bly came up and talked
6 to the judge, but was informed to come back and talk on the
7 record after lunch.)

8 (11:50 a.m. Whereupon the prospective jurors are
9 excused and leave the courtroom, and proceedings continue in
10 their absence, as follows:)

11 THE COURT: All right.

12 All right. The record will show the absence of our
13 prospective jurors, the presence of both counsel. Mr. Coghill
14 is with us as well.

15 You said you had a few motions in limine that you
16 wanted to take up before --

17 MR. EUCHNER: Yes, Your Honor. It's actually one
18 motion with three provisions, and some of them we just wanted
19 to make clear before we started, and some of them haven't been
20 addressed yet. And I have my motion in here someplace. I
21 haven't found it.

22 But I know the first one was just any references to
23 adult pornography outside of what we had discussed on JE3-MM,
24 and then in the motions hearing that had already been
25 discussed, and we wanted to discuss certain parts of that a

PIMA COUNTY SUPERIOR COURT

1 little further later.
2   But just to essentially put into effect what the
3 Court of Appeals ruling was in this case, just no adult
4 pornography comes in unless there is somehow a connection to
5 child pornography.
6   THE COURT: All right. Mr. Jensvold.
7   MR. JENSVOLD: That's fine, as long as it goes for
8 both Mr. Franks and Mr. Coghill. I've done my best to redact
9 everything that, well, some of it's going to be interpretation
10 as to who was responsible for which particular files in the
11 KaZaA log. But as long as it goes both ways, I don't have a
12 problem.
13   MR. EUCHNER: And, Your Honor, the way I'm
14 interpreting your ruling from a couple of weeks ago, which is,
15 if there is some probative value of the adult pornography,
16 where it has some sort of connection to child pornography,
17 such as the links that had Lolitas, and other things that
18 could possibly refer to child pornography, that that was the
19 probative value. So that's our understanding of the ruling.
20   THE COURT: That's correct.
21   So, no adult pornography, subject to the ruling that
22 I already made will come in as to either the defendant or to
23 Mr. Franks.
24   MR. EUCHNER: Okay. The second one we put in was
25 any reference to files or folders found on the CD labeled as

PIMA COUNTY SUPERIOR COURT

JE3-MM, that reference adult pornography, including the name of the folder, porn, and all of those links that did not have any connection to child pornography. And that is what we had discussed a couple of weeks ago as well.

MR. JENSVOLD: The only difficulty I have with that is the folder labeled porn, because a number of these charged files that Detective Englander is going to talk about, his forensic analysis shows that they were found within that folder. And that folder was created on a particular date which I think becomes relevant. It's not going to make any mention of adult pornography, but the fact that there's a folder titled porn within JE3-MM, I think, has some connection to the fact that there was a similar folder on the computer, on the hard drive, where some of these files were found.

MR. EUCHNER: And, Your Honor, just to make sure it's clear, I think Mr. Jensvold understands, but it might not be clear to the Court, that this is a different porn folder on the CD than the porn folder that Detective -- former Detective Englander will talk about.

Englander is going to talk about a porn folder on the hard drive which was more than two years after this CD was created. So there is no connection to the two porn folders, other than they both have the name porn. And given that the word porn is such a part of common parlance now, that I don't think that just merely having the name porn in both places is enough.

Basically, if the jury is going to hear that there are five or six child pornography describing sites on this, we don't want them hearing that it's going to be the only things within a porn folder. That seems to be just as misleading as if they got to hear that there were 166 links.

THE COURT: So, my understanding, though, is that some of the links that I was going to allow the State to get into on JE3-MM were saved under this file called porn.

MR. EUCHNER: But in a folder called porn, which was in a folder called favorites. So we have no objection to it being described as these were within the folder called favorites, which is correct. On the CD they're actually within a subfolder of favorites. But it would not be misleading to the jury to say they were within the favorites directory.

And Detective Mawhinney, as well as Tami Loehrs, can talk about how the favorites folder would exist and how it would have been created on the CD. And there's no disagreement that these files are the kind of files that would be created when you're surfing an internet explorer and you click "add to favorites".

The question is only are they in the main directory of favorites, or are they in a subdirectory. And because the subdirectory is called porn, that's why we don't want that

1 mentioned.
2   THE COURT: Well, I think what it's titled goes to
3 knowledge, and the defendant's knowledge. So I'm going to
4 allow the State to simply name that, the files that they want
5 to get into under the JE3-MM, that I've allowed them to get
6 into, was under the subcategory called porn in the favorites
7 thing.
8   But the other items in there that you want to keep
9 out --
10   MR. EUCHNER: On numbers three and four, I don't
11 think Mr. Jensvold is going to have any objection. We just
12 put them in there to be safe because the witness might say
13 something on his own.
14   THE COURT: Any objection?
15   MR. JENSVOLD: I'm sorry, what were they?
16   MR. EUCHNER: That was reference to genital
17 mutilation, and that James Coghill had a sexual interest in
18 minor children. This stuff came out during the interview we
19 did a couple of months ago, that Jacob Franks said these
20 things.
21   And this also goes to number seven as well, any
22 reference by Jacob Franks that James Coghill was molested as a
23 child. Franks testified to that in the first trial.
24   THE COURT: Any objection, Mr. Jensvold, to three?
25   MR. JENSVOLD: Well, the only thing is Mr. Franks'

PIMA COUNTY SUPERIOR COURT

response to that question during the first trial was, the question that was asked to him in which he gave that answer was: Did Mr. Coghill ever tell you why he watched child pornography?

That, according to Mr. Franks, was Mr. Coghill's answer.

Mr. Coghill disputes that was the case. He never told Jacob that.

MR. EUCHNER: I remember the question, but I think that was elicited by the State as well. But either way, that, that particular reference to possible molestation has no bearing on this case, and there is no evidence that it happened. It's just Jacob Franks talking.

THE COURT: Okay.

MR. JENSVOLD: That's fine. I guess as long as it's not going to be used to impeach Jacob, then --

MR. EUCHNER: We don't want to elicit that.

THE COURT: Okay. Let's be real clear, item three, four, and seven, we're in agreement, will be precluded.

MR. EUCHNER: Yes.

THE COURT: Yes? Okay.

MR. EUCHNER: Going back then to five and six are basically the same grouping, and these are things that were disclosed to us by Mr. Jensvold. Mr. Jensvold went on web sites and found writings of, at least that purport to be those of James Coghill. The web sites were entitled, letters from prison, and it talked about this case. And it, basically it's opinions. It's nothing at all.

It talks about the evidence of the first trial and how it went. But it's nothing more than opinions of a non -- well, even if it was an expert, there is nothing -- this is for the jury. So we would ask for five, as well as six, which are, Mr. Jensvold has got a copy of a letter that Mr. Coghill sent to people that he was in prison with that also talked about this case.

THE COURT: All right. What about five to start with, Mr. Jensvold?

MR. JENSVOLD: I don't have a problem with five.

THE COURT: All right.

Five is precluded then.

What about six? Letters written by Mr. Coghill to other inmates.

MR. JENSVOLD: Well, I think there are portions of that letter that could be valid impeachment of Mr. Coghill, presuming he testifies. It covers a lot of different things. It covers his opinion of what's going on with the case. And in particular it talks about how he makes his, his case, C's differently than the ones that appear on the CDs.

THE COURT: So why don't I do this. If Mr. Coghill testifies, and he testifies in a manner that you think makes

1 that letter somehow relevant to impeach him, then we can take
2 it up outside the presence of the jury and decide at that
3 point whether or not you'd be allowed to impeach Mr. Coghill
4 with that letter. Is that right --
5   MR. JENSVOLD: Yes.
6   THE COURT: -- Mr. Euchner?
7   MR. EUCHNER: Yes, Your Honor.
8   THE COURT: And eight, any reference that Mr. Franks
9 or Mr. Coghill smoked marijuana.
10   MR. JENSVOLD: That's fine.
11   THE COURT: That's precluded then.
12   Any other motions?
13   MR. EUCHNER: Well, that's the only, those are the
14 only motions we have.
15   Then what I would like to do is move on to the KaZaA
16 logs that are going to be admitted to the jury in this case.
17 The question that we'll have is how much needs to be redacted.
18 I know Mr. Jensvold has already given the clerk his
19 redactions. However, I think our redactions might be fewer
20 than Mr. Jensvold's, and I'll explain.
21   Based on the Court's ruling on the JE3-MM CDs, any
22 title of a file or anything within the file that purports to
23 be child pornography, has any connection whatsoever to child
24 pornography, has probative value and the jury can hear.
25   Within the KaZaA logs there is, there are some

indicators within these file names and file descriptions that some of these are child pornography. So even if it turns out that they weren't, they don't turn out to be child pornography, but, for example, if I were to download something, I don't know what it is for sure until I open it. I get it, and I open it, and I view it.

But at the time I click on, when I do a search in KaZaA and I click on it, when I'm getting it, I have a description, I have a file name in hand, and I'm downloading it based on what limited information I have at that point.

And the KaZaA logs have references to, not just to what would clearly be adult pornography, but also some references that would be to child pornography, very similar to the file names on JE3-MM. Some of them talk about 15-year-old girl, some of them say under age, 16-year-old girl, 17-year-old girl. One, I think one of them says illegal. Some of them just say young or teen.

And what I would like to do is get a ruling from the Court as to which ones do purport to be child pornography sufficiently that we can use them, because these particular records are downloaded very close in time to when Jacob Franks is downloading his music.

THE COURT: All right. And --

MR. EUCHNER: And I can provide an unredacted copy, for purposes of the record, of the KaZaA logs.

1   THE COURT: Is the redacted copy 12-C, Mr. Jensvold?
2   MR. JENSVOLD: That was the State's redacted copy,
3 yes.
4   THE COURT: And what is the significant -- are there
5 significant differences between what the State has redacted
6 and what you want redacted?
7   MR. EUCHNER: I think that there is just going to be
8 the first set of -- there's actually what looks to be three
9 different logs. One of them has, if the Court sees at the top
10 under decoding database, there's, each one of these records
11 that's separated by lots of equal signs, says record number
12 equal zero. And that's the only thing that's sequential about
13 these KaZaA logs. Everything else in terms of the download
14 date or the file date, those are not sequential, so it
15 requires a lot of effort to follow the order they're going in.
16   But the first set that goes up to approximately
17 record number 184, I think it is, don't, I think at most there
18 might be one pornographic, but all of them are either music or
19 something else that doesn't even appear to be pornographic.
20 Then there's --
21   THE COURT: Stop right there. Let's just take this
22 in stages. So you don't have any problem with the State's
23 redactions up until record 184, through record 184?
24   MR. EUCHNER: Your Honor, I haven't even looked at
25 the State's redactions yet, but chances are they might have

redacted one or two of those. I don't think there are going to be a lot of redactions in that group.

What I'm saying is right after you get to 184, the next grouping after that, it starts again, decoding data base, and honestly, I'm not really sure what the difference is between the two sets of logs, but based on the data contained therein, there are two sets of logs.

And then there is another set that starts with decoding data base record number equals zero. And most of these are pornographic. Like record number two is ritual music of Tibetan Buddhism. 44 and 45 appear to be music videos. But just about everything else seems to be, and zero is, looks like a music video, too.

But starting with record number one, it appears to be all pornographic. And some of them show no indicator of child pornography. But then I get to what's record number 12, teen audition, part two. Record number 13, voluptuous teen redhead does it all.

THE COURT: Let me go back to record 12. I mean, it might be helpful if you actually look at the redactions that Mr. Jensvold proposes, because I don't see on the record number 12 that's in front of me, anything that says anything about teens.

MR. JENSVOLD: That's been redacted.

MR. EUCHNER: And, Your Honor, like I said, there's

```
 1  two sets.  You might be looking at the first record number 12.
 2         THE COURT:  No, I'm looking at the second record
 3  number 12.
 4         MR. EUCHNER:  Oh, okay.
 5         THE COURT:  Yeah.
 6         MR. EUCHNER:  Right, I expect, and that's why like,
 7  for example, if it refers to teen, that is suggestive of child
 8  pornography.
 9         Record number --
10         THE COURT:  No, not necessarily.  I'm dealing with
11  teens, teens that are under the age 15.  And I think my ruling
12  was something that could be, clearly could be linked to
13  prepubescent.  Something that is reflective of a video of
14  somebody under the age of 15.
15         MR. EUCHNER:  But, Your Honor, my understanding of
16  the ruling is that it's basically what's legal versus what's
17  illegal, and children are under 18.
18         THE COURT:  Okay.
19         MR. EUCHNER:  So then there are some that, for
20  example, number 13 just says teen; number 15 refers to a young
21  girl.
22         THE COURT:  All right.  And the record that I'm
23  looking at, so let's -- why don't we do this.  I'm looking at
24  Mr. Jensvold's records on page 47.  On record number 13, I
25  don't see any reference whatsoever to --
```

PIMA COUNTY SUPERIOR COURT

1   MR. JENSVOLD: Those have been redacted, Your Honor.
2 So you're looking, unfortunately, you're looking at what we
3 redacted from it. So you're not seeing what Mr. Euchner's --
4   THE COURT: Right. But this is what you propose the
5 jury have.
6   MR. JENSVOLD: Correct. We left the record number
7 in there. I, through my legal assistant, had her redact out
8 the information that would reference it as pornography.
9   MR. EUCHNER: Your Honor, so what the defense is
10 asking, things that are not actually in front of the Court's
11 eyes, but some of these others that the jury should have.
12   So this says college teens, so presumably that would
13 be the 18 or 19 year old.
14   Then a number, let's see --
15   THE COURT: Have you --
16   MR. EUCHNER: Three teen, number 18 is three teen
17 Lolitas squirting juices.mpeg. Sorry, that's Lolitas, that
18 goes to the same ruling as what was on the CD.
19   THE COURT: It looks like that's redacted in
20 Mr. Jensvold's version.
21   MR. JENSVOLD: Wait, number 18?
22   MR. EUCHNER: Correct (indicating).
23   THE COURT: Let me make a proposal. I don't know if
24 you and Mr. Jensvold have gotten together to try to see if you
25 can come to some consensus about what should be redacted and

what should not be redacted, but I think it would be a better use of everyone's time if the two of you could go through these logs together, determine what you agree on, and then I can take up what you disagree on.

MR. EUCHNER: Well, Your Honor, what we're looking for first is just a preliminary ruling that, if it says, for example, says Lolita, that that would be fair game for us to use because the State gets to use Lolitas from the CD.

THE COURT: What do you mean, fair game for the defense to use?

MR. EUCHNER: That we would prefer to have a copy that's redacted, but less redacted, that would actually have some of these records in that the jury could see. Because these download times in these records, are pretty much the exact time that Jacob Franks is downloading his music.

THE COURT: So you want a more encompassing KaZaA report to go back than the State's proposing.

MR. EUCHNER: Yes, Your Honor. And we haven't discussed this yet with Mr. Jensvold. We were working on a lot of other things. But if we just know which ones we can get and which ones we can't by their names, then we can go back and do the redactions based on the Court's ruling.

THE COURT: All right. I think I have tried to be very limited in what I allowed the State to get into in regard to the names of the files on that J3-MM -- I'm sorry, I don't know the full name of it.

But if, but if for some reason it's relevant to your defense and relevant to show that these were really Mr. Franks' files, and you want to get into the names of more of those files than the Court was originally willing to let the State get into, that's fine.

But I think it would probably be better if you and Mr. Jensvold figured out which you agree on, and then we can take up if there are disagreements.

It seems like Mr. Jensvold's redactions were very generous and sweeping. But if there are files that are relevant based on dates and times that similarly reflect Lolitas that you think could demonstrate that it was really Mr. Franks that possessed these items versus Mr. Coghill, I don't have an issue with that.

Mr. Jensvold?

MR. JENSVOLD: No, I don't either. It's just that this whole thing again raises the same issues that we had during the first trial. Which, you know, at some point, when does the fact that the entirety of what either Mr. Franks or Mr. Coghill was watching become relevant?

I mean, I don't want to get in a fight with the Court of Appeals again since I lost the first time, but there is a line here that the, I don't think the Court of Appeals really understood that is hard to draw down here as opposed to down the street.

THE COURT: Well, I'll draw the line, if it's adult pornography as both gentlemen, it just doesn't come in. If it's titles or images that are clearly child pornography, for lack of a better word, I think that it's relevant as to both, provided that it's at a time and in a space where Mr. Franks would similar, have similar access as Mr. Coghill did.

MR. JENSVOLD: It's just that, you know, if I ask Mr. Franks, what were you searching for, what were you watching? Oh, I was watching, you know, adult porn stuff. And, you know, he has a particular affinity for redheads, at least at this time, and that's what a lot of these files are, and I have to go back with either Detective Mawhinney or Englander to see if they found any of these files in the KaZaA logs that we're talking about actually on the hard drive itself. I don't remember the answer to that question.

But that's another area that I'm probably going to go into if that's allowed. And the fact is that none of the files, none of the web sites from JE3-MM were actually located, so it's just the files themselves.

But I am perfectly willing to be fair here. It's just when we do this, it opens the door to going other places, and then it's not the easiest issue to resolve because it's all interlinked.

THE COURT: Well, if you want to bring it in to

Mr. Franks as well, as long as it doesn't come in to Mr. Coghill; that was the issue that brought us all back here. So I guess y'all can do what you want with Mr. Franks, I mean, with regard to the adult pornography.

MR. JENSVOLD: I know.

THE COURT: But I just want to make sure that it absolutely doesn't come in as to Mr. Coghill.

MR. EUCHNER: Well, Your Honor, just like Mr. Jensvold, we want the rules to be the same for both. And if it's got a title of a file or anything within the file that is indicative of even purporting to be child pornography, if it comes in on JE3-MM, then it comes in on the KaZaA logs.

And I don't know what Mr. Englander or Detective Mawhinney did, but our expert had done this work and it's in the report that was disclosed.

THE COURT: That sounds fair to me, Mr. Jensvold, if they want it to come in so they can demonstrate it is at a time when Mr. Franks had access to that computer, and if they are titles suggestive of child pornography, then I think that it's fair game to come in on the KaZaA logs.

MR. JENSVOLD: Yeah, I understand.

Let me think about it over the lunch hour and see if there is a way to come up with it. At this point, I just think it opens up a can of worms. And I again, I'll say the same thing I said last time, I don't think it's fair to have

Mr. Franks talk, up there talking about him watching adult pornography when Mr. Coghill admitted the same thing.

Just, you know, we're talking about two people, nobody else, at least as far as I know, that's going to be alleged to have downloaded any of these things. So that was the issue in the first trial, and it's just that we're getting back to that same point.

THE COURT: But here's the deal though. I ruled if you wanted to keep adult pornography out with regard to Mr. Franks, and I think that was part of the defense motion as well, all adult pornography stays out as to both gentlemen.

So, I mean, it's up to you. If you want to start bringing it in as to Mr. Franks for some strategic reason, we need to know that now.

But, I mean, my ruling is no adult pornography period as to either gentleman, only the titles that relate to the children as to both.

I see Mr. Euchner's smiling.

MR. EUCHNER: Nodding.

THE COURT: Nodding, correct, and smiling.

MR. EUCHNER: Because I'm always smiling.

MR. JENSVOLD: And just, I mean, now that I'm thinking this through, if we eliminated the ruling on JE3-MM and we just didn't go there --

THE COURT: You mean to keep out all of those

titles?

MR. JENSVOLD: -- to keep out all of those titles, I mean, they're basically titles of -- the distinction I see here is that we're talking about titles of files that don't necessarily have actual images or movies to go with them. Now, that may not be the case on some of these in the KaZaA logs. I'm not positive. Do you know the answer?

MR. EUCHNER: I'm sorry, what was the question exactly?

MR. JENSVOLD: The answer of where did Tami find evidence of the actual files that were named in the KaZaA logs? Some of the ones that you're talking about here.

MR. EUCHNER: Yes.

MR. JENSVOLD: Okay.

MR. EUCHNER: It was in the report. If you look at the -- in fact, some of them were in the list of the 312 files that Mr. Englander corrupted, well, he didn't corrupt, he contaminated them.

THE COURT: So let's, let's do this. I need to give my staff a break here because we have to be back on the record at 1:00 for another thing.

Mr. Jensvold, if you want to re-examine your position about whether any of the files under JE3-MM come in, come in, I mean, Mr. Euchner moved to preclude those, so I don't know that it would hurt his feelings if you decided not

1 to bring any of those things. And I guess I should be a
2 little bit more legal sounding. I don't think he would have a
3 problem if you reversed your opinion on those. And we could
4 maybe take this up before, at some later point this afternoon
5 when you have a better chance to think these things through.
6   MR. EUCHNER: And, Your Honor, for the record I can
7 mark the unredacted copy of the KaZaA logs as Defense A, I
8 guess we're up to.
9   THE CLERK: I just want that before I mark that one.
10   THE COURT: Anything else you want to take up before
11 we break?
12   MR. EUCHNER: No, Your Honor.
13   THE COURT: All right. I'll see you all back here
14 maybe 1:10-ish. We'll have the jury out in the hall at 1:15.
15 Make sure nothing happened over the lunch hour.
16   All right. We're off the record.
17   (Whereupon proceedings were recessed.)
18   (Whereupon the proceedings continued, as follows:)
19   THE COURT: The record will show the absence of our
20 prospective jurors, the presence of both counsel, and
21 Mr. Coghill is here as well.
22   Any reason why we can't bring the jurors back in?
23   MR. EUCHNER: Well, Judge, we have a very brief
24 record we would like to make.
25   Mr. Jensvold and Mr. Skitzki and I talked over the

PIMA COUNTY SUPERIOR COURT

break, and I think we have an agreement as to what we discussed before the break, which is, we will not introduce any of the KaZaA logs in terms of what we were talking about before, and we'll stick with the State's redacted copy, which I have not yet looked at, but I have no reason to doubt, as I speak right now, that Mr. Jensvold redacted as well.

But that we'll stick with the State's redacted copy in exchange for not showing or introducing evidence of any of the names of those links from JE3-MM, or that there was a porn folder.

THE COURT: Is that your understanding?

MR. JENSVOLD: That's fine.

THE COURT: Okay. So by stipulation of the parties, and subject to Mr. Euchner actually having a chance to meaningfully review State's 12-C, the KaZaA logs will come in.

However, what did you say, the names of the files and the fact that they were kept in a folder called porn, will not?

MR. EUCHNER: On JE3-MM, correct.

THE COURT: Correct. Okay.

MR. EUCHNER: And then on the KaZaA logs, the State's redacted copy, subject to review, will be what we agree to as well.

THE COURT: Okay. Great.

All right. We'll bring the jurors in.

PIMA COUNTY SUPERIOR COURT

1	And, counsel, Ms. Bly approached
2	MR. EUCHNER: Yes.
3	THE COURT: And I am going to go ahead and bring her
4	up to the bench, because my thought is I don't want jurors to
5	think over the lunch hour ways to get out of jury duty. So I
6	don't want to empower them with any ideas.
7	(Prospective jurors now present.)
8	THE COURT: Counsel, thanks.
9	You can be seated.
10	We have a juror missing in action, Mr. Korinko.
11	We'll go ahead and wait for him. We can't really
12	start without him.
13	(Brief pause in proceedings.)
14	THE COURT: We're back on the record.
15	The record will show the presence of all our jurors,
16	the presence of both counsel, the presence of Mr. Coghill.
17	Hope you all had a good lunch.
18	I have a handful more questions to ask you.
19	Have any of you, any members of your family, or any
20	close friends, ever been arrested, charged, or convicted of
21	any offense other than a minor traffic violation?
22	All right. Ms. Tucker, Mr. Bagwell, Ms. Ouimette.
23	Anybody else in the back row?
24	Okay. Middle row, I have Ms. Graves, Mr. Buntin.
25	PROSPECTIVE JUROR BUNTIN: Yes.

PIMA COUNTY SUPERIOR COURT

THE COURT: And in the front I have Ms. Knew, Ms. Crawford, and Mr. --

PROSPECTIVE JUROR LESCHAK: Leschak.

THE COURT: Leschak. Just like it looks. Okay. Ms. Tucker -- oh, I'm sorry, and Mr. Kinsella. Okay.

PROSPECTIVE JUROR KINSELLA: Yes.

THE COURT: Okay.

PROSPECTIVE JUROR TUCKER: I have a sister who was arrested 30 years ago, on a cocaine charge. And I have a nephew who is now serving time for sexual misconduct with a minor.

THE COURT: All right. Did you follow either of those cases as they progressed through the system? Meaning, did you come to the trial? Did you talk to parties about the case?

PROSPECTIVE JUROR TUCKER: My nephew, no. My sister, I actually paid for her attorney. But I was never, I never went to court with her, never knew any of her information.

THE COURT: All right. Anything about either your sister's or your nephew's experience that would make it difficult for you to sit fairly in this case?

PROSPECTIVE JUROR TUCKER: No.

THE COURT: And the reason we ask this question, is

PIMA COUNTY SUPERIOR COURT

because your decision in this case, if you are selected as a juror in this case, needs to be based solely on the evidence that's produced in this trial.

I mean, everybody comes with life experiences and everyone comes with things that have occurred in their lives. But what's really important for both the State and Mr. Coghill is that any decision you make is based only on what happens in court, and not based on something that may have happened in your life, and not influenced by something that may have happened in your life.

Ms. Tucker, anything about your experiences that would make it difficult for you to decide this case just based on the evidence presented here in court?

PROSPECTIVE JUROR TUCKER: Not at all.

THE COURT: Okay.

Mr. Bagwell.

MR. BAGWELL: 30 years ago, myself, stupid college mistake, arrested for shoplifting. Never prosecuted, never carried through.

THE COURT: Anything about that experience that would make it difficult for you to sit fairly for both sides in this case?

PROSPECTIVE JUROR BAGWELL: No, ma'am.

THE COURT: Ms. Ouimette.

PROSPECTIVE JUROR OUIMETTE: Post-college, 1983, I

believe, I had a DUI. But they lost my file, so I don't think it's in the record.

THE COURT: Okay. Anything about that experience that would make it difficult for you to sit fairly in this case?

PROSPECTIVE JUROR OUIMETTE: No.

THE COURT: Ms. Graves.

PROSPECTIVE JUROR GRAVES: My son, about seven years ago, got a DUI.

THE COURT: Anything about that experience make it hard for you to be fair to both sides in this case?

PROSPECTIVE JUROR GRAVES: No.

THE COURT: Mr. Buntin.

PROSPECTIVE JUROR BUNTIN: My son, five years ago, DUI.

THE COURT: Anything about that experience that would cause you any difficulty being fair to both sides in this case?

PROSPECTIVE JUROR BUNTIN: No.

THE COURT: Ms. Bly, I forgot, as soon as I get the answers to this, we'll bring you up and discuss what you wanted to talk with me about; okay? I apologize.

Ms. Knew.

PROSPECTIVE JUROR KNEW: Two things. A few years ago my son had a shoplifting, minor shoplifting thing. And

PIMA COUNTY SUPERIOR COURT

myself a few years ago, I had a bad check. That's it. Neither one of those pertain to anything.

THE COURT: So you think you'd be able to give both sides a fair trial in this case?

PROSPECTIVE JUROR KNEW: Yeah, no problem.

THE COURT: Mr. Kinsella?

PROSPECTIVE JUROR KINSELLA: I had a shoplifting misdemeanor, about 25 years ago.

THE COURT: Anything about that experience --

PROSPECTIVE JUROR KINSELLA: No.

THE COURT: -- that would make it difficult for you to give both sides a fair trial here?

PROSPECTIVE JUROR KINSELLA: (Shakes head.)

THE COURT: You need to answer out loud because she takes down everything you say.

PROSPECTIVE JUROR KINSELLA: No.

THE COURT: Okay. Thanks.

Ms. Crawford.

PROSPECTIVE JUROR CRAWFORD: Sister-in-law back in New York, and I think a cousin in Texas. And I'm not close with either.

THE COURT: All right. And so I take it that neither one of those experiences would make it difficult for you to give both sides a fair trial in this case?

PROSPECTIVE JUROR CRAWFORD: No problem.

PIMA COUNTY SUPERIOR COURT

1	THE COURT: And Mr. Leschak.
2	PROSPECTIVE JUROR LESCHAK: I had a minor in
3	possession when I was under 21.
4	THE COURT: Anything about that make it hard for you
5	to give both sides a fair trial?
6	PROSPECTIVE JUROR LESCHAK: No.
7	THE COURT: Does anybody think that because of
8	something that has happened, either to yourself or to a close
9	friend or family member, that you would absolutely not be able
10	to set that aside and decide this case just based on the
11	evidence produced in court?
12	(No response.)
13	THE COURT: All right.
14	Ms. Bly, why don't you come on up.
15	Counsel.
16	(Whereupon the Court and counsel and prospective
17	juror confer at the bench, on the record, as follows:)
18	THE COURT: You wanted to take something up?
19	PROSPECTIVE JUROR BLY: I just decided that if it
20	came to me being the last one deciding if he was innocent,
21	that I couldn't fairly do that.
22	THE COURT: Okay. Help me understand.
23	PROSPECTIVE JUROR BLY: If I were to make a
24	decision, I already made -- but I'm just split, so, I mean,
25	there is no reason, I couldn't decide.

PIMA COUNTY SUPERIOR COURT

1   THE COURT: Well, I haven't explained to you any of
2 the constitutional principles that apply. So maybe when we
3 get to that part, if you still think that you're sitting
4 here --
5   PROSPECTIVE JUROR BLY: I'm willing to be, you
6 know --
7   THE COURT: Because as he sits here right now, he's
8 absolutely innocent. Absolutely innocent. He's presumed
9 innocent.
10   PROSPECTIVE JUROR BLY: Yeah.
11   THE COURT: And if you had to render a verdict right
12 now, it would have to be not guilty, because you don't have a
13 shred of evidence; do you understand that?
14   PROSPECTIVE JUROR BLY: Yeah.
15   THE COURT: Do you have any problem with that
16 concept?
17   PROSPECTIVE JUROR BLY: No.
18   THE COURT: Okay. All right. So tell you what, is
19 there something else that's making you --
20   PROSPECTIVE JUROR BLY: No.
21   THE COURT: All right. So --
22   PROSPECTIVE JUROR BLY: Just the nature of the case,
23 just makes me --
24   THE COURT: Okay. And I'm going to venture a guess
25 that it's probably new to you as to everyone else on the jury.

PIMA COUNTY SUPERIOR COURT

1 Is it something about the nature of the case that you think is
2 just going to make it --
3 　　　　　PROSPECTIVE JUROR BLY: No. I can, I will be able
4 to hear out the rest and, you know --
5 　　　　　THE COURT: You're not going to have to see anything
6 in this case. You're not going to have to view a single
7 image.
8 　　　　　I think the only issue in this case is whether
9 Mr. Coghill actually knew that that stuff was at his home and
10 possessed it. There is not any dispute. As long as you don't
11 view the videos, you're not going to have to see a single
12 thing about that. Does that make any difference to you?
13 　　　　　PROSPECTIVE JUROR BLY: That's fine.
14 　　　　　THE COURT: Are you sure?
15 　　　　　PROSPECTIVE JUROR BLY: Um-hum.
16 　　　　　THE COURT: All right.
17 　　　　　Any questions, Mr. Skitzki?
18 　　　　　MR. SKITZKI: No, not right now.
19 　　　　　THE COURT: Mr. Jensvold?
20 　　　　　MR. JENSVOLD: No.
21 　　　　　THE COURT: All right. Ms. Bly, you can have a
22 seat. Thanks.
23 　　　　　(Whereupon proceedings continued in open court, on
24 the record, as follows:)
25 　　　　　THE COURT: Is there anybody who had a "yes" answer

```
 1   that I didn't get on that last question?
 2          Mr. Flores.
 3          PROSPECTIVE JUROR FLORES: Yes. I had a
 4   brother-in-law that was in jail for drug trafficking. And the
 5   case was in California. After all the case was done, we went
 6   through, and I saw it, the law was soft in many situations
 7   like those, and I have been thinking about what you say about
 8   those videos and movies about this person, and kind of made up
 9   my mind that a person just by possessing something is already
10   guilty.
11          THE COURT: Well, let me -- I usually talk about
12   this at the end, but let's talk about it right now.
13          There's some really, really important constitutional
14   principles and constitutional rights that everybody in this
15   country has, including Mr. Coghill. Okay.
16          As Mr. Coghill sits before you right now, he is
17   absolutely innocent. Our Constitution says everybody,
18   everybody is presumed innocent. Simply because the State has
19   filed a piece of paper and says that he's done something
20   wrong, doesn't mean a thing. It does not mean a thing. It's
21   just a way to put someone on notice that the State is alleging
22   that they think he's done something wrong. Okay.
23          The presumption of innocence is so powerful, it is
24   so powerful that Mr. Coghill can sit in this courtroom, as
25   anybody that is a citizen, or not even a citizen but, you
```

know, a non-citizen, that's accused of a crime in this country, they can sit here and they don't have to produce a shred of evidence. They don't have to utter a single word. That's how strong that presumption of innocence is.

Through every second of this trial, through every word that is spoken by both counsel for the State and counsel form Mr. Coghill, he's absolutely presumed innocent.

The only time that presumption lifts and you can even begin contemplating that he's anything other than innocent, is when you get this case as a juror and you retire to the jury room to begin your deliberations. Up to that second in time he's absolutely innocent of what he's been charged with.

The State has to prove he's guilty beyond a reasonable doubt. That's the highest burden that we have in the law.

Does anybody have any problem with any of the constitutional principles that I've just discussed with you?

(No response.)

THE COURT: Does anybody think people shouldn't be presumed innocent, people should have to produce evidence, people should have to testify on their own behalf?

Anybody believe any of that?

(No response.)

THE COURT: Does anybody think the burden of proof

PIMA COUNTY SUPERIOR COURT

is too high? That the State shouldn't have to prove someone guilty beyond a reasonable doubt, that's just way too high.

All right. I see no hands.

So, if Mr. Coghill through his trial exercises his constitutional rights and doesn't present a shred of evidence, and doesn't say a word, does not utter a word, are any of you going to hold that against him and say, well, he must be guilty because he didn't give me any evidence, and he didn't tell me anything? Anybody feel that way?

(No response.)

THE COURT: All right. So Mr. Flores, with that, I guess background information, are you willing to afford Mr. Coghill every constitutional right that he has by virtue of being charged with a crime in this country?

PROSPECTIVE JUROR FLORES: Yeah, I think I do. But I have an opinion that many people use some kind of right and some kind of the law sometimes in many cases just to get around and get a very low punishment, very little punishment for it.

THE COURT: So if you're a juror in this case, what you're going to be deciding is simply whether or not the State has proved its case against Mr. Coghill beyond a reasonable doubt. You don't have to decide punishment. In fact, you'll be instructed you are not even to consider punishment. Your sole duty is to determine what the facts are and apply the law that I give you to see whether or not the State has met its burden of proof.

I mean, so there's lots of opinions that people have about the system and what happens that's good in the system, and what happens that may not be so good in the system. The real question is, setting all those opinions and thoughts aside, can you follow the law that I give you, afford Mr. Coghill every presumption that he is entitled to in this country, and simply decide whether the State has met its burden of proof in this case?

PROSPECTIVE JUROR FLORES: Yeah, I probably wouldn't be fair for me, because I already have, have made my mind up already.

THE COURT: Any objection, Mr. Jensvold?

MR. JENSVOLD: No.

THE COURT: Mr. Skitzki?

MR. SKITZKI: No.

THE COURT: Thank you, Mr. Flores. I appreciate your candor. You can step down and go back down to the first floor and check in with them, sir. Thanks.

THE CLERK: What was his name?

THE COURT: Mr. Flores, Juror number 16.

THE CLERK: Juror number 16, Colleen Boyce.

THE COURT: Did you have any "yes" answers so far?

PROSPECTIVE JUROR BOYCE: Yes. A few years ago I

1 was arrested for misdemeanor assault.

2 THE COURT: Could you step forward just a little
3 bit. The acoustics in this room aren't very good.

4 PROSPECTIVE JUROR BOYCE: Yeah, I have an arrest for
5 domestic violence assault.

6 THE COURT: Anything about that fact that would make
7 it difficult for you to sit fairly in this case?

8 PROSPECTIVE JUROR BOYCE: No.

9 THE COURT: Any other "yes" answers?

10 PROSPECTIVE JUROR BOYCE: No.

11 THE COURT: Okay. Great. Then if you want to take
12 a seat, then, next to Ms. Bly.

13 Have any of you ever served as a member of a grand
14 jury, whether it's federal, state, county? Anybody a grand
15 juror?

16 All right. Ms. Crawford, how long ago was that?

17 PROSPECTIVE JUROR CRAWFORD: My best guess it was
18 back in the 90s. I know for certain it was when the Oklahoma
19 building blew up, because we were in there that day, so that
20 would tell you the year. But I don't recall the date.

21 THE COURT: Anything about that service that would
22 make it difficult for you to be a fair juror in this case?

23 PROSPECTIVE JUROR CRAWFORD: No.

24 THE COURT: Was your grand jury service here in Pima
25 County, or in a different -- here in Pima County?

PIMA COUNTY SUPERIOR COURT

1   PROSPECTIVE JUROR CRAWFORD: Correct.
2   THE COURT: Do any of you, or are any of you,
3 members of your family, or close friend, currently law
4 enforcement officers, or have served as a law enforcement
5 officer?
6   Think broadly, think Customs, Border Patrol,
7 Corrections.
8   All right. Ms. Tucker, Ms. Lane, thank you.
9 Mr. Buntin, Mr. Winkenwerder, Ms. Padilla, Ms. Boyce,
10 Ms. Knew, and Ms. Crawford.
11   Anybody else? I got you, Ms. Knew, thank you.
12   All right. Ms. Tucker, who do you know?
13   PROSPECTIVE JUROR TUCKER: I have a friend who is
14 the Field Operations Supervisor for Homeland Security.
15   THE COURT: Anything about that relationship that
16 would make it difficult for you to sit fairly in this case?
17   PROSPECTIVE JUROR TUCKER: No.
18   THE COURT: And I tell you a lot about why we ask
19 questions, so here's another one where why I tell you why we
20 ask this question. When a law enforcement officer testifies,
21 they are not entitled to any greater weight or believability,
22 or any lesser weight or believability, simply because they're
23 a law enforcement officer.
24   We ask this question to make sure that no matter who
25 the witness is that's testifying before you all, whether a law

PIMA COUNTY SUPERIOR COURT

enforcement officer, a civilian, who ever they are, that you will judge their testimony, and all of their testimony, using the same test for each witness. So no one will have a leg up, and no one will have a leg down, just based on where they work.

Will you be able, Ms. Tucker, to be able to judge all the witnesses in this case using the same test of credibility?

PROSPECTIVE JUROR TUCKER: Yes.

THE COURT: Ms. Lane, who do you know?

PROSPECTIVE JUROR LANE: I had an ex-husband that was a police officer.

THE COURT: Was that here in town, or some other place?

PROSPECTIVE JUROR LANE: I don't know. It was 30 years ago.

THE COURT: Anything about that, that would make it difficult for you to sit fairly in this case?

PROSPECTIVE JUROR LANE: No.

THE COURT: Do you think you'd be able to judge every witness that came before us and use the same test of credibility, regardless of how they're employed?

PROSPECTIVE JUROR LANE: Yes, sir. Yes, ma'am.

THE COURT: Okay.

Ms. Boyce.

                PROSPECTIVE JUROR BOYCE: I have an uncle in New
Jersey who's a cop.
                THE COURT: Does he ever talk about his work with
you?
                PROSPECTIVE JUROR BOYCE: I am not close to him at
tall.
                THE COURT: So I'm guessing that nothing about that
relationship would make it difficult for to you sit fairly
here?
                PROSPECTIVE JUROR LANE: No.
                THE COURT: And do you think you'd be able to judge
all witnesses using the same test of credibility?
                PROSPECTIVE JUROR LANE: Absolutely.
                THE COURT: Mr. Buntin.
                PROSPECTIVE JUROR BUNTIN: My brother works at the
Sheriff's Department for Corrections, and he's a supervising
probation officer in the field.
                THE COURT: Does he ever discuss his work with you?
                PROSPECTIVE JUROR BUNTIN: None of his cases that he
has.
                THE COURT: Anything about that, how your brother --
you said your brother, right?
                PROSPECTIVE JUROR BUNTIN: Yes.
                THE COURT: -- how he's employed, that would make it
difficult for you to sit fairly in this case?

PIMA COUNTY SUPERIOR COURT

1   PROSPECTIVE JUROR: No.
2   THE COURT: Would you be able to listen to all the
3   witnesses and judge them using the same test of credibility?
4   PROSPECTIVE JUROR BUNTIN: Yes.
5   THE COURT: Mr. Winkenwerder.
6   PROSPECTIVE JUROR WINKENWERDER: Yes. My daughter
7   was a special agent for the F.B.I.
8   THE COURT: Okay.
9   PROSPECTIVE JUROR WINKENWERDER: No longer in that
10   position though.
11   THE COURT: All right. Anything about that
12   experience or where your daughter was employed that would make
13   it difficult for you to sit fairly here?
14   PROSPECTIVE JUROR WINKENWERDER: No.
15   THE COURT: Do you think you'd be able to judge all
16   the witnesses using the same test?
17   PROSPECTIVE JUROR WINKENWERDER: Yes, ma'am.
18   THE COURT: Ms. Padilla.
19   PROSPECTIVE JUROR PADILLA: Yes.
20   THE COURT: Who do you know?
21   PROSPECTIVE JUROR PADILLA: My daughter was a
22   Corrections Officer. And I have a cousin that's actually a
23   Corrections Officer now.
24   THE COURT: Anything about those relationships that
25   would make it difficult for you to be a fair juror in this

PIMA COUNTY SUPERIOR COURT

case?

PROSPECTIVE JUROR PADILLA: No.

THE COURT: And do you think you would be able to judge all the witnesses using the same test?

PROSPECTIVE JUROR PADILLA: Yes.

THE COURT: Ms. Crawford.

PROSPECTIVE JUROR CRAWFORD: Two uncles and a cousin back east. We never spoke. I didn't have any exchange on that issue. And two cousins out here, their husbands were in, one was Corrections, and I think the other might have been TPD, but I'm not close.

THE COURT: So I'm taking it that since you're not real close to those folks, that nothing about those relationships would make it hard for you to be a juror here?

PROSPECTIVE JUROR PADILLA: No.

THE COURT: And would you be able to judge all the witnesses using the same test of credibility?

PROSPECTIVE JUROR PADILLA: Yes.

THE COURT: And Ms. Knew.

PROSPECTIVE JUROR KNEW: I know it might be a little broad, but my daughter is a security officer, but she does do drug busts in connection with TPD.

THE COURT: Anything about how your daughter is employed that would make it difficult for you to sit fairly here?

PIMA COUNTY SUPERIOR COURT

1   PROSPECTIVE JUROR KNEW: No.

2   THE COURT: Would you be able to judge all the
3   witnesses using the same test of credibility?

4   PROSPECTIVE JUROR KNEW: Yes.

5   THE COURT: Is there anyone on the jury who doesn't
6   feel like they would be able to judge every witness using the
7   same test?

8   (No response.)

9   THE COURT: Have any of you ever been a witness in a
10   criminal case? No witnesses. Okay.

11   Oh, I am sorry, Ms. Graves.

12   PROSPECTIVE JUROR GRAVES: It was a long time ago.
13   It was a young man, it was a juvenile case, he had broken into
14   our house. And I guess I wasn't a witness per se, but the
15   judge asked me to come up and speak to how disappointed we
16   were with him and everything else. It was a long, long time
17   ago.

18   THE COURT: Anything about that experience that
19   would make it hard for you to sit fairly in this case?

20   PROSPECTIVE JUROR GRAVES: No.

21   THE COURT: Have any of you, any members of your
22   family, ever been a victim of a crime?

23   All right. Ms. Graves, and Ms. Knew, just one
24   second, let me get all the hands first. And Ms. Tucker,
25   Ms. Ouimette, Mr. Winkenwerder.

PIMA COUNTY SUPERIOR COURT

```
 1              Anybody else?  Mr. Korinko, and Mr. Kinsella.
 2              We'll start with you, Mr. Korinko.
 3              PROSPECTIVE JUROR KORINKO:  Breaking and entering of
 4   our house.
 5              THE COURT:  How long ago?
 6              PROSPECTIVE JUROR KORINKO:  Ten years ago.
 7              THE COURT:  Any prosecution at all?
 8              PROSPECTIVE JUROR KORINKO:  Yes.
 9              THE COURT:  And was it a situation, I guess not,
10   where you had to come down to court and testify?  Or was it?
11              PROSPECTIVE JUROR KORINKO:  No, we didn't have to
12   come to court and testify.  It was done without our -- we
13   didn't have to do anything.
14              THE COURT:  Anything about that experience make it
15   difficult for you to sit fairly in this case?
16              PROSPECTIVE JUROR KORINKO:  I don't think so.
17              THE COURT:  Ms. Tucker.
18              PROSPECTIVE JUROR TUCKER:  Breaking and entering,
19   theft.
20              THE COURT:  How long ago was that?
21              PROSPECTIVE JUROR TUCKER:  Thirty years ago.
22              THE COURT:  Do you remember if there was a
23   prosecution?
24              PROSPECTIVE JUROR TUCKER:  There wasn't.  They never
25   found anybody.
```

PIMA COUNTY SUPERIOR COURT

1 THE COURT: Is there anything about that experience
2 that would make it difficult for you to sit fairly here?
3 PROSPECTIVE JUROR TUCKER: No.
4 THE COURT: Ms. Ouimette.
5 PROSPECTIVE JUROR OUIMETTE: My mother was a victim
6 of a purse snatching. There was no one arrested.
7 I was burglarized twice going back about 15 or 20
8 years. And then a couple of years ago, I had an intruder in
9 my house, but it turned out to be a very inebriated college
10 student that my dog took care of, so I didn't press charges.
11 THE COURT: Anything about any of those experiences
12 that would make it difficult for you to sit fairly in this
13 case?
14 PROSPECTIVE JUROR TUCKER: No.
15 THE COURT: Ms. Graves.
16 PROSPECTIVE JUROR GRAVES: I was broken into when I
17 was home, and they never caught him.
18 THE COURT: Anything about that experience make it
19 hard for you to sit as a juror here?
20 PROSPECTIVE JUROR GRAVES: No.
21 THE COURT: Mr. Kinsella.
22 PROSPECTIVE JUROR KINSELLA: I got stabbed a couple
23 of times from a neighbor. I called the police about his
24 music, and they busted him and they took his drugs and stuff,
25 and he got mad.

PIMA COUNTY SUPERIOR COURT

```
 1              THE COURT:  How long ago was that?
 2              PROSPECTIVE JUROR KINSELLA:  That was about 10
 3   years.
 4              THE COURT:  Was there a prosecution?
 5              PROSPECTIVE JUROR KINSELLA:  Yes.
 6              THE COURT:  Anything about that experience make it
 7   hard for you to sit fairly in this particular case?
 8              PROSPECTIVE JUROR KINSELLA:  No.
 9              THE COURT:  Okay.
10              Mr. Winkenwerder.
11              PROSPECTIVE JUROR WINKENWERDER:  Several
12   occurrences.  I had a car broken into about 45 years ago.  I
13   owned a business for a while, it was broken into three times.
14   And then, just a couple of years ago, internet fraud in terms
15   of credit card, where a credit card was fraudulently used.
16              THE COURT:  Anything about those experiences make it
17   hard for you to sit fairly in this case?
18              PROSPECTIVE JUROR WINKENWERDER:  No.
19              THE COURT:  And Ms. Knew.
20              PROSPECTIVE JUROR KNEW:  We just had a prowler for
21   two years that followed us around from three places we lived
22   and we were never able to find.
23              THE COURT:  Anything about that experience make it
24   hard for you to be a juror here?
25              PROSPECTIVE JUROR KNEW:  No.
```

PIMA COUNTY SUPERIOR COURT

THE COURT: The first 26 folks that are seated up here with us, if you could take a look around at your fellow 26 and see if you know anybody. And I always hope I get two hands, because if I don't it's awkward. All right. Everybody is strangers.

All right. At this time, folks, we are going to do the questions that Christina is going to turn around on the board. The bad news is that you're going to have to stand to answer these questions because the acoustics are really poor and the court reporter is going to need to be able to hear everything you say.

When you get to question two that talks about your residence, you don't need to tell us your address. Just give us the general area of town, eastside, northwest, Oro Valley.

And since Mr. Korinko is in lucky seat number one, you get to start us off.

PROSPECTIVE JUROR KORINKO: Okay.

My name is Joseph Korinko. I was born and raised in Chicago, Illinois. Now I live in Vail, Arizona. I have a Bachelor's degree in electrical engineering, and working on a Master's degree in systems engineering currently. Married; I am married with a spouse. My spouse's occupation is a registered nurse. I have five children, two under 21, both are 17. Employed at Raytheon Missile Systems. Past occupation, same sort of work. I worked down in Fort

1 Huachuca. Interests, outdoor activities hiking, fishing,
2 physically active things, sports.
3   Responsibilities, active organizations, memberships.
4 Well, I am active in my church. I don't have any other
5 memberships. Magazines, newspapers read regularly. Probably
6 some outdoor magazines; I don't really subscribe to any. But
7 I get the newspaper on Sunday, the Tucson citizen.
8   Bumper stickers, don't have any. I've never served
9 on a jury.
10   THE COURT: All right. Thank you.
11   Ms. Tucker.
12   PROSPECTIVE JUROR TUCKER: Rosalie Ann Tucker. I
13 was born in Townsend, Massachusetts. Grew up most of my life
14 here in Tucson. I have a Bachelor's degree in communications.
15 Single; no children. Presently I'm a marketing rep for an
16 auto glass and window tint company. Previously I was employed
17 with the phone company; retired after 37-and-a-half years.
18   Interests, I like to play golf, work in the yard,
19 play games on the internet. I am actually an active volunteer
20 for Habitat for Humanity, building homes. I don't read
21 anything regularly except the Parade magazine and the funnies
22 on Sunday. I don't do bumper stickers. And never served on a
23 jury before.
24   THE COURT: Thank you.
25   Mr. Madlambayan. How much closer was that?

1 PROSPECTIVE JUROR MADLAMBAYAN: It was very close;
2 Joel Madlambayan. I was born in the Philippines. And I live
3 like close central. Education, Bachelor of Science in
4 mechanical engineering. Marital status, single. No children.
5 Employment, GHL Architects and Engineers. Hobbies,
6 working out, hiking. I will read like, on the internet,
7 CNN.com.
8 And no bumper stickers. No prior jury service.
9 THE COURT: Great. Thank you.
10 Ms. Syverson.
11 PROSPECTIVE JUROR SYVERSON: Brenda Syverson. I was
12 born in Blue Earth, Minnesota. And I live on the eastside of
13 town. I am pursuing my Bachelor's in Human Services right
14 now. And I am single. I have zero children.
15 I'm employed at Canyon Ranch in Tucson. And my
16 hobbies, pretty much hiking, biking, outdoor activities. And
17 I do not read any magazines or newspapers. And I do not have
18 any bumper stickers.
19 And I served on a jury about four years ago.
20 THE COURT: What kind of case was it?
21 PROSPECTIVE JUROR SYVERSON: It was a drug case.
22 THE COURT: Do you remember your verdict?
23 PROSPECTIVE JUROR SYVERSON: It was not guilty.
24 THE COURT: Okay. Thank you.
25 Ms. Goldsmith.

PIMA COUNTY SUPERIOR COURT

PROSPECTIVE JUROR GOLDSMITH: I am Patricia Goldsmith. I live in the -- I was born in New Jersey, and I live now in Catalina Foothills. I have a Master's degree in nursing. I am married, and my husband is a lawyer. I have three sons under 21, age 12, 14, and 18.

I am presently employed as an assistant professor at the College Of Nursing. And my interest are my children, and their hobbies are my hobbies. I don't have any independent hobbies like most parents.

I do have some professional organizations, including the American and Arizona Public Health Association that I'm a member of. I read the New York Times on line, at night. And Gresham novels. And I have no bumper stickers and no prior jury service.

THE COURT: Thank you.

Ms. Horton.

PROSPECTIVE JUROR HORTON: Hi, I'm Eleanor Horton. I was born in Buffalo, New York, and I now live in Oro Valley. I have a BA in math. I am a widow. I have two children over 21.

Let's see, I'm a retired nuclear analyst. And hobbies are golf, and bridge, and reading. Newspapers and magazines are Newsweek, the Daily Star, USA Today, I read regularly. And I was on a jury a few years ago.

THE COURT: Do you recall what kind of case?

PIMA COUNTY SUPERIOR COURT

PROSPECTIVE JUROR HORTON: It was with a civil case against Walmart.

THE COURT: All right. And do you know if you found for the plaintiff or for the defendant?

PROSPECTIVE JUROR HORTON: For the plaintiff.

THE COURT: Okay. Thank you.

Mr. Bagwell.

PROSPECTIVE JUROR BAGWELL: My name is Donald Bagwell. I was born and raised in Michigan. I currently live in Tucson on the west side of town. I am married, with no children. My spouse's occupation, she also works for IBM. So my employment is IBM, past 25 years. I do technical training, technical support, and technical authorship.

Interests, motorcycle riding. Newspapers and magazines, no subscriptions. I get news and information from the internet, wide variety of different sources there.

No bumper stickers. No prior jury service.

THE COURT: Great. Thank you.

Ms. Ouimette.

PROSPECTIVE JUROR OUIMETTE: I apologize for the sunglasses. I'm under oath, my dog did eat my glasses.

THE COURT: Okay.

PROSPECTIVE JUROR OUIMETTE: Susan Ouimette. I was born in New Hampshire. And right now I live about two miles north of the university. I graduated from the University with a Bachelor's degree in political science. I'm single. No children.

I work in the Eller College Of Management at the University as an academic advisor, and I sometimes teach.

Hobbies, I have to be honest, reality shows and tabloid magazines. I admit to People Magazine at times as well. Well, I think I have a, I have something on my license plate that says, run with the big dogs. And I haven't been on a jury before.

THE COURT: See, most people leave out the People, and the reality type TV.

PROSPECTIVE JUROR OUIMETTE: I am under oath.

THE COURT: We hear a lot of National Geographic.

Ms. Lane.

PROSPECTIVE JUROR LANE: My name is Bess Lane. I was born and raised in South Dakota. And I got smart and moved to where it was warm. I am the slum dog of education. I have a high school plus maybe a year's worth of college. Single, no children. English bulldog.

Employment, 20 years with the phone company, and about 20 years in the travel business. I work at home, though, most of the time. My interests is travel, travel, travel. I watch the news more, and I don't read a lot of magazines at this point in my life. No bumper stickers. And I've never been asked to stay on the jury.

1 THE COURT: Okay.

2 PROSPECTIVE JUROR LANE: Thank you.

3 THE COURT: Thanks, Ms. Lane.

4 Mr. Ratliff.

5 PROSPECTIVE JUROR RATLIFF: My name is Michael
6 Ratliff. I was born and raised here in Tucson. I live on the
7 north side. I finished high school. I'm working on an
8 Associates for automotive tech. I'm single; no kids.

9 I'm a service attendant at a service station. I'm
10 into cars, basketball, hiking, mountain biking. Pretty much
11 the same type of magazines. I don't really read newspapers.
12 No bumper stickers. No prior jury duty.

13 THE COURT: Did you fill out your bracket for like
14 the NCAA thing? Has that come out yet? You didn't fill one
15 of those out?

16 PROSPECTIVE JUROR RATLIFF: No.

17 THE COURT: That's all right. I thought since you
18 were into basketball, I'm sorry, Mr. Ratliff.

19 Did anybody fill one out? A few.

20 Ms. Yoho.

21 PROSPECTIVE JUROR YOHO: My name is Karen Yoho. I
22 was born here in Tucson. I've lived here all my life. I live
23 on the eastside of town. I am a graduate of Rincon. I am
24 widowed. I have three stepchildren. I am a clerk at St.
25 Joe's Hospital.

PIMA COUNTY SUPERIOR COURT

1   My interests would be paper crafts. I am the
2   treasurer and secretary of my homeowner's association.
3   Magazines, Reader's Digest, Women's Magazine, Crafting
4   Magazine. No bumper stickers. No prior jury service.
5   THE COURT: Thank you.
6   PROSPECTIVE JUROR YOHO: You're welcome.
7   THE COURT: Mr. Kinsella.
8   PROSPECTIVE JUROR KINSELLA: My name is Mike
9   Kinsella. I was born in Montana, and raised on Air Bases all
10   across the country. I'm working on a molecular biology
11   Bachelor's in college. Not married. No children. Not
12   employed.
13   I like geology and minerals. I read the on-line
14   news. I don't drive. And I've never been on a jury.
15   THE COURT: All right. Thank you, sir.
16   Mr. Sawyer.
17   PROSPECTIVE JUROR SAWYER: My name is Clark Thomas
18   Sawyer. Born in Fargo, North Dakota. I reside in the central
19   part of Tucson, Arizona. I'm married with one son.
20   I'm the team leader and head mechanic over at Penske
21   Truck Leasing here in Tucson, Arizona.
22   My interests are, I'm a six-time national champion.
23   I have won NHRA and NASCAR. Cam-painting new car in the NHRA
24   magazines, chiefly high performance. I have one next month.
25   And I read National Dragster and NAS Dragster.

PIMA COUNTY SUPERIOR COURT

                 THE COURT: NAS Dragster--
                 PROSPECTIVE JUROR SAWYER: National Dragster.
                 THE COURT: I'm a little slow.
                 PROSPECTIVE JUROR SAWYER: I don't do bumper
stickers. And I've never had any prior service.
                 THE COURT: Thank you, sir.
         Mr. Buntin.
                 PROSPECTIVE JUROR BUNTIN: William Buntin. Tucson
native. I live on the east side. I have got two years of
college. I am married. My wife is a sales director. I have
one child under 21.
         I work for the Groundskeeper. Prior occupation was
for Pima County Department of Transportation. I was a Public
Works manager.
         My interests are outdoor activities. No magazines
or newspapers. I subscribe to on-line news, that type of
thing. No bumper stickers. And no prior jury service.
                 THE COURT: Great. Thank you.
         Ms. Bly.
                 PROSPECTIVE JUROR BLY: My name is Lindsay Bly. I
live in Tucson. I was born in Los Angeles. I was raised in
Tucson. I am single. I went to the University of Arizona,
degree in graphic design. I have no children.
         I am self-employed as a freelance photographer. I
am interested in the human psyche and our affects on one

PIMA COUNTY SUPERIOR COURT

another.

I don't --subscribe to, I subscribe to Esquire Magazine. And no bumper stickers. No prior jury service.

THE COURT: Great. Thank you.

Ms. Boyce.

PROSPECTIVE JUROR BOYCE: Colleen Boyce. I was born in New Jersey. I grew up here in Tucson. I currently live on the east side. I have a Bachelor's degree in English from NAU. I am married; no children.

My husband is a receiving clerk at a local manufacturing company. I am a substitute teacher for Marana Unified School District.

I enjoy working out, reading, being an aunt. I read the weekend newspaper, the New Yorker, Esquire. I have no bumper stickers, and no prior jury service.

THE COURT: Thank you.

Ms. Abrogast? Is that close?

PROSPECTIVE JUROR ABROGAST: Uh-huh.

THE COURT: Did I say it right? Abrogast.

PROSPECTIVE JUROR ABROGAST: My name is Amanda Abrogast. I was born and raised in Pittsburgh, Pennsylvania. I moved out here 10 years ago. I am currently in school for, I just changed my major to business. Third year in school. Single with no children.

I currently work as a pharmacy technician for the

1 last couple of years.
2   My interests would be probably snow boarding and
3 hiking. The only magazines I really read are newspapers and
4 ones that deal with medications, since that's what I do. And
5 then I don't have any bumper stickers or prior jury service.
6   THE COURT: Ms. Graves.
7   PROSPECTIVE JUROR GRAVES: I'm Nina Graves. I was
8 born in Biloxi, Mississippi. I was raised all over the United
9 States and in two foreign countries. I live on the eastside.
10   I have a Bachelor of Science, Business and
11 Administration, and Personnel and Labor Management. I am
12 divorced. I have one son that's over 21 years of age.
13   I work as a sales representative for Standrum (ph)
14 Millworks here in Tucson, construction sales. I am happy I
15 have a job. I love bird watching, gardening, hiking.
16   And magazines, I read the Daily Star. I read AARP
17 Magazine, Tucson Lifestyle. I do like the trash magazines,
18 too, thank you.
19   I do have four bumper stickers. One is political
20 and three of them are military. And I have never served on a
21 jury before.
22   THE COURT: Can you please give us an idea of the
23 one military and ones political.
24   PROSPECTIVE JUROR GRAVES: Sure. One say, I love my
25 soldier. My son is in Afghanistan right now in the Army. And

the political is an Obama Biden ticket.

THE COURT: Great. Thank you.

Ms. Weinstein.

PROSPECTIVE JUROR WEINSTEIN: My name is Laura Weinstein. I was born and raised in Ohio. And I live on the eastside now. I went to school for a diploma program for nursing. I am divorced. I have three children, all over the age of 21.

I work as a home health nurse.

Hobbies and interests, nothing specific. I do read the weekend newspaper. No bumper stickers. And no prior jury service.

THE COURT: Thank you.

And see, now you're going to be mad that I didn't say that before you stood up, you guys in the front row don't necessarily have to stand because we can hear you. But I know those seats are really uncomfortable, so if you want to stand, please do. Feel free.

PROSPECTIVE JUROR WEINSTEIN: Yeah.

THE COURT: You'd have got up anyway, right?

Ms. Kauk.

PROSPECTIVE JUROR KAUK: My name is Rebecca Kauk. I'm originally from South Dakota. I am currently on the eastside. High school grad. Single; no kids.

I work for Skywest Airlines as a fleet service

attendant.

My interests right now are basically to sleep, because I work nights. And my, and the magazines, basically whatever I find on the airplane, because we clean them. No bumper stickers and no prior jury service.

THE COURT: Okay.

Mr. Winkenwerder.

PROSPECTIVE JUROR WINKENWERDER: I'm going to take advantage of the stretch.

Hi. My name is Charles Winkenwerder. I was born in Chicago, Illinois and raised in the suburbs. I hold -- I have a Bachelor's degree in physical sciences, a Master's degree in aviation safety. Married. Three children, all over 21.

I'm retired. Two significant jobs. I'm a retired Air Force Officer, pilot for 24 years. Then I went to work for the Federal Aviation Administration, and I'm retired out of that occupation as the manager in Fargo, North Dakota business, too.

Hobbies, aviation. We like to square dance. We also travel extensively in our RV. I belong to the American Legion, Military Officer's Association, and we read those magazines regularly. Watch the news a lot. Read the news off of the internet. No bumper stickers, and no prior jury service.

THE COURT: Did you ever have to sit on a court

martial proceeding in your time in the military?

PROSPECTIVE JUROR WINKENWERDER: No, I did not.

THE COURT: Okay. Thank you, sir.

Ms. Padilla.

PROSPECTIVE JUROR PADILLA: My name is Stella Padilla. I was born in Tucson. I live on the southwest side. I graduated from high school. I am married.

My spouse works for Zeemax (ph) as a driver. I've got two children over the age of 21. And I'm a guardian, too. One is two, and the other one is nine years old.

I'm employed with Pima County. And I've had a number of, numerous different jobs.

My interests are horses and roping. We only have one newspaper or magazine that we read, and that's the Super Duper. No bumper stickers. And I've never served on a jury.

THE COURT: Do you own horses?

PROSPECTIVE JUROR PADILLA: Yes.

THE COURT: How many?

PROSPECTIVE JUROR PADILLA: Too many. We sell them.

THE COURT: We have an ongoing record here. I know this is totally irrelevant to what's going on, but we have a guy that we think holds the record in our potential jurors. How many do you have?

PROSPECTIVE JUROR PADILLA: We have four.

THE COURT: Okay. He had nine. So I think he still

is our champion. But I have to ask.

Mr. Leschak.

PROSPECTIVE JUROR LESCHAK: My name is Paul Leschak. I'm born and raised in Tucson, Arizona. I currently live on the northwest side of town.

Education, Associate's degree from Pima. Marital status, I'm married. My wife is a stay-at-home mom. We have two kids and an adopted son who is eight, and a little girl who is two.

And I am a real estate agent in a wonderful market. Before that I worked at a restaurant downtown for 10 years.

Interests, I am a graphic designer, own my own T-shirt company and baby gymnastics.

Magazines and newspapers, don't really pay attention to either. My bumper sticker says, begin within. And I've never been on a jury before.

THE COURT: Thank you sir.

PROSPECTIVE JUROR LESCHAK: Yeah.

THE COURT: Mr. Sarikas.

PROSPECTIVE JUROR SARIKAS: My name is Mike Sarikas. I was born and raised in down state Illinois, which is a long way from Chicago.

My education, my undergraduate major was accounting. I have a Master's in an advanced tax degree. I am married. My wife is a volunteer. I have one son who is almost 16 years

1 old.
2   I work as a trustee for the Murphy Trust. My
3 interests are sports and reading. I read the Arizona Daily
4 Star and the Wall Street Journal, New York times, and the
5 Durango Herald on-line. I read Fine magazine, Sports
6 Illustrated, and three or four car magazines. I have no
7 bumper stickers. And I have never been on a jury before.
8   THE COURT: Great. Thank you.
9   Ms. Crawford.
10   PROSPECTIVE JUROR CRAWFORD: My name is Dawn
11 Crawford-Rogers. I am born and raised on Long Island, New
12 York. I live out in Rita Ranch. I've been in Tucson about
13 19-and-a-half years. I have a Bachelor's and Master's in
14 social work. I am married. My husband is now medically
15 retired, but had been an elementary school teacher. I have
16 two children under 21, ages 16 and 18.
17   I am currently employed by CODAC Behavioral Health
18 Services as a social worker. I enjoy spending time with
19 family and friends, reading, being outside, walking, spending
20 time with my animals. And I like to read. I don't subscribe
21 right now to any magazines or newspapers. No bumper stickers.
22   And I was on a Federal Grand Jury back in the mid
23 90s.
24   THE COURT: Ms. Knew.
25   PROSPECTIVE JUROR KNEW: My name is Jayne Knew. I

PIMA COUNTY SUPERIOR COURT

was born in Bedford, Ohio. I was raised in Ohio and here in Tucson. I live over near Rita Ranch. I have some college. I'm married. My husband works for the phone company. He's a splicer. I have five children; they are all over the ages of 21.

I am not working. I am disabled. We do camping and hiking and traveling. We don't belong to any memberships or anything. I don't read any magazines. The only newspapers that I read are on-line when I get a chance, and when, they are the Las Vegas newspaper, the Cleveland newspaper, and the Phoenix and Tucson newspapers.

I have a bumper sticker for the military, a little ribbon.

And I served on a jury in Las Vegas, criminal.

THE COURT: What kind of charges were they?

PROSPECTIVE JUROR KNEW: Kidnapping.

THE COURT: Do you recall your verdict?

PROSPECTIVE JUROR KNEW: Guilty.

THE COURT: All right. Thanks.

So at this time, folks, the lawyers have the opportunity to ask you some questions. They certainly are not required to, but they may if they wish.

Mr. Jensvold, any questions by the State?

MR. JENSVOLD: Yes, Your Honor. Thank you.

I don't have very many in follow-up.

PIMA COUNTY SUPERIOR COURT

1   Mr. Sarikas, you mentioned you know, professionally
2   or personally, Mr. Hirsh and Mr. Unklesbay?
3   PROSPECTIVE JUROR SARIKAS: I just know them around
4   town for some years. I played basketball with Rick some years
5   ago on a team together.
6   MR. JENSVOLD: He never hit you or anything that you
7   would hold --
8   Does anybody as they sit here today think they know
9   what the definition of beyond a reasonable doubt is here in
10 Arizona?
11 PROSPECTIVE JUROR OUIMETTE: That we do?
12 MR. JENSVOLD: Yeah. Do you have an idea of what
13 you think the definition is?
14 PROSPECTIVE JUROR OUIMETTE: Yes.
15 MR. JENSVOLD: Yes, Ms. Ouimette.
16 PROSPECTIVE JUROR OUIMETTE: Oh, gosh, now I'm
17 tongue tied. I knew what it was for a while. A reasonable
18 doubt would mean a witness. So, to me, beyond a reasonable
19 doubt, I can't phrase it any other way, but in percentage.
20 Everything is always possible. So nothing can be proven
21 always an absolute. So I think it's probably a fine line to
22 have to walk between. You never know absolutely, positively,
23 but you have to live with your conscience. And so it boils
24 down to me to letting my conscience lead me at that point.
25 MR. JENSVOLD: Okay. You said some things that were

actually going to be pretty close to what Judge Godoy is going to read you later. However, that's not exactly that there is a definition in Arizona what beyond a reasonable doubt is. In some states they don't give you a definition. They let you all figure it out on your own.

There is a definition, I'm not going to tell you what it is now. But do you have any difficulty in following the specific instruction that Judge Godoy is going to give you as to what beyond a reasonable doubt means?

PROSPECTIVE JUROR OUIMETTE: Me?

MR. JENSVOLD: Yes?

PROSPECTIVE JUROR OUIMETTE: No.

MR. JENSVOLD: Can you set aside whatever you think it might mean today?

PROSPECTIVE JUROR OUIMETTE: Exactly. No, I would follow her lead.

MR. JENSVOLD: Does anybody else think they know what the definition is as you sit here today?

(No response.)

MR. JENSVOLD: Anybody going to have any problem with following the instructions that Judge Godoy is going to give you?

(No response.)

MR. JENSVOLD: Okay.

I want to ask each of you a question. And I'm not

just doing this because I'm just nosey, it does have some
relevance to this. I'm going do ask you what kind of music
you listen to. You'll see why it plays some role here later.
But I just want to ask you know to get an idea. You don't
have to go into a whole bunch of depth, I don't want to know
your whole CD collection or what's on your Ipod.

    Let's start with you, Mr. Korinko?

    PROSPECTIVE JUROR KORINKO: I listen a lot to Christian rock.

    MR. JENSVOLD: Okay. And Ms. Taylor -- Tucker.

    PROSPECTIVE JUROR TUCKER: Jazz, easy listening, contemporary music.

    MR. JENSVOLD: Mr. Madlambayan.

    PROSPECTIVE JUROR MADLAMBAYAN: Alternative rock.

    MR. JENSVOLD: KFMA, that kind of thing?

    PROSPECTIVE JUROR MADLAMBAYAN: Yeah.

    MR. JENSVOLD: Ms. Syverson.

    PROSPECTIVE JUROR SYVERSON: Country, and easy listening.

    MR. JENSVOLD: Ms. Goldsmith?

    PROSPECTIVE JUROR GOLDSMITH: Americana and jazz.

    MR. JENSVOLD: Ms. Horton.

    PROSPECTIVE JUROR HORTON: I like the oldies stations and jazz.

    MR. JENSVOLD: Mr. Bagwell.

1   PROSPECTIVE JUROR BAGWELL: 70s classic rock and
2 Frank Sinatra.
3   MR. JENSVOLD: Ms. Ouimette.
4   PROSPECTIVE JUROR OUIMETTE: Very close. 70s and 80
5 rock. And I have E Street Radio programmed into my car.
6   MR. JENSVOLD: On Sirius?
7   PROSPECTIVE JUROR OUIMETTE: Yes.
8   MR. JENSVOLD: Ms. Lane.
9   PROSPECTIVE JUROR LANE: Easy rock, and then
10 sometimes I like the metaphysical spiritual stuff.
11   MR. JENSVOLD: Mr. Ratliff.
12   PROSPECTIVE JUROR RATLIFF: Mostly rock.
13   MR. JENSVOLD: And Ms. Graves.
14   PROSPECTIVE JUROR GRAVES: Alternative music, new
15 age type stuff, and classic rock.
16   MR. JENSVOLD: Ms. Abrogast.
17   PROSPECTIVE JUROR ABROGAST: A bit of R and B, and
18 country.
19   MR. JENSVOLD: Ms. Boyce.
20   PROSPECTIVE JUROR BOYCE: All country.
21 Experimental, like an alternative version of rock.
22   MR. JENSVOLD: What is all country, just like--
23   PROSPECTIVE JUROR BOYCE: Like an alternative
24 version of rock.
25   MR. JENSVOLD: More rock version.

PIMA COUNTY SUPERIOR COURT

PROSPECTIVE JUROR BOYCE: Well, yeah. So it's like the alternative rock, but country. Like it wouldn't be on the radio.

MR. JENSVOLD: Okay. I got you.

Ms. Bly.

PROSPECTIVE JUROR BLY: Modern pop, rock, easy listening. I used to listen to the Christian station.

MR. JENSVOLD: Mr. Buntin.

PROSPECTIVE JUROR BUNTIN: Yes, sir. County, jazz, classic rock.

MR. JENSVOLD: Mr. Sawyer.

PROSPECTIVE JUROR SAWYER: Classic rock.

MR. JENSVOLD: Like 107, that kind of stuff?

PROSPECTIVE JUROR SAWYER: Yeah. Exactly.

MR. JENSVOLD: Mr. Kinsella.

PROSPECTIVE JUROR KINSELLA: I don't really listen to music. I have some kinds, but that's about it.

MR. JENSVOLD: Ms. Yoho.

PROSPECTIVE JUROR YOHO: Anything but rap.

MR. JENSVOLD: All right. I promise not to play any for you.

PROSPECTIVE JUROR YOHO: Just don't do any.

MR. JENSVOLD: That will definitely never happen.

Ms. Weinstein.

PROSPECTIVE JUROR WEINSTEIN: Country western,

1 classic rock.
2   MR. JENSVOLD: Ms. Kauk.
3   PROSPECTIVE JUROR KAUK: I listen to pretty much
4 anything, but it's mainly rock or alternative.
5   MR. JENSVOLD: Mr. Winkenwerder.
6   PROSPECTIVE JUROR WINKENWERDER: Country music. The
7 50s and 60s, some nice easy listening.
8   MR. JENSVOLD: Ms. Padilla.
9   PROSPECTIVE JUROR PADILLA: I very, very rarely
10 listen to music, but if I do, it's country.
11   MR. JENSVOLD: Mr. Leschak.
12   PROSPECTIVE JUROR LESCHAK: Bob Marley, Jack
13 Johnson, underground, hip hop, stuff like that.
14   MR. JENSVOLD: Underground hip hop.
15   PROSPECTIVE JUROR LESCHAK: Tri-Poled Qwest (ph),
16 just stuff, yeah.
17   MR. JENSVOLD: Mr. Sarikas.
18   PROSPECTIVE JUROR SARIKAS: 50s or 70s, and country
19 western.
20   MR. JENSVOLD: And Ms. Crawford-Rogers.
21   PROSPECTIVE JUROR CRAWFORD-ROGERS: I enjoy jazz,
22 some rock, and have the Mountain on.
23   MR. JENSVOLD: 92.9 FM radio?
24   PROSPECTIVE JUROR CRAWFORD-ROGERS: Uh-huh.
25   MR. JENSVOLD: Ms. Knew.

PIMA COUNTY SUPERIOR COURT

1   PROSPECTIVE JUROR KNEW: I get pretty specific.
2   John Denver, Peter, Paul and Mary, Beach Boys.
3   MR. JENSVOLD: Nothing 80s on?
4   PROSPECTIVE JUROR KNEW: No.
5   MR. JENSVOLD: I think that's all I have.
6   Thank you.
7   THE COURT: Thank you.
8   Mr. Skitzki.
9   MR. SKITZKI: Ladies and gentlemen, I know that the
10   judge asked you early on when we put everybody on the panel,
11   but I think we've had some changes on the panel since then.
12   I want to go back to one of the Judge's questions,
13   which was, is there anybody on the panel in the 26 of you, who
14   doesn't, you know, have any kind of interaction on a daily
15   basis with a computer? Is there anybody in the 26?
16   PROSPECTIVE JUROR: That does not?
17   MR. SKITZKI: That does not. So everybody,
18   everybody has got some connection, either work or at home,
19   with a computer.
20   Is there anybody on the panel who doesn't have a
21   computer at home? So there is Ms. Ouimette and Ms. Graves,
22   you don't have computers at home.
23   Are there people on the panel, and if you could
24   raise your hand, who have never, I don't know, let's say,
25   downloaded anything onto the computer? Is there anybody on

PIMA COUNTY SUPERIOR COURT

1 the panel who's never done anything like that? And that would
2 be Ms. Tucker?
3   PROSPECTIVE JUROR TUCKER: Uh-huh.
4   MR. SKITZKI: You've not downloaded anything?
5   PROSPECTIVE JUROR TUCKER: Well, could you be more
6 specific with your question?
7   MR. SKITZKI: Well, and, you know, let me tell you
8 that my experience with computers is very limited. Everybody
9 apparently here, with the exception of Judge Godoy who
10 volunteered that, is much more -- has a lot more experience by
11 way of computers.
12   I'm impressed if I get -- somebody e-mails me a
13 photograph and I can actually make it show up on my computer.
14 I think that that's an incredible technical accomplishment.
15 So, if you can do anything beyond that, that's what I'm asking
16 for.
17   PROSPECTIVE JUROR TUCKER: I've downloaded programs
18 for work and stuff like that, is what I'm talking about.
19   MR. SKITZKI: Okay. Well, I'm lucky to turn the
20 thing on and have something coming up on the screen.
21   PROSPECTIVE JUROR TUCKER: Okay.
22   MR. SKITZKI: So that's --
23   So everybody on the panel has experience, let's say,
24 surfing the web, would that be fair to say?
25   And, I guess for the record, the majority of the

PIMA COUNTY SUPERIOR COURT

panel nodded their heads to indicate that they do indeed have experience surfing the web.

I know that there were some of you on the panel that talked about getting your news in part via the internet, or reading the newspaper via the internet.

For those of you who do read newspapers and things of that nature on the internet, are there some of you who read, let's say in the local paper where they, you can comment on the articles, or are there people who are familiar with that? If you could raise your hands.

A VOICE: I've seen them.

MR. SKITZKI: Okay. So, I'd say that half of the panel that's indicated that they have experience doing that. And unfortunately I guess I'm going to have to pick somebody to ask the follow-up question to.

Mr. Winkenwerder, you raised your hand and indicated that, you know, that you've read articles where they have the comment section on-line. Have you ever had any experience in yourself commenting on those articles that you've read?

PROSPECTIVE JUROR WINKENWERDER: No, I don't comment on those.

MR. SKITZKI: Do you read the comments?

PROSPECTIVE JUROR WINKENWERDER: Some; limited amounts.

MR. SKITZKI: For entertainment purposes, or just to

```
 1  see if there is some kind of further in depth discussion of
 2  what's going on in that?
 3          PROSPECTIVE JUROR WINKENWERDER: Well, for example,
 4  my central interest is aviation. So if I see an aviation
 5  article that talks about, most recently like the crash in the
 6  river, in New York City, and there'll be some comments on-line
 7  there. I'm looking for the technical aspects of what
 8  happened. So I'll read those comments by folks that I feel
 9  are technically qualified to comment on what really happened
10  to the airplane.
11          MR. SKITZKI: So when you're looking for something
12  like that, you are looking to see if, you know, you're getting
13  some technical insight from some of the readers of the
14  article.
15          PROSPECTIVE JUROR WINKENWERDER: That's correct.
16          MR. SKITZKI: Is there anyone who raised their hand
17  about reading articles where, you know, on-line comments can
18  be made, who's personally gone on-line and entered a comment?
19          And that would be about five or six of you.
20          Mr. Bagwell, can you give us an example of an
21  article that you might have gone on-line and offered a comment
22  on?
23          PROSPECTIVE JUROR BAGWELL: Political web sites,
24  people get into engagements and disagreements back and forth.
25          MR. SKITZKI: So you read those political arguments,
```

1   and then you're sort of interested in the comments to see how
2   the discourse plays back and forth among the commentators.
3   PROSPECTIVE JUROR BAGWELL: Correct.
4   MR. SKITZKI: I'm going to shift gears for a little
5   bit, and I know the Judge asked this question earlier. But is
6   there anyone on the panel who in the course -- if you're asked
7   to sit as a juror on this case, and we get to the end of the
8   case, and Mr. Coghill hasn't testified, is there anyone on
9   this panel who is going to be disturbed or have a problem with
10   the fact that Mr. Coghill did not testify in this case?
11   If I can have a hand if anybody would be
12   uncomfortable with that.
13   Mr. Korinko.
14   PROSPECTIVE JUROR KORINKO: Yes.
15   MR. SKITZKI: Can you tell us why, why would you
16   have a problem with that?
17   PROSPECTIVE JUROR KORINKO: Assuming Mr. Coghill
18   understands the charges against him, I don't see why he
19   wouldn't be ready to refute them and defend himself and put
20   his side of the story on it.
21   MR. SKITZKI: So it's your position that, you know,
22   somebody who's charged with something like this, if they have
23   nothing to hide, they're going to get up on the stand and
24   they're going to testify?
25   PROSPECTIVE JUROR KORINKO: Absolutely.

PIMA COUNTY SUPERIOR COURT

MR. SKITZKI: And if he choses not to do that, is that something that you're going to hold against him back in the jury room afterwards?

PROSPECTIVE JUROR KORINKO: Depending on what I heard as evidence if I'm chosen as a juror, I think that could be the case. If it appears that he could testify and is not willing to, like I say, it depends on some of the evidence presented.

MR. SKITZKI: Okay. Is there anybody else who has that concern?

Ms. Bly.

PROSPECTIVE JUROR BLY: I have very identical concerns.

MR. SKITZKI: So, depending on what the evidence is, if Mr. Coghill choses not to testify, that might be something that you'd hold against him?

PROSPECTIVE JUROR BLY: Depending on the evidence.

MR. SKITZKI: Mr. Madlambayan.

PROSPECTIVE JUROR MADLAMBAYAN: Same.

MR. SKITZKI: Same thing?

PROSPECTIVE JUROR MADLAMBAYAN: Yes.

MR. SKITZKI: Okay.

Ms. Goldsmith.

PROSPECTIVE JUROR GOLDSMITH: Yes.

MR. SKITZKI: Same thing?

PIMA COUNTY SUPERIOR COURT

1	PROSPECTIVE JUROR GOLDSMITH: Same thing.
2	MR. SKITZKI: Okay. Is there anyone else?
3	Okay. Ms. Horton, same reason?
4	PROSPECTIVE JUROR HORTON: I think I might be
5	slightly prejudiced, yes.
6	MR. SKITZKI: And Ms. Lane.
7	PROSPECTIVE JUROR LANE: I would probably question
8	it a little bit, but I would try to be really open-minded and
9	listen to what you advise us, and go by that. I think it
10	would be more my own personal, what -- basically he's trying
11	to hide something. But if I'm instructed not to listen to
12	that, and that's what she already told us, then I would want
13	to go with what I was instructed to do.
14	THE COURT: If I could jump in just a second here?
15	MR. SKITZKI: Sure, Judge.
16	THE COURT: What Ms. Lane brings up is a very good
17	distinction. I mean, I think as individuals we all have ways
18	that we would personally deal with the situation, depending on
19	our personality, depending on how we think about things. But
20	everybody is different, and simply because personally you
21	think, well, you know, I think that should occur, I think
22	someone should testify, doesn't mean that that's what the law
23	is. And, in fact, the law is absolutely contrary to that.
24	It doesn't, what it means is that it goes back to
25	that very, very important principle of being presumed

PIMA COUNTY SUPERIOR COURT

innocent. Because you're presumed innocent, you don't have to do any of that. It's not because you're afraid to. It's not because you're hiding something. It's not for any other reason than you have that right. You can just say, no, I don't want to. And it means nothing more than you have exercised that right.

Folks do that for any number of reasons. Not the least of which is they confer with their lawyers and they said, you know what, and I'm not saying that's the case here, but, based on everything we heard, you know, you shouldn't do this. Sometimes it's based on the advice of counsel, sometimes it's a personal choice.

But at the end of the day what's important is that whatever feelings you have about what somebody should or should not do in terms of being a defendant charged in a case, if I told you the law was you absolutely cannot consider that, you cannot let that affect your choice, your deliberations in any way in this case, would anybody not be able to do that?

In other words, I don't care what you say, I'm going to think about it. I'm going to hold it against him. I don't care what that Constitution says, it's just, I'm done, stick a fork in me.

PROSPECTIVE JUROR KORINKO: I stick with my original answer.

THE COURT: Anybody else? Okay.

1   Ms. Bly. You, too.
2   I'm sorry, Mr. Skitzki.
3   MR. SKITZKI: That's fine.
4   The only other thing I have, are there folks on the
5   jury who watch CSI? If you could raise your hands. About six
6   or seven.
7   Are there folks -- you can lower your hands.
8   Are there folks on the panel who watch lawyer shows?
9   A little more than that.
10   Is there anybody on the panel who is going to expect
11   the lawyers in this case to put on a show like they do on the
12   TV? Because I want to warn you beforehand, that we are going
13   to disappoint you.
14   And there is no hands expecting us to put on a TV
15   show for you. Okay.
16   I don't have any other questions.
17   THE COURT: Counsel want to approach the bench, on
18   the record.
19   (Whereupon the Court and counsel confer at the
20   bench, out of the hearing of the jurors, as follows:)
21   THE COURT: Are you going to have a motion?
22   MR. SKITZKI: I'm going to ask Mr. Korinko and
23   Ms. Bly be excused for cause.
24   MR. JENSVOLD: I have no objection.
25   THE COURT: Anybody else for cause at this point?

PIMA COUNTY SUPERIOR COURT

1   MR. SKITZKI: No.

2   THE COURT: Okay. Thanks.

3   (Whereupon proceedings continued in open court, on
4   the record, as follows:)

5   THE COURT: Mr. Korinko and Ms. Bly, you are both
6   excused. Check back down on the first floor. I think there
7   is still trials going on, so see what they have going on for
8   you, okay.

9   (Whereupon the prospective jurors were excused from
10   service and leaves the courtroom.)

11   THE CLERK: For juror seat number one, Jessica
12   Snider.

13   THE COURT: Hi. You thought it was winding down,
14   didn't you?

15   PROSPECTIVE JUROR SNIDER: The only answer I have a
16   "yes" to is I'm a full-time student, so starting Monday it's
17   going to be difficult.

18   THE COURT: Why don't you come on up. I can't hear
19   you very well, I'm sorry.

20   PROSPECTIVE JUROR SNIDER: I am a full-time student,
21   so come Monday I'm not able to miss classes.

22   THE COURT: All right. What are your class
23   schedules like on Tuesday and Wednesday?

24   PROSPECTIVE JUROR SNIDER: I'm taking seven classes,
25   so I'm busy all day.

PIMA COUNTY SUPERIOR COURT

```
 1          THE COURT:  Okay.
 2          Mr. Jensvold, any objection?
 3          MR. JENSVOLD:  No.
 4          THE COURT:  Mr. Skitzki?
 5          MR. SKITZKI:  No.
 6          THE COURT:  You're excused, Ms. Snider.
 7          Head back down to the first floor, ma'am.
 8          (Whereupon the prospective juror was excused from
 9   service and leaves the courtroom.)
10          THE CLERK:  For seat number one, Zanley Fonoti.
11          THE COURT:  Is Zanley Fonoti here?
12          Mr. Fonoti, did you have any "yes" answers, sir?
13          PROSPECTIVE JUROR FONOTI:  No.
14          THE COURT:  Okay.  Great.  Why don't you come up and
15   take that seat over there next to Ms. Tucker, and I'll get
16   back to you in just a minute.  Okay.
17          THE CLERK:  For seat number 15, William Trawick.
18          THE COURT:  Mr. Trawick?
19          PROSPECTIVE JUROR TRAWICK:  Trawick.
20          THE COURT:  Hi, Mr. Trawick.  How are you?
21          PROSPECTIVE JUROR TRAWICK:  Good.  How about you?
22          THE COURT:  I'm doing well, thank you, sir.
23          Did you have any "yes" answers, Mr. Trawick?
24          PROSPECTIVE JUROR TRAWICK:  I did.  Actually
25   several.
```

PIMA COUNTY SUPERIOR COURT

```
 1          THE COURT:  Why don't you come on up so we can hear
 2   you a little bit better.
 3          PROSPECTIVE JUROR TRAWICK:  First one, same as
 4   Ms. Snider, I'm a full-time student, going for my teaching
 5   credentials, last semester.
 6          THE COURT:  So you need to be there?
 7          PROSPECTIVE JUROR TRAWICK:  Yeah.
 8          THE COURT:  Any objection, Mr. Jensvold?
 9          MR. JENSVOLD:  No.
10          THE COURT:  Mr. Skitzki?
11          MR. SKITZKI:  No, Your Honor.
12          THE COURT:  Well, good luck, Mr. Trawick.
13          PROSPECTIVE JUROR TRAWICK:  Thank you.
14          THE COURT:  Report back down to the first floor.
15   Thank you, sir.
16          THE CLERK:  Seat number 15, Larry Olson.
17          PROSPECTIVE JUROR OLSON:  How are you?
18          THE COURT:  I'm well.
19          Did you any "yes" answers?
20          PROSPECTIVE JUROR OLSON:  Work.  I'm a contractor
21   and we have a house starting in St. David on Monday, so I've
22   got to get my guys down there.
23          THE COURT:  And if you don't show up for work, do
24   you get paid for being there?
25          PROSPECTIVE JUROR OLSON:  I haven't been paid in a
```

PIMA COUNTY SUPERIOR COURT

```
 1  month, so yes, that's --
 2          THE COURT:  Well, you head on down to St. David.
 3          Unless counsel have an objection?
 4          MR. JENSVOLD:  No.
 5          MR. SKITZKI:  No.
 6          THE COURT:  No objection by either.  But first,
 7  before you go to St. David, go back and check in with the Jury
 8  Commissioner, okay.  They might have a different idea of where
 9  you're going to be.
10          THE CLERK:  Wendy Weiss.
11          THE COURT:  Hi, Ms. Weiss.
12          PROSPECTIVE JUROR WEISS:  Hi.
13          THE COURT:  How are you?
14          PROSPECTIVE JUROR WEISS:  I have a few yeses.
15          THE COURT:  Okay.
16          PROSPECTIVE JUROR WEISS:  The first is in connection
17  with the lawyer.  My husband is an attorney.  He's retired,
18  faculty member for the U of A, and he's working part-time for
19  a firm, not in criminal.
20          Yes, to anybody close ever accused or convicted of a
21  crime.  A cousin of mine, also an attorney, went to jail for,
22  I don't know if it was embezzling, but, anyway, that was that.
23          Yes, I have been on prior juries.  Do I respond to
24  those?
25          THE COURT:  Not the board yet.
```

PIMA COUNTY SUPERIOR COURT

```
 1              PROSPECTIVE JUROR WEISS:  And I think, in terms of
 2   having an opinion about this case, what you asked early on, as
 3   I understood it this case is about internet stuff.  It's not
 4   about, the internet stuff is not about victims on the spot.
 5              THE COURT:  Correct.
 6              PROSPECTIVE JUROR WEISS:  Then I think I can be
 7   fair.
 8              THE COURT:  Two questions for you.
 9              PROSPECTIVE JUROR WEISS:  Yes.
10              THE COURT:  The fact that I think you said your
11   spouse is an attorney.
12              PROSPECTIVE JUROR WEISS:  Yes.
13              THE COURT:  Anything about that cause you any
14   difficulty in this case?
15              PROSPECTIVE JUROR WEISS:  I don't think so.
16              THE COURT:  You would be able to follow the law that
17   I give you?
18              PROSPECTIVE JUROR WEISS:  I think so.
19              THE COURT:  And then I think you said that you knew
20   someone who had been charged with an offense.
21              PROSPECTIVE JUROR WEISS:  Yes.
22              THE COURT:  Anything about that experience make it
23   difficult for you to sit as a juror here?
24              PROSPECTIVE JUROR WEISS:  Unh-uh.
25              THE COURT:  I'm not sure which seat we have on
```

PIMA COUNTY SUPERIOR COURT

1 there. It's the hardest one to get to. I'm sorry, Ms. Weiss.
2   All right. Mr. Fonoti, we need you to do the board,
3 sir. Can you see it where you're seated? Because I can turn
4 it for you, if you want.
5   PROSPECTIVE JUROR FONOTI: My name Zanley Fonoti. I
6 reside on the eastside. I was born in Hawaii, raised in
7 Afega, Samoa. I have a Bachelor's in psychology. I am
8 married. My wife is a RN. No children. I am a contractor.
9   Hobbies are hunting. I don't read magazines or
10 newspapers. No bumper stickers. And no prior jury service.
11   THE COURT: All right. Great.
12   And, Ms. Weiss, if you could do the board as well.
13   PROSPECTIVE JUROR WEISS: Wendy Weiss. Born in the
14 Philadelphia area, raised there. Been in Tucson for 16 years,
15 live in Sabino Canyon. I have a Master's in social work. I
16 am married, as I said. My kids are all, two kids, and,
17 they're all over, close to 40.
18   I'm retired. I was a clinical social worker, family
19 and marriage therapist in private practice, retired about
20 two-and-a-half years ago. Previously a social work director
21 when we lived in New Jersey in private practice.
22   Interests, hobbies; outdoor cycling, hiking, travel.
23 Doing some volunteer work now, some with hospice, some with
24 the local family services agency, Family and Children.
25   Still a member of social work organizations and

PIMA COUNTY SUPERIOR COURT

family therapy organization. Read the Star, the Journal periodically, the New Yorker, occasionally stuff on-line. No bumper stickers on my car.

And I have been on two previous juries, one criminal, one, I guess civil, medical malpractice. Medical malpractice was settled, and that was in New Jersey. And the criminal one here was a student at U of A, DUI charge, and it was not guilty.

THE COURT: All right. So this is the last question, I promise. Well, I hope it's the last question. We've asked you lots of questions here this morning and this afternoon.

Are any of you sitting there thinking, wow, there is something these folks need to know about me, but they just haven't asked the right question? Something that you think could touch on your qualifications, or you think that we need to know about you but we just simply haven't asked you the right question.

Because in about 30 seconds I'm going to make these folks in the back really excited, because I'm going to let them all go back down to the first floor and check in.

Ms. Goldsmith?

PROSPECTIVE JUROR GOLDSMITH: I don't want to whine. But I have a, feel a strong sense of urgency to be at work next week. I mean, you can have my whole Spring break. But to not be at work next week, I have students that are, the rest of the semester is depending on decisions we make next week, so I am really panicked right now.

And I feel that I'm going to be just wanting to do whatever I can to get it done. So as much as I want to give an honest and a fair trial, I am just really panicked.

THE COURT: Okay. Counsel approach, please.

(Whereupon the Court and counsel confer at the bench, out of the hearing of the jurors, as follows:)

THE COURT: Do you guys have an opinion of Ms. Goldsmith?

MR. SKITZKI: I think if she doesn't want to be here, she's going to want to get out of here quick. I would be much more comfortable if we would excuse her.

MR. JENSVOLD: That's fine with me.

THE COURT: Okay. Great.

(Whereupon proceedings continued in open court, on the record, as follows:)

THE COURT: All right, Ms. Goldsmith, we are going to excuse you, ma'am. Head back down to the first floor. They might have another trial that they'll send you to, okay. No guarantees.

(Whereupon the prospective juror was excused from service and leaves the courtroom.)

THE CLERK: For seat number five, Angelita Doss.

```
 1          THE COURT:  Ms. Doss.  You were about to be really
 2   happy, huh?
 3          Ms. Doss, did you have any "yes" answers?
 4          PROSPECTIVE JUROR DOSS:  I have about seven yeses,
 5   Your Honor.
 6          THE COURT:  Okay.  Why don't you come up a little
 7   closer so we can all hear you, okay?
 8          PROSPECTIVE JUROR DOSS:  First one is financial
 9   hardship.  Your Honor, I'm self-employed.  I'm a real estate
10   agent and I do have a client that wants to make an offer on a
11   house.  And if I can't make it in, I lose a client.
12          THE COURT:  Mr. Jensvold?
13          MR. JENSVOLD:  I don't have an objection.
14          THE COURT:  Mr. Skitzki?
15          MR. SKITZKI:  No objection.
16          THE COURT:  Thank you, Ms. Doss.
17          We will excuse you, ma'am.  Head back down to the
18   first floor.
19          PROSPECTIVE JUROR DOSS:  Thank you.
20          (Whereupon the prospective juror was excused from
21   service and leaves the courtroom.)
22          THE CLERK:  For seat number five, Lester Josephson.
23          THE COURT:  Hi, Mr. Josephson.  You have some "yes"
24   answers for us?
25          PROSPECTIVE JUROR JOSEPHSON:  No, I don't.
```

PIMA COUNTY SUPERIOR COURT

1   THE COURT: We have a seat for you then. The second
2 hardest one to get to, I'm so sorry.
3   And we won't let you get comfortable, sir. We'll
4 have you do the board as soon as you get there. Okay?
5   PROSPECTIVE JUROR JOSEPHSON: Thank you.
6   THE COURT: Thank you.
7   PROSPECTIVE JUROR JOSEPHSON: Okay. My name is
8 Lester Josephson. Born and raised in Minnesota. I live on
9 the northwest side. I have a Bachelor's degree in education,
10 as well as about a year-and-a-half of law school. Married.
11 My wife is retired. We have three kids, all over 21. And
12 nine grandkids.
13   Presently I'm a loan officer in the mortgage
14 business. In many years past, played professional football.
15 Play golf. I'm active on the church council of Our Saviors
16 Lutheran Church here in town. Read the Daily Star, as well as
17 numerous on-line papers. No bumper stickers.
18   And I've been on, I believe, five juries.
19   THE COURT: Any of those criminal?
20   PROSPECTIVE JUROR JOSEPHSON: Yeah. One of them
21 was.
22   THE COURT: Do you recall what the charges were?
23   PROSPECTIVE JUROR JOSEPHSON: I'll be honest with
24 you, no. It's been six or seven years ago.
25   THE COURT: Do you recall your verdict?

PIMA COUNTY SUPERIOR COURT

```
 1        PROSPECTIVE JUROR JOSEPHSON:  Convicted.
 2        THE COURT:  All right.  And you said you played pro
 3   football?
 4        PROSPECTIVE JUROR JOSEPHSON:  Yeah.
 5        THE COURT:  Where did you play?
 6        PROSPECTIVE JUROR JOSEPHSON:  Los Angeles, when they
 7   had a team.
 8        THE COURT:  So you were, were they the Rams?  You
 9   were a Ram?
10        PROSPECTIVE JUROR JOSEPHSON:  Yeah.
11        THE COURT:  And you said you went to law school for
12   about a year-and-a-half.  Anything about that experience make
13   it hard for you to sit fairly here?
14        PROSPECTIVE JUROR JOSEPHSON:  Not really.  There is,
15   there is some frustrating parts of law school, as you're well
16   aware of.
17        THE COURT:  I still haven't forgotten.
18        PROSPECTIVE JUROR JOSEPHSON:  It was a conflict with
19   my professional athletic career that, well, I had too many
20   surgeries.  I couldn't keep up with law school.
21        THE COURT:  Okay.
22        Does anybody have a "yes" answer to what I call the
23   magic question?  Something that we just haven't asked you
24   about, but you think we need to know about you.
25        Ms. Lane.
```

PIMA COUNTY SUPERIOR COURT

1   PROSPECTIVE JUROR LANE: I think I need to say this
2   because everybody has a right to make their own decision. I
3   get psychic pictures, and I do do some, some psychic reading.
4   And, you know, I just don't want that to be an issue.
5   THE COURT: And so long as you promise us that you
6   will make your decision in this case just based on what you
7   hear in the courtroom, and the law that I give to you.
8   PROSPECTIVE JUROR LANE: Yes, I will.
9   THE COURT: Okay. All right.
10   Anybody else?
11   Ms. Padilla.
12   PROSPECTIVE JUROR PADILLA: I'm a guardian of two
13   kids, and one of them was molested. And that's why I ended up
14   with a two year old. I just wanted to make sure that it
15   doesn't involve young children.
16   THE COURT: It involves nothing involving molest of
17   young children that they have alleged that this defendant did.
18   It's of nothing like that. It's simply the possession of
19   images, for lack of a better word, are child pornographic type
20   images. That's what it is.
21   Any other any other "yes" answers?
22   Mr. Ratliff.
23   PROSPECTIVE JUROR RATLIFF: You said that this might
24   go into next week, to Wednesday?
25   THE COURT: Potentially.

PIMA COUNTY SUPERIOR COURT

1   PROSPECTIVE JUROR RATLIFF: I might find it
2 difficult to concentrate. I have exams next week when school
3 starts up again.
4   THE COURT: All right. When do your exams start?
5   PROSPECTIVE JUROR RATLIFF: Tuesday evening. It's
6 going to be after this.
7   THE COURT: All right. There's a really good chance
8 that the evidence will wrap up on Friday of this week, but at
9 the very latest you will hear arguments on this and be
10 deliberating. So Wednesday is just kind of a cautious day
11 that we're letting you know of. If you have to come back on
12 Wednesday, it would simply be to continue to deliberate in the
13 event that you haven't reached a verdict. Does that help you
14 out at all? Wednesday is pretty much just, a just in case. I
15 know that's a lot of justs, but does that help you out?
16   PROSPECTIVE JUROR RATLIFF: Yeah.
17   THE COURT: All right.
18   So, you folks whose names have not been called --
19 wait, before I do that, does the State pass the panel?
20   MR. JENSVOLD: Your Honor, could I ask a question
21 based on what I think Ms. Weiss said, and Ms. Padilla raises a
22 question that I had.
23   THE COURT: Why don't you come on up.
24   Counsel approach.
25   (Whereupon the Court and counsel confer at the

PIMA COUNTY SUPERIOR COURT

bench, out of the hearing of the jurors, as follows:)

MR. JENSVOLD: Just the way that Ms. Padilla stated, and the way that Ms. Weiss said, that as long as there are no actual victims they'll be okay. Well, it just made me think of what about the reverse, whether anybody doesn't think that the mere possession of these things should be illegal. The way Ms. Weiss asked it just made me a bit concerned. Not necessarily Ms. Padilla.

THE COURT: All right. I'll ask that.

(Whereupon proceedings continued in open court, on the record, as follows:)

THE COURT: So this is the last question.

Do any of you sitting there -- are any of you sitting there thinking that someone should be allowed to possess child pornography? That that should be legal? Any of you feel that it should be legal; that you should be allowed to possess it if you want to?

Ms. Ouimette.

PROSPECTIVE JUROR OUIMETTE: I'm not saying that it should be allowed, but I am fussy on -- obviously you would explain the law.

THE COURT: Yes.

PROSPECTIVE JUROR OUIMETTE: That's all.

THE COURT: All right. And you don't need to know what the law is relating to it, we just wanted to know if

PIMA COUNTY SUPERIOR COURT

anybody has an opinion. Like some people think marijuana should be legal. This is the same kind of question. Do any of you think possessing child pornography should be legal?

All right. I see no hands.

Mr. Jensvold, pass the panel?

MR. JENSVOLD: Yes.

THE COURT: Yes, Mr. Madlambayan.

PROSPECTIVE JUROR MADLAMBAYAN: Could you define child pornography? Everybody has a different definition.

THE COURT: Well, I'll define it if you're a juror in this case. I'll let you know what it is. Essentially, it is, in this case it would be a visual depiction, either a movie, or a video, or an image that was somehow taken from a computer, showing people that are under a certain age engaged in either exploitive exhibition or in some sort of sexual conduct.

All right, Ms. Padilla?

PROSPECTIVE JUROR PADILLA: Yeah, I would assume that would be against the law, wouldn't it?

THE COURT: Well, it is. But I'm asking you -- some people think certain things shouldn't be against the law. And I'm wondering if anybody thinks this is one of the things that people believe shouldn't be against the law.

PROSPECTIVE JUROR PADILLA: Oh.

THE COURT: Okay.

PIMA COUNTY SUPERIOR COURT

1   All right. Mr. Jensvold, pass the panel?
2   MR. JENSVOLD: Yes.
3   THE COURT: Mr. Skitzki?
4   MR. SKITZKI: Yes.
5   THE COURT: So you folks in the back, I'm going to
6   go ahead and excuse you. You have to report back down to the
7   first floor, check in with the Jury Commissioner.
8   Thank you all for your time and attention.
9   JURORS: You're welcome.
10 (Whereupon the nonselected prospective jurors are
11 excused and leave the courtroom.)
12 THE COURT: And for the 26 of you that are here,
13 passing the panel essentially means both sides have found you
14 to be fair and impartial jurors. So what they are going to do
15 over the course of the next -- do you guys need about 30
16 minutes?
17 MR. JENSVOLD: Yes.
18 THE COURT: 30 minutes, are make selections about
19 who is actually going to be the jurors that hear the case. So
20 why don't I excuse you until about 3:15. Meet outside where
21 we've been having you meet.
22 Remember not to talk about the case. Don't speak
23 with anyone about the case. And I'll see you back in about 30
24 minutes or so. Okay.
25 (2:45 p.m. Whereupon the prospective jurors are

excused and leave the courtroom, and proceedings continue in their absence, as follows:)

THE COURT: All right. Show the absence of the jury, the presence of both counsel and Mr. Coghill.

Anything we need to take up before you do your strikes?

MR. JENSVOLD: I don't think so.

THE COURT: We'll see you in a bit then.

We're off the record.

(2:45 p.m. Whereupon proceedings were recessed while counsel exercised their right of peremptory challenge.)

(Whereupon proceedings resumed, as follows:)

THE COURT: Back on the record in James Prentiss Coghill, 2004-2573.

The record will show the absence of the jury. The presence of both counsel, and Mr. Coghill is present as well.

Before we bring the jurors back in, any objection to the preliminary instructions, Mr. Jensvold?

MR. JENSVOLD: No, Your Honor.

THE COURT: Mr. Euchner?

MR. EUCHNER: No, Your Honor.

THE COURT: And I just want to make sure that I have the correct -- when I read the indictment to the jury, do you want me to read the file that it was located in, which really isn't part of the charge? Can I just say located in the

```
 1  listed file?
 2          MR. JENSVOLD: I think that's fine.
 3          MR. EUCHNER: Yes, Your Honor. That's fine.
 4          THE COURT: Great. Bring in the jury then.
 5          (3:20 p.m. Prospective jurors now present.)
 6          THE COURT: Come on in folks and have a seat in the
 7  back.
 8          Counsel, thanks. You can be seated.
 9          Mr. Coghill.
10          All right, folks, what's going to happen now is the
11  clerk is going to call the names of the jurors who have been
12  selected to try this case, or hear this case actually.
13          When your name is called, please come forward and
14  Christina will show you where you need to be seated.
15          THE CLERK: Zanley Fonoti.
16          THE COURT: Come on up, sir.
17          THE CLERK: Rosalie Tucker. Lester Josephson.
18  Donald Bagwell. Karen Yoho. Clark Sawyer. William Buntin.
19  Colleen Boyce. Charles Winkenwerder. Paul Leschak. John
20  Sarikas. Dawn Crawford-Rogers, and Jayne Knew.
21          THE COURT: All right.
22          For you folks whose names were not called, we truly
23  thank you for your time and attention in answering all our
24  questions today. You're excused.
25          Please go down to the first floor and check in.
```

PIMA COUNTY SUPERIOR COURT

1 They might still have a place where they need you to be.
2   Thank you.
3   (Whereupon the nonselected prospective jurors are
4 excused and leave the courtroom.)
5   THE COURT: All right. And for the 16 folks, can
6 you hear me without the microphone? For the 16 folks who have
7 been selected to be trial jurors, if you would all please
8 stand, and we are going to administer the trial juror oath.
9   (Whereupon the jurors were duly sworn to try the
10 case.)
11   THE COURT: Go ahead and take your seats.
12   All of you should have found on your chairs your
13 juror notebooks. Inside the juror notebooks are some things
14 that we're going to go over right now.
15   The first thing I'm going to do is I'm going to read
16 the indictment to you, and I'm going to tell you the
17 defendant's plea to these charges.
18   Again, remember this indictment is not evidence
19 whatsoever against the defendant and he's plead not guilty to
20 all of these charges.
21   Omitting the formal caption:
22   The Grand Jurors of the County of Pima, and in the
23 name of the State of Arizona, and by its authority accuses
24 James Prentiss Coghill, and charge that in Pima County: Count
25 one, sexual exploitation of a minor under 15, a dangerous

crime against children; on or about the 1st day of April, 2003, James Prentiss Coghill knowingly committed sexual exploitation of a minor by possessing, receiving, or exchanging any visual depiction in which a minor under 15 years of age is engaged in exploitive exhibition or other sexual conduct, to wit: a video and/or movie showing an adult male, perhaps female, performing oral sex on a prepubescent girl, and an adult male engaging in penile/vaginal intercourse with a prepubescent female, located on the listed file.

Count Two, sexual exploitation of a minor under 15, a dangerous crime against children. On or about the 1st day of April, 2003, James Prentiss Coghill knowingly committed sexual exploitation of a minor by possessing, receiving, or exchanging any visual depiction in which a minor, under 15 years of age, is engaged in exploitive exhibition or other sexual conduct, to wit: a video and/or movie depicting a prepubescent female performing oral sex on an adult male, contained on the listed file.

Count three, sexual exploitation of a minor under 15, a dangerous crime against children. On or about the 1st day of April, 2003, James Prentiss Coghill knowingly committed sexual exploitation of a minor by possessing, receiving, or exchanging any visual depiction in which a minor under 15 years of age is engaged in exploitive exhibition or other sexual conduct, to wit: a video and/or movie depicting a prepubescent girl masturbating and having a dildo inserted into her anus, contained on the listed file.

Count four, sexual exploitation of a minor under 15, a dangerous crime against children. On or about the 1st day of April, 2003, James Prentiss Coghill knowingly committed sexual exploitation of a minor by possessing, receiving, or exchanging any visual depiction in which a minor under 15 years of age is engaged in exploitive exhibition or other sexual conduct, to wit: a video and/or movie depicting an adult male attempting to vaginally penetrate a prepubescent female, contained on the listed file.

Count five, sexual exploitation of a minor under 15, a dangerous crime against children. On or about the 1st day of April, 2003, James Prentiss Coghill knowingly committed sexual exploitation of a minor by possessing, receiving, or exchanging any visual depiction in which a minor under 15 years of age is engaged in an exploitive exhibition or other sexual conduct, to wit: a video and/or movie depicting two prepubescent males masturbating each other, and an adult male, contained on the listed file.

Count six, sexual exploitation of a minor under 15, a dangerous crime against children. On or about the 1st day of April, 2003, James Prentiss Coghill knowingly committed sexual exploitation of a minor by possessing, receiving, or exchanging any visual depiction in which a minor under 15 years of age is engaged in exploitive exhibition or other sexual conduct, to wit: a video and/or movie depicting a prepubescent female performing oral sex on an adult male, contained on the listed file.

Count Seven, sexual exploitation of a minor under 15, a dangerous crime against children. On or about the 1st day of April, 2003, James Prentiss Coghill knowingly committed sexual exploitation of a minor by possessing, receiving, or exchanging any visual depiction in which a minor under 15 years of age is engaged in exploitive exhibition or other sexual conduct, to wit: a video and/or movie depicting an adult male ejaculating into the mouth of a prepubescent female, contained on the listed file.

Count eight, sexual exploitation of a minor under 15, a dangerous crime against children. On or about the 1st day of April, 2003, James Prentiss Coghill knowingly committed sexual exploitation of a minor by possessing, receiving, or exchanging any visual depiction in which a minor under 15 years of age is engaged in exploitive exhibition or other sexual conduct, to wit: a video and/or movie depicting a prepubescent female masturbating, then performing oral sex on an adult male, contained on the listed file.

Count nine, sexual exploitation of a minor under 15, a dangerous crime against children. On or about the 1st day of April, 2003, James Prentiss Coghill knowingly committed

PIMA COUNTY SUPERIOR COURT

sexual exploitation of a minor by possessing, receiving, or exchanging any visual depiction in which a minor under 15 years of age is engaged in exploitive exhibition or other sexual conduct, to wit: a video and/or movie depicting a prepubescent female stripping, displaying her genitals, and performing oral sex on an adult male, contained on the listed file.

Count 10, sexual exploitation of a minor under 15, a dangerous crime against children. On or about the 1st day of April, 2003, James Prentiss Coghill knowingly committed sexual exploitation of a minor by possessing, receiving, or exchanging any visual depiction in which a minor under 15 years of age is engaged in exploitive exhibition or other sexual conduct, to wit: a video and/or movie depicting an adult male ejaculating into the mouth of partially clothed prepubescent female, contained on the listed file.

Count 11, sexual exploitation of a minor under 15, a dangerous crime against children. On or about the 1st day of April, 2003, James Prentiss Coghill knowingly committed sexual exploitation of a minor by possessing, receiving, or exchanging any visual depiction in which a minor under 15 years of age is engaged in exploitive exhibition or other sexual conduct, to wit: a video and/or movie depicting a bound prepubescent female vaginally, anally, and digitally penetrated by an adult male, contained on the listed file.

PIMA COUNTY SUPERIOR COURT

Sexual exploitation of a minor under 15, a dangerous crime against children, count 12. On or about the 1st day of April, 2003, James Prentiss Coghill knowingly committed sexual exploitation of a minor by possessing, receiving, or exchanging any visual depiction in which a minor under 15 years of age is engaged in exploitive exhibition or other sexual conduct, to wit: a video and/or movie depicting a prepubescent female performing oral sex on an adult male, contained in the listed file.

Count 13, sexual exploitation of a minor under 15, a dangerous crime against children. On or about the 1st day of April, 2003, James Prentiss Coghill knowingly committed sexual exploitation of a minor by possessing, receiving, or exchanging any visual depiction in which a minor under 15 years of age is engaged in exploitive exhibition or other sexual conduct, to wit: a video and/or movie depicting a prepubescent female performing oral sex on an adult male, contained in the listed file.

Count 14, sexual exploitation of a minor under 15, a dangerous crime against children. On or about the 1st day of April, 2003, James Prentiss Coghill committed sexual exploitation of a minor by possessing, receiving, or exchanging any visual depiction in which a minor under 15 years of age is engaged in exploitive exhibition or other sexual conduct, to wit: a video and/or movie depicting a prepubescent female taking off her underwear, masturbating, and being vaginally penetrated by an adult male, contained in the listed file.

Count 15, sexual exploitation of a minor under 15 in the second degree, a preparatory crime against children. On or about the 1st day of April, 2003, James Prentiss Coghill knowingly committed sexual exploitation of a minor in the second degree by attempting to receive, exchange, or possess, any visual depiction in which a minor under 15 years of age is engaged in exploitive exhibition or other sexual conduct, to wit: a video and/or movie depicting multiple scenes of prepubescent males and females engaged in various sexual acts with each other, contained on the listed file.

To each of these counts, members of the jury, the defendant has pled not guilty.

Now, also contained in your notebook are the preliminary jury instructions, and I'm going to read those for you now.

PRELIMINARY JURY INSTRUCTIONS

To help assure a fair trial, you are required to follow the Court's instructions. You will receive preliminary instructions at the beginning of trial, and additional instructions after you have heard all the evidence. If you have any questions about these instructions, do not hesitate to ask for clarification.

PIMA COUNTY SUPERIOR COURT

Juror conduct. This is what I call the admonition. The following rules govern your conduct as jurors. Keep an open mind. Do not form any opinions until you have heard all the evidence, the final instructions, and the closing arguments.

Do not discuss the case. You will be expected to discuss the case openly with your fellow jurors during deliberations. Until that time, do not discuss the case with anyone. Also, do not let anyone discuss the case with you or in your presence.

If you are approached by someone or accidentally overhear something, please report it to the bailiff.

Avoid contact with lawyers, parties, and witnesses. While it is natural and acceptable to say "Hello", anything beyond that might be construed as evidence of bias on your part.

Wear your juror badges. Wear your badges in and around the courthouse so people will recognize you as jurors.

Do not conduct an independent investigation. Do not visit any scene or location to inspect it for yourself. Do not conduct any research or experiments. I'm going to expand a little bit. Don't get on the internet. Don't look up stuff in the dictionary. Don't go to encyclopedias. Everything you need to decide this case you're going to get right here in the courtroom.

Avoid media coverage. Do not read, watch, or listen to any newspaper, internet, television, or radio accounts of this trial. If you inadvertently see, hear, or read something about the case, please let me know.

Notebooks and pencils have been provided for your use in taking notes. Take as many or as few notes as you wish to help you remember the testimony.

Transcripts will not be provided, nor is testimony likely to be repeated after a witness has been excused from the witness stand.

During deliberations you may share your notes with your fellow jurors. At all times the notes will be kept confidential. No one but you and the bailiff will have access to them.

After you have reached your verdict, the bailiff will destroy the notes unless you choose to keep them.

Order of trial. Criminal trials usually proceed in this order:

Opening statements. The prosecutor will make an opening statement to you previewing the case. The defendant's attorney may give an opening statement, either immediately afterward, or after the State has presented it evidence, or may chose not to give one at all.

Evidence. The State will present its evidence. The defense is not required to present any evidence, but may do so. The State may then present rebuttal evidence. Each witness is subject to direct examination, cross-examination, and redirect examination.

Final instructions. After all the evidence is in, I will read the final instructions which contain the rules of law that you must follow in deciding this case.

Closing arguments. The attorneys will present their closing arguments. The State is given the right to argue first and last because the State has the burden of proof.

Deliberations. You will deliberate in the jury room. Once you agree on a verdict, you will be brought into court where the clerk will read the verdict in the presence of the parties.

Duties of jurors. You have two major duties:

A. Determine the facts; and,

B. Reach a verdict by applying the law to the facts.

In fulfilling these duties, you must not be concerned with any opinion you may feel I have about the facts. You are the sole judges of the facts.

Also, you must not be influenced by sympathy or prejudice.

Finally, do not consider the possible punishment.

You must determine the facts from the evidence produced in court. Evidence includes the testimony of witnesses, exhibits admitted by the Court, and stipulations which are agreements between the parties. Evidence does not include lawyers' statements. The statements and arguments of the attorneys may help you understand the law and the evidence, but they are not evidence in and of themselves.

Objections. If I sustain a lawyer's objection to a question, you must disregard the question and any answer given.

Stricken testimony. If I order certain testimony stricken from the record, you should disregard that testimony.

Questions put to witnesses. A lawyer's question is not by itself evidence. However, it may be used to give meaning to a witness' answer.

Rejected exhibits. If I do not allow a particular exhibit to be received as evidence, that exhibit is not evidence for you to consider.

Credibility of witnesses. It is up to you to decide what testimony to believe and how much weight to give it. In determining the credibility of witnesses, take into account such things as their ability and opportunity to observe, their memory, their manner while testifying, any motive or prejudice they might have, and any inconsistent statements they may have made.

The rules of evidence ordinarily do not permit the opinion of a witness to be received as evidence. However, a witness may give an opinion on a subject upon which the witness has become an expert because of education, study, or experience. Give the expert opinion the weight that you believe it deserves.

Questions by jurors. Jurors are not permitted to ask questions directly of witnesses. The examination of witnesses is left to the attorneys. You may wonder why a certain question is not asked by the attorneys. The answer may very well be that the question you have in mind is prohibited under our laws of evidence, or I have ruled prior to the start of the trial that the lawyers may not get into that particular area.

However, in the event that you have an important question you want brought to the Court's attention, raise your hand during the trial when I ask if are there any questions from the jury. The question must be in writing or it cannot be considered. Please do not put your name on the question. I will review the submitted question just as I review each of the lawyers' questions, and decide if it is relevant and proper under our laws and rules of evidence.

If I determine that the question can be asked, it will be referred to the lawyers or asked of the witness before that person is excused. If your question arises after that witness has been excused by the Court, the witness will not be asked to return. If I decide the question is not relevant or proper and do not ask it, you may not speculate as to what the answer might have been.

Presumption of innocence. The law does not require a defendant to prove his innocence or to present any evidence. A defendant is presumed by law to be innocent. The State must prove a defendant guilty beyond a reasonable doubt. This means the State must prove each element of the charge beyond a reasonable doubt. The burden of proving the defendant guilty beyond a reasonable doubt rests upon the State. This burden never shifts throughout the trial.

If the State does not meet the burden of proof, you must find the defendant not guilty. A verdict of guilty cannot stand on mere suspicion, probability, or supposition. A verdict of not guilty cannot stand on sympathy.

The charge against the defendant is not evidence. You must not think that the defendant is guilty just because he has been accused. Every defendant in a criminal case is presumed by law to be innocent. The State must prove every part of the charge beyond a reasonable doubt before a guilty verdict may be returned.

The crime of sexual exploitation of a minor under the age of 15 requires proof of the following:

One, the defendant knowingly possessed or received any visual depiction in which an actual minor is engaged in exploitive exhibition or other sexual conduct; and,

Two, the actual minor depicted in any visual depiction was under the age of 15 at the time.

The crime of attempted exploitation of a minor under 15 requires proof of one of the following:

The defendant intentionally engaged in conduct which would have been a crime if the circumstances related to the crime as the defendant believed them to be; or,

Two, the defendant intentionally committed any act which was a step in a course of conduct which the defendant planned would end, or believed would end in the commission of a crime; or,

Three, the defendant engaged in conduct intended to aid another person to commit a crime in a manner which would make the defendant an accomplice had the crime been committed or attempted by the other person.

Visual depiction includes each visual image that is contained in an undeveloped film, videotape or photograph, or data stored in any form and capable of conversion into a visual image.

"Exploitive exhibition" means the actual or simulated exhibition of the genitals or pubic or rectal areas of any person for the purpose of sexual stimulation of the viewer.

"Sexual conduct" means actual or simulated sexual intercourse, including genital to genital, oral to genital, anal to genital, or oral to anal, whether between persons of the same or opposite sex; or,

Penetration of the vagina or rectum by any object; or,

Three, masturbation for the purpose of sexual stimulation of the viewer.

"Knowingly" means with respect to conduct or to a circumstance described by a statute defining an offense that a person is aware of or believes that his conduct is of that nature or that the circumstance exists. It does not require any knowledge of the unlawfulness of the act or omission.

The offense of sexual exploitation of a minor requires that the minor participating in the film or video must be an actual person and not a computer generated image, or a representation of a person.

Counsel, have I neglected to read any of the instructions I told you I would read?

MR. EUCHNER: No, Your Honor.

MR. JENSVOLD: No.

THE COURT: At this time, Mr. Jensvold, does the State have an opening statement?

MR. JENSVOLD: Yes.

THE COURT: Please proceed.

STATE'S OPENING STATEMENT

MR. JENSVOLD: Where was Jacob Franks? More

specifically, where was Jacob Franks between March 2nd and March 19th of 2003?

That's the question I'm going to ask you to keep in mind as you hear the evidence over the next few days, and when you listen to the closing arguments, and when you go back into deliberations.

The reason -- I'm not going to argue the case now, obviously that's for the end of the case -- but I want you to keep that in mind as you listen, because the evidence in this case will key in on those particular dates. In particular, March 4th through March 6th. All of these dates associated with the files that are at issue in this case, the 15 files.

There is, you will actually see a stipulation between the parties, that there were over 200 child pornography files found within Mr. Coghill's motor home on April 1st of 2003 that were later analyzed. And they were on multiple CDs, over at least 20 different CDs on which these video images were stored. But the 15 files that you're going to be dealing with, you will hear evidence that will correlate those files with those particular dates between March 2nd and March 19th of 2003.

Now, let me just briefly describe to you what the evidence will show regarding how this case came about.

On April 1st of 2003, early in the morning, Jacob Franks, from the pay phone, called the police to report that

1 Mr. Coghill was in possession of child pornography.
2   Now, there was a back story behind why Mr. Coghill
3 (sic) chose to do that on the morning of April 1st of 2003.
4   To go back a little further, Mr. Coghill and
5 Mr. Franks had known each other for a number of years, since,
6 I believe, memories may differ a little bit on this, but at
7 least since 1999, perhaps as early as 1998.
8   The two men met in Phoenix at a job site. They were
9 working for a telemarketing company. They became friends.
10 Perhaps they will differ on exactly how that came about, but
11 they became friends.
12   And actually, Mr. Franks would end up moving into,
13 on a couple of different occasions, and there may be some
14 disagreement about when those dates occurred, but Mr. Franks
15 certainly lived in the motor home that Mr. Coghill had parked
16 at his parents' house in Moon Valley, in the Moon Valley area
17 in Phoenix. So all of that is before April 1st of 2003.
18   Their relationship goes back and forth, and they'll
19 describe to you, Mr. Franks will testify, I believe tomorrow
20 morning. You'll hear statements probably attributed to
21 Mr. Coghill as well.
22   But more specifically, on March 31st of 2003, is
23 sort of the, of the event and the events that caused Mr.
24 Franks to finally call in and report Mr. Coghill.
25   Mr. Franks will tell you that he knew about

1 Mr. Coghill's, that he had possessed and viewed child
2 pornography over a number of years, but chose never to call in
3 and report Mr. Coghill because, well, he was friends with
4 Mr. Coghill. He was living with Mr. Coghill. Mr. Coghill was
5 doing him favors. Mr. Franks, you will, it will be crystal
6 clear to you that Mr. Franks is not the most, let's say,
7 consistent employee in the world.
8   You will hear that Mr. Franks has been to prison a
9 number of times, nothing sexually related; car theft,
10 burglary, I think disorderly conduct. He's been to prison a
11 few times. He had several felony convictions.
12   And he will, you will hear that Mr. Coghill often
13 took Mr. Franks in, let him live with him, helped him try to
14 find a job. That's one of the things that sparked this whole
15 incident. But that's what Mr. Franks will tell you as to why
16 he waited until April 1st of 2003 to finally report
17 Mr. Coghill.
18   On March 31st of 2003, Jacob Franks, while
19 Mr. Coghill was at work, Mr. Coghill was an aircraft mechanic,
20 and he was at work. That day he had his motor home parked at
21 a motor home lot on East Benson Highway. Now, Mr. Franks was
22 there. And so, on March 31st, he took what's called a Goped,
23 basically a scooter with a motor. And it had lights on it, I
24 guess.
25   Mr. Coghill allowed Mr. Franks to use the Goped to

go around and look for jobs. He didn't give him permission to go all the way downtown to Broadway and Fourth Avenue, which is where Mr. Franks had gone. And on March 31st, he got hit by a car as he was riding this Goped. The Goped was trashed.

Mr. Franks had to go to Kino Hospital. He had to find his way back from Kino Hospital to the motor home park where he was living with Mr. Coghill.

Needless to say, Mr. Coghill wasn't real happy about the fact that, one, Mr. Franks had gone way father away than he was supposed to, and, two, that his Goped was now, you know, basically wrecked. So they were not happy with each other, and Mr. Coghill is not happy with Mr. Franks on March 31st.

Well, the next morning Mr. Franks is supposed to go to a job interview that Mr. Coghill had set up with him at Hamilton Aerospace or something along those lines, something along those lines. And Mr. Coghill says -- Mr. Franks -- said he put on this huge red T-shirt that looked like it was five or six sizes too big for him. Mr. Coghill tells him, you can't go to the job interview like that, tells him to put on this white colored shirt. Mr. Franks doesn't like that. He thinks Mr. Coghill is still upset at him over the day before, and they get into an argument, and Mr. Franks takes off after Mr. Coghill says something to the effect of, I'm just going to take you back up to Phoenix and leave you there.

PIMA COUNTY SUPERIOR COURT

Mr. Franks doesn't like that. He will tell you that he left. He walked around. He's angry. And he debates it for a certain period of time, and then finally decides to call the police. And that's when the police are called.

Two deputies show up to talk to Mr. Franks at his location. And then I believe both of those deputies, Schupbach and Judd -- they'll be some of your first witnesses after Mr. Franks, they go to the motor home where Mr. Coghill and Mr. Franks were living.

Now, based on the information they got from Mr. Franks, they knew what, kind of what they were looking for based on what Mr. Franks had told them. They were looking for CD's that were next to the computer, some of them marked K-P for kiddie porn, and they indeed find several CDs that are labeled K-P.

There are numerous CDs. I haven't counted them. You guys can count them later if you want. I don't know if you want to get an official count. But there is six or seven different spindles of CDs that you're going to see pictures of. You're actually going to see some of the actual CDs that were taken. And, specifically, you're going to be, you're not going to be able to take a computer back and open the CDs, but you're going to be able to see what's been written on the outside of the CDs. And I will get to that in a minute.

But JE3, you might want to mark that down, that's

the spindle; spindle, basically a rod that the CDs stack on top of each other on, that's the key spindle at issue in this case, because all of the files, the 15 files that are at issue in this case, were found on one or more of those CDs.

Now, the top CD, there will be some question about whether that CD was on the top when the deputies arrived or not, but, anyway, JE3-A, is labeled, "dirty". Now, that is not one of the CDs from which these files, the 15 files that you're dealing with were taken.

What Mr. Franks will tell you about that CD, is that when he got down to Phoenix -- Tucson, I'm sorry, he was on the computer and that there was some files that he noticed that appeared to be child pornography. And he asked Mr. Coghill what he was supposed to do with them, because he wanted to get them off the hard drive so he could download some of his own stuff.

And Mr. Franks will tell you that at Mr. Coghill's discretion, he told him to burn those files onto the CD which would later be identified as JE3-A, and write "dirty" on it. So you're going to see that CD. You will be able to look at the handwriting that says "dirty" on it, and compare that with a known sample of Jacob Franks' handwriting, as well as a known sample of Mr. Coghill's handwriting.

Alan Kreitl is going to talk to you about handwriting. He'll tell you what his opinion was based on;

PIMA COUNTY SUPERIOR COURT

some of the stuff that he reviewed. You'll be able to judge Mr. Kreitl's testimony like any other witness, and you'll be able to look at the CDs themselves as well. But below JE3-A are JE3-B, all the way to, it goes all the way down to like four letters. I can't remember the exact end of it. But I think between JE3-B and JE3-Q are the 15 CDs in which the 15 files that you are dealing with were taken from.

And you'll see the labels on those files. Some of them are labeled K-P, some of them are K-P porn movies, something else similar to that. But even below those CDs, you're also going to see some others, and you'll be able to judge and compare the handwriting of the CDs that contain the 15 pornography files in this case with other CDs. Compare the handwriting on those and see what you think.

You will see some CDs that are labeled, "my pictures complete." From that CD, which was below the child pornography CDs, you will see some photographs of Mr. Coghill and his family members that were on that CD.

There were others. There were actually three or four, at least three other CDs that were below the child pornography CDs that have handwriting on the top of them, and that have Mr. Coghill's pictures and his family members or friends on them as well. So that's what you'll be able to evaluate in a nutshell.

You're going to hear from two primarily computer

forensic witnesses in this case. The first person that the State will call, his name is Jefford Englander. He was the lead detective on the case at the time that this case was issued and the time the investigation began.

He's been a private computer forensic analyst for a number of years. He works in Phoenix for a company called Lighthouse Solutions. He will tell you about his investigation into the computer that was taken from the motor home; about the two hard drives that were on it, about his analysis of the hard drives. And then he went through virtually, I think he went through every single CD left in the motor home that was seized by the police, by the Sheriff's Department.

He'll talk to you about burn dates on the CDs, about when the particular CDs were burned, about which software was present on the computer inside the motor home that was used to burn the CDs. And so I want you to listen to that.

I'm certainly not going to go in and summarize all of it right now. But he will tell that you there was evidence on the hard drive of several of the 15 files, not all of them. I believe six or seven of the files that are on there were, there is evidence that -- when I say "evidence," I'll explain in just a little bit, but evidence that those files perhaps were present on the hard drive between the dates of March 2nd and March 19th, in particular March 4th, March 6th, March

PIMA COUNTY SUPERIOR COURT

19th. Keep those three dates in mind.

Now, when he talks about evidence, he's not going to be able to tell you that all 15 files he was able to go to the hard drive, click on it, and play it.

What he will tell you is that what his forensic software allowed him to do was to see traces of file names that were present. Either they were deleted by other files and overwritten, but he will be able to tell you that there were several of those files that were charged that were found on the CDs on that spindle, JE3. That there were traces of those files on the hard drives.

And he will tell you that there is at least one file which he could play using his software and actually play the file itself. He'll also tell you about burn dates on March 25th of 2003. March 25th of 2003 is when JE3-A, the CD labeled "dirty" was burned. And he'll tell you that as part of his report he printed out a KaZaA log.

Maybe some of you are familiar with that web site. It allows for, well, frankly, illegal activity, illegal downloading, sharing files between users. But you'll hear from Jacob Franks that he was downloading music during that time that he was there.

Pay attention when you see that KaZaA log. Look at, we'll talk about it during closing arguments, but look at what was going on between March 25th of 2003 and April 1st of 2003.

And then I want you also to look at what is going on prior to that.

And why I say that, is because Jacob Franks will tell you that he came to Tucson about a week prior to April 1st, 2003. Which would mean he wasn't there, according to Mr. Franks, between March 2nd and March 19th of 2003.

You'll also hear what Mr. Coghill told Detective Englander on April 1st of 2003. You'll actually hear the tape of the interview. And you will hear Mr. Coghill say that he picked up Jake one week ago from April 1st of 2003. Now a little later on in that interview, Detective Englander asked him a question about what's been going on the last two weeks, and Mr. Coghill says, well, over the last two weeks I haven't been able to get on the computer because Jake's been monopolizing it.

But Mr. Coghill doesn't say one word to Detective Englander on April 1st of 2003 about Jake being in Tucson between March 2nd and March 9th of 2003, or between March 18th and March 19th of 2003.

It's not until April of 2006 at a prior hearing in which Mr. Coghill was under oath, that he says for the first time, at least publically, that now he remembered that he went back up to Phoenix and picked Jake up on March 2nd and brought him down to Tucson, and he spent here on March 9th; this is Mr. Coghill's birthday, and that he took him back up to

PIMA COUNTY SUPERIOR COURT

Phoenix, and then he went and got him again on March 18th. That's what Mr. Coghill said in 2006, under oath.

But he did not say that to Detective Englander on April 1st of 2003. So you'll be able to decide for yourself whether you, whether you believe Mr. Franks or Mr. Coghill. And you'll be able to look at the forensic evidence to help you make that determination.

The Judge is going to give you a stipulation. She's already told you about the fact that you're not going to see these images. So the parties have agreed that you're not, we're not going to play the images for you. So basically, you're going to -- basically it's already going to be established for you. It's already going to be not disputed at all that these images were child pornography images; that they meet the statutory definition. So that's not what you're going to be debating.

You're going to be debating whether Mr. Coghill or Mr. Franks, which one of those two persons, basically, was responsible for downloading and burning these child pornography files to CDs.

You're going to hear from Tami Loehrs who is the defense computer forensic person. And she's going to talk to you about, about a number of things. But she's going to talk to you about the date of May 14th of 2003. Now, May 14th of 2003 is important because on the second hard drive, which is called the slave drive on this computer, there was a master drive and a slave drive. I didn't make those words up by the way.

She's going to tell you that they found, and she found in her analysis, that there were 312 files in which the last access date of those files was May 14th of 2003. Now, none of those files are going to be the 15 files that we're dealing with in our case.

They're not even known child pornography files, but they are certainly not the 15 files that we're dealing with in our case that were found on CDs.

She will tell you that, in her opinion, because that last access date happened after April 1st of 2003, while the hard drives were in the possession of the Sheriff's Department, that somehow that that means that at least the hard drive, the secondary drive was not handled in a forensically sound manner.

Now, Mr. Englander is going to give you his opinion as to what may have happened during that time. He will tell you that he had taken both hard drives out of evidence between that period of time between May and July of 2003. I don't believe he's going to be able to tell you exactly why some of those last access dates had changed.

But I want you to listen to the evidence carefully when you get to Mr. Englander, and then you get to Ms. Loehrs' opinion as to what happened and how last access dates can be changed, and whether it really matters to you. Especially the file, the 15 charged files in this case which last access dates had not changed. And there is no evidence that, that the burn dates on the CDs had been changed. You'll hear about how burn dates on CDs are created and those kind of things.

And I also want you to keep in mind when Ms. Loehrs testifies about what her purpose was when she was doing her analysis. Compare her purpose with Mr. Englander's purpose.

Because Ms. Loehrs will tell you that, based on her conversations with defense counsel, she had a very targeted purpose. And one of those purposes that she had was to find any evidence that Mr. Franks had been using the computer, or during particular periods of time. She won't say that she was looking for evidence of Mr. Coghill's use, but she'll tell you that one of her purposes was to look for evidence that Mr. Franks was using the computer. So keep that in mind.

And also keep in mind the fact that Ms. Loehrs didn't look at the KaZaA logs as part of her evaluation. She didn't look at all the evidence. She didn't look at the handwriting. She's going to tell you that she had a narrow purpose in looking at only the computer to make sure particular conclusions. But keep those in mind.

And, ladies and gentlemen, I believe that when you put all of this together, particularly when you compare the handwriting, I want you to look closely, listen carefully to Mr. Kreitl and what he's going to tell you about how particular words are formed in handwriting, and then compare his opinions with your own common sense.

When you see the handwriting, you're going to see a number of CDs, and you're going to be able to look at that handwriting on those CDs and compare the burn dates of those CDs that have particular handwriting with other CDs that have different styles of handwriting.

And, ultimately, ladies and gentlemen, what you're going to conclude, and I believe the evidence will show, is that Jacob Franks was not in Tucson until April 25th, 2003, and, therefore, Mr. Coghill was the person responsible for the 15 charged files. And I'm going to ask you to find a verdict of guilty on all 15 counts.

Thank you.

THE COURT: Mr. Skitzki, or Mr. Euchner.

MR. EUCHNER: Thank you, Your Honor.

THE COURT: Please proceed.

MR. EUCHNER: I told him he should never make me angry. Those were among the first words out of Jacob Franks' mouth when Deputy Schupbach showed up at the Circle K after he called 9-1-1. Jacob Franks didn't call the police about child pornography in this case out of any sense of civic duty, and he will be the first one to admit that. He called the police out of vengeance against our client, James Coghill.

Why was Jacob Franks so angry with Jim Coghill? Well, Mr. Jensvold went over a lot of the story. They met four, five years earlier. Jake Franks was at a job with Jim Coghill. Jim was in between jobs at the time as an aviation mechanic, and he was working at a call center.

Jake Franks got the job at a call center, and shortly thereafter violated his probation. When he gets out, he needs a helping hand. And he's burned enough bridges in his time that he needs somebody to turn to. And lo and behold, there's Jim Coghill. Somebody who cares about another human being. And says, you know, you need a leg up. I'll help you out. You need a place to stay, I can give you a place to stay. You need help finding a job. I'll help you find a job.

For at least a couple of years Jim Coghill lived in a recreational vehicle, because a lot of the airline mechanic jobs are all over the country. They might last only a couple of weeks and the contract ends. So it's easier for Jim to drive around the country in the RV.

So, on occasion, when Jake would say, I need a place to live, can you help me out, Jim would say, sure, you can have the couch in my RV. It's certainly not the most, most luxurious of quarters for a guest house, but if your choice is either sleep on the couch in an RV or sleep on the streets,

Jake Franks took the opportunity that Jim Coghill offered him, and chose not to sleep on the streets, and to put his head down in Jim Coghill's place.

And Jim also was not just offering a place to stay, and on occasion tried to help him find a job, he also said, Jake, feel free to use my computer. You'll hear evidence, not only from the defense expert Tami Loehrs, but also from all of the State's witnesses including Mr. Englander, there was no password protections on this computer. Anybody can come in and sit down on the computer and log on to the internet and surf, download whatever you want, go to whatever web site you want.

And Jake Franks had free access to this computer every time that he visited Jim Coghill. Sometimes he stayed a weekend, sometimes he stayed several months.

On April 1st, 2003, Jake Franks had been in Tucson for about a week. Sometime around March 25th, maybe a day earlier give or take, Jake had e-mailed Jim because Jake was not only without a place to stay, he didn't even have a phone. He'd go to some place where he would have free internet access whether it be a library or a friend. And he sent Jim an e-mail saying, basically, I'm on the streets, what can I do.

James says, I'll come and pick you up. I'll bring you down to Tucson. I'll help you find a job. And this is one of the only times that Jake Franks had ever even been to

PIMA COUNTY SUPERIOR COURT

Tucson. Jim had only been in Tucson for about a month-and-a-half at this point. They both generally lived in Phoenix. So this, most of the evidence you'll hear about in this case is Phoenix related. But for this month-and-a-half Jim is in Tucson, and now Jake comes to Tucson in that last week.

And Jake is going to find a job and Jim is going to help him. And what Jake does the minute he gets in to Tucson is, he immediately gets on the computer and spends all day and all night downloading. That's all he does when he is there, is he stays up all night downloading. And you'll hear a lot of evidence in this case about a lot of downloading, some of which was done by Mr. Coghill, some of which was done by Mr. Franks.

But there is somewhere in excess, as Mr. Jensvold says, I don't know the exact count, but somewhere in excess of maybe 600 CDs that are burned that are all on the computer desk in various spindles of approximately a hundred each. And most of it is sci-fi such as Star Trek, X-Files, Voyager, other TV shows and movies. Both of them download a lot.

However, there is only about 20 CDs out of all of these that contained child pornography. And coincidentally, when the police meet up with Jake Franks and then go over to Jim Coghill's RV, and they ask if they can come in, and Jim invites them in, they find all of those child porn CDs right

PIMA COUNTY SUPERIOR COURT

at the top of one of the spindles in broad daylight.

Now when Jim invites Deputies Judd and Schupbach into his RV, he said, come on in. They ask if they can look around. He says, sure. Can we look at your VHS collection? Sure. Can look at your photo album collection? Sure. Can we look at your computer and your CDs? Sure, go ahead.

When Deputy Judd looks at some of these CDs and he notices CDs that are marked K-P, just like Jake Franks said that the police would find, Jim Coghill says, some of these CDs are Jake's. I don't know what those are.

Then Deputy Judd says: Do you mind, if you would, would you mind speaking with detectives? Sure, no problem. And then, back then, Detective Englander, now Mr. Englander, comes to the scene and he knows nothing about the case other than there is a report of child pornography.

The very first thing he does after getting a few seconds of a briefing from one of the deputies, is he talks to Mr. Coghill. And he says: Do you mind talking to me? Sure, not a problem. And you'll hear the recording of the conversation between Jim Coghill and Mr. Englander. And Jim Coghill sat there in the air conditioned car and he spoke with Mr. Englander, and he said I don't know about any child pornography. Jake has free access to the computer.

Mr. Coghill told Detective Englander the story of March 31st and April 1st, and you'll hear it at length later, about the Goped accident, and the shirt that Jake Franks thought was suitable to wear to a job interview.

But what Mr. Jensvold said, at no time did Mr. Coghill volunteer that March 2 and March 6 Jake Franks was here. And when you hear the tape, you'll know that the reason why he didn't volunteer is because the question was never asked.

Detective Englander, when he gets to the scene, he doesn't know what questions to ask because he hasn't done any investigation yet. He's just trying to find more information. What can you tell me? And he tells him what he thinks he can.

While Detective Englander is talking to Jim Coghill at the RV park, Jake Franks is giving another interview to another detective at the substation, the Sheriff's substation.

At the end of the interview Detective Englander goes in and says to Jake Franks, I just talked to Coghill, and what he's telling me is that if I find anything, it's going to be yours. How do I know who it belongs to? And Jake Franks says, it's going to be his because I saw the RYGOLD files.

Now, you have the indictments before you and you will see a lot of words that are spelled R@YGOLD. Some of them are just spelled simply R-Y-G-O-L-D. Jake Franks knows how to pronounce that. Jake Franks knows that that's RYGOLD. And he tells Detective Englander. Based on this amount of information, this is the extent of the interviews that

Detective Englander conducted. Then after he seized all of the evidence with the search warrant, and he spent over a year going through all of the hard drives and going through the CDs, he decided that the evidence that he had suggested that it pointed to Jim Coghill and not to Jake Franks.

Now, there is going to be a lot of questions about what Detective Englander at the time, now Mr. Englander, what he did with the case. How did he come to these conclusions that he drew? How did he decide that it was Jim Coghill and not Jake Franks?

You're going to hear that when it came to the dirty CD that Mr. Jensvold talked about, the one that Jake Franks said, yeah, I burned that CD because Jim told me to burn it, that they didn't even charge any of the files that were on that CD, because Detective Englander isn't sure that those belonged to Mr. Coghill; those might be Jake Franks.

And what the defense submits to you and will submit to you at the end of the case, is that all of these files are Jake Franks.

Now, Mr. Jensvold mentioned a stipulation that we entered into. There is three different stipulations. One of them is that these files are child pornography. There is no question about it. You don't need to see any of this. It's graphic enough just to hear it, but you don't need to see this.

PIMA COUNTY SUPERIOR COURT

And the reason why we are willing to stipulate to that, is not just because we don't want you to see it, although that certainly is a concern, but because you don't need to see it. It is totally irrelevant in this case whether what is on those CDs is child pornography technically, or if it's a close call. Because the real question in this case has nothing to do with whether Mr. Coghill knew that was child pornography. The real question in this case is whether Mr. Coghill even knew of the existence of those CDs in the first place.

As I just said earlier, those CDs were found at the top of a stack of other CDs that were Mr. Coghill's personal CDs, such as "my pictures complete." And given that this is Mr. Coghill's house, you would expect to find CDs of his personal property.

One of the other stipulations that the State and the defense have entered into relates to fingerprint evidence. And there are, there were all the fingerprints -- I'm sorry, excuse me, all of the CDs were dusted for fingerprints, and sometimes they found Jim Coghill's fingerprints, sometimes they found Jake Franks' fingerprints. And sometimes they found each of their fingerprints on CDs in the stack that is labeled JE3.

And you'll hear a lot about this JE3. And JE stands for Jefford Englander. And JE1 is the hard drive, I mean,

PIMA COUNTY SUPERIOR COURT

excuse me, the computer. I forget what JE2 is. And I think he numbered all of the spindles he seized JE4, JE5, JE6, et cetera.

JE3 is the spindle that contains all of Mr. Coghill's personal photos, and other things such as his word documents, things of that nature. But this CD, this spindle has a hundred CDs on it. None of the CDs that contain child pornography have Jim Coghill's fingerprints. Also none of them have Jake Franks' fingerprints. So the fingerprint evidence isn't going to help us one way or the other in this case.

So then we have to turn to the forensic evidence. And the State seized all of the forensic evidence, all of the digital evidence, and this was a lot, this was 600 CDs, and a couple of pretty large hard drives, a 15 gig hard drive and a 5 gig hard drive, which in 2003 was a lot larger than it would be today.

And Detective Englander looked through the KaZaA logs to see what the downloading, what kind of downloads was done during that period. And the KaZaA logs only have about one month worth of dates that were -- because the log only holds so many entries.

And the KaZaA log in this case is largely going to be a red herring, if that much, because there is no child pornography on any of the KaZaA logs. It wouldn't point to

Jake Franks, and it wouldn't point to Jim Coghill. So the KaZaA logs aren't going to help you in this case.

Then the question is what kind of activity is on this? When were the CDs burned that had the child pornography? And when were the files created? And Mr. Jensvold already wrote up here a lot of dates, and he's going to, I don't know if he's going to want to show this at the end of the case, but I'm going to want to show you this at the end of the case. Because I'm going to come to you at the end and tell you that Mr. Jensvold was not able to prove what he told you in his opening that he could.

He's not going to, first, he's not going to be able to prove that Jake Franks was in Phoenix between March 2nd and March 9th. There are child pornography CDs that were burned on these dates.

The defense, on the other hand, will be able to prove to you that Jake Franks was in Tucson. These dates that Mr. Jensvold is showing, I'm not really sure why he wrote them up here, because you'll find at the end of the case that these are not important. This is an important date, March 3rd, 2003, and these are important dates, and then there will be dates that go so far back to 2002 that nobody recalls.

Now, Mr. Jensvold has to prove to you beyond a reasonable doubt that, on all of those dates where child pornography was proved, that Jake Franks could not have had access to the computer. We can't prove to you that Jake Franks had access or did not have access on some of those dates that go far enough back, because we don't know.

But what we can do is we can prove to you in this case that on these dates, these are probably the most crucial dates in this case, and Jake Franks was in Tucson. Jake Franks was on Jim Coghill's computer, and Jake Franks was burning CDs, and he was active on the computer during those dates.

All Tami Loehrs is going to do when she testifies for the defense, is she's not going to say that she can prove that Jake Franks burned those CDs. All she's going to do is say that we don't know who did burn them, and we can say that Jake Franks was on the computer, that's basically all we can say about this.

Other things that we can't prove in this case, what the evidence doesn't show, the evidence will not show that any of these CDs were ever played on this computer. It's possible at some point they were, but there's no evidence of it anyplace. The evidence won't show the Jim Coghill was ever at the computer at any time when the child pornography was downloaded or burned to CDs. He might have been nearby. He lives in the house where the computer is, but so did Jake Franks during all those important dates.

What it's going to come down to is the digital

evidence is not going to give you any guidance as to who did it in this case.

And, finally, Mr. Jensvold talked about the handwriting. You will get a chance to see Jake Franks' handwriting, Jim Coghill's handwriting, and what the CDs look like.

But the handwriting that purports, that the K-P handwriting, it's just two letters on a CD. It's not going to be something that any expert in handwriting analysis will be able to tell you conclusively, that's definitely his handwriting, or that's definitely his handwriting. The handwriting expert is not going to be able to provide you much guidance in this case.

So, basically what it comes down to, is what Mr. Jensvold said it's not going to come down to. Because it really is all going to be about Jake Franks' credibility. It's all going to be about whether Jake Franks called the police on April 1st, 2003, and said something and he couldn't take it back, because if he tried to take it back, then he put it out there already, he has to follow through on his story.

And as Mr. Jensvold told you, Jacob Franks has multiple felony convictions. He's been in and out of jail. He does not have credibility. You'll get a chance to judge it for yourself when he's on the witness stand.

Now, Mr. Jensvold talked briefly about what beyond a

reasonable doubt means, and the Judge talked to you during voir dire about beyond a reasonable doubt. It is the highest standard that we have --

MR. JENSVOLD: Objection, argumentative.

THE COURT: He can finish his thought.

MR. EUCHNER: This isn't a civil case where it's you're deciding 51 percent whether to side with the plaintiff or the defendant like in a fender bender. The State has to prove beyond a reasonable doubt that you'll be certain, you will be firmly convinced that Mr. Coghill was the one that was downloading and possessing that child pornography.

And I submit to you now, and I'll submit to you again at the end of the case, that the State will not be able to meet that burden.

And at the end of this case, we'll ask you to return verdicts of not guilty on all counts, because Jim Coghill is guilty of only one thing; he trusted the wrong person.

Thank you.

THE COURT: All right, folks, what we're going to do is we're going to take our evening recess right now. You have been here since 7:30 this morning. There are some matters that Christina needs to take about 10 or 15 minutes with you showing you the jury room, explaining some things that you are going to need to know. So we are going to go ahead and excuse you for the evening.

PIMA COUNTY SUPERIOR COURT

```
 1           Remember the admonition.  Please keep your juror
 2   badges on.  If you could reconvene in the jury room that she's
 3   going to take you to at about 10:15 in the morning, and we're
 4   going to try to get started as close to 10:30 as we can.
 5           Have a good night, and we'll see you back in the
 6   morning.
 7           (Whereupon the jurors are excused and leave the
 8   courtroom, and proceedings continue in their absence, as
 9   follows:)
10           THE COURT:  The record will show the absence of the
11   jury, the presence of both counsel, the presence of
12   Mr. Coghill.
13           Anything we need to take up before the recess?
14           MR. EUCHNER:  No, Your Honor.
15           MR. JENSVOLD:  No.
16           THE COURT:  Hopefully we can get started really
17   close to 10:30 tomorrow.  We'll see you back then.
18           Good night, Mr. Coghill.
19           THE DEFENDANT:  Good night.
20           (Whereupon proceedings were adjourned in this
21   matter.)
```

PIMA COUNTY SUPERIOR COURT

C E R T I F I C A T E

STATE OF ARIZONA   )
)
COUNTY OF PIMA   )

      I, BONITA ROBERTSON, Certified Court Reporter in and for the State of Arizona, do hereby certify that the foregoing transcript of the proceedings held on the 17th day of March, 2009, in Pima County Superior Court, is a true and accurate record of the proceedings had.

Bonita Robertson

BONITA ROBERTSON, RMR

CERTIFIED REPORTER, #50454

Day One of Trial

March 17th, 2009

Motions in Limine

Page 81-8-9 Judge states, "[m]y ruling is no adult pornography period."

Voir Dire

Page 86-9   Rogue juror's name is Tucker. She states she has a nephew who is serving time on a sex charge.

Day Two

```
 1         IN THE SUPERIOR COURT OF THE STATE OF ARIZONA
 2                     IN THE COUNTY OF PIMA
 3
 4   STATE OF ARIZONA,           )
                                 )
 5          PLAINTIFF,           )
                                 )
 6   vs.                         )    CR-2004 2573
                                 )
 7                               )    2-CA-CR 2009-0247
     JAMES PRENTISS COGHILL,     )
 8                               )
                                 )
 9          DEFENDANT.           )
                                 )
10   _____)
11
12
13   BEFORE:   THE HONORABLE TERESA GODOY
               JUDGE OF THE SUPERIOR COURT
14
15                                        FEB 23'10 PDA PM 4:27
16
17
18
                        JURY TRIAL - DAY TWO
19
                          MARCH 18, 2009
20
                          TUCSON, ARIZONA
21
22
     REPORTED BY:                       COPY
23
24                       BONITA ROBERTSON, RMR
                         CERTIFIED REPORTER #50454
25
```

PIMA COUNTY SUPERIOR COURT

APPEARANCES:

> SHAWN JENSVOLD, ESQ.,
> DEPUTY COUNTY ATTORNEY,
> APPEARING ON BEHALF OF THE STATE.
>
>
> DAVID EUCHNER & PAUL SKITZKI, ESQS.,
> APPEARING ON BEHALF OF THE DEFENDANT.

PIMA COUNTY SUPERIOR COURT

```
                              INDEX


WITNESS NAME                                              PAGE


JACOB FRANKS
    DIRECT EXAMINATION BY MR. JENSVOLD                       4
    CROSS-EXAMINATION BY MR. SKITZKI                        41
    REDIRECT EXAMINATION BY MR. JENSVOLD                    59


JACE JUDD
    DIRECT EXAMINATION BY MR. JENSVOLD                      75
    CROSS-EXAMINATOIN BY MR. SKITZKI                        94


BRENDA SCHUPBACH
    DIRECT EXAMINATION BY MR. JENSVOLD                     110
    CROSS-EXAMINATION BY MR. SKITZKI                       119


WILLIAM KNUTH
    DIRECT EXAMINATION BY MR. JENSVOLD                     129
    CROSS-EXAMINATION BY MR. SKITZKI                       136


BRIAN MARK McGRAW
    DIRECT EXAMINATION BY MR. JENSVOLD                     145
    CROSS-EXAMINATION BY MR. EUCHNER                       151


JOHN MAWHINNEY
    DIRECT EXAMINATION BY MR. JENSVOLD                     157
    CROSS-EXAMINATION BY MR. EUCHNER                       166
    REDIRECT EXAMINATION BY MR. JENSVOLD                   175
    RECROSS EXAMINATION BY MR. EUCHNER                     179


GERARD MORETZ
    DIRECT EXAMINATION BY MR. JENSVOLD                     186
    CROSS-EXAMINATION BY MR. SKITZKI                       192
    REDIRECT EXAMINATION BY MR. JENSVOLD                   199
```

PIMA COUNTY SUPERIOR COURT

```
 1                    P-R-O-C-E-E-D-I-N-G-S
 2
 3          (10:30 a.m.  Whereupon proceedings commence, as
 4   follows:)
 5          THE COURT:  All right.  The record will show the
 6   presence of the jury.  Be seated.  Thank you.
 7          The presence of both counsel, and Mr. Coghill.
 8          All right.  Mr. Jensvold, the State have a witness?
 9          MR. JENSVOLD:  Yes.  The State calls Jacob Franks.
10          THE COURT:  Mr. Franks, step forward, sir.  The
11   clerk is going to swear you in.
12
13                         JACOB FRANKS,
14   having been first duly sworn, was examined and testified, as
15   follows:
16
17                      DIRECT EXAMINATION
18   BY MR. JENSVOLD:
19       Q.   Mr. Franks, will you please state your name and
20   spell your last name.
21       A.   Jacob Franks, F-R-A-N-K-S.
22       Q.   And, Mr. Franks, where do you live now?
23       A.   Anthem.
24       Q.   And where specifically is that?
25       A.   It's north of Phoenix.
```

PIMA COUNTY SUPERIOR COURT

1	Q.	And where do you live?
2	A.	In a home, house.
3	Q.	Do you have roommates?
4	A.	Yes.
5	Q.	And how long have you lived there?
6	A.	Um, since September.

7 Q. And let's just go ahead and get this out of the way.
8 You have had a number of different felony convictions over the
9 past, I don't know, how long has it been?

10 A. From a span of to, 1999 to 2006.
11 Q. And you've been to prison, the Department of
12 Corrections a couple of times?
13 A. Yes.
14 Q. When was the most recent time?
15 A. Um, up until February of '08.
16 Q. And so, how long were you there?
17 A. Six months on like a parole violation.
18 Q. And how long had you been there previously at
19 different times?
20 A. Off and on, total about seven years.
21 Q. When was the first time that you went, do you know?
22 A. 2001.
23 Q. And which month, do you remember?
24 A. Um, I'm going to say April.
25 Q. How long were you there the first time?

PIMA COUNTY SUPERIOR COURT

1	A.	Probably like three months.
2	Q.	And was, what about the second time?
3	A.	Um, second time I did three years.
4	Q.	And what was the time frame?
5	A.	I did about 30 months, or three years, so I would say from, actual DOC, December 8th of '03 until January, early January of '06.
8	Q.	Okay. And these convictions, they were related to burglaries of cars?
10	A.	Yeah.
11	Q.	And there were other violations that you had?
12	A.	Yes.
13	Q.	None of them sexually related?
14	A.	No.
15	Q.	None of them related to child pornography or anything related to that?
17	A.	No.
18	Q.	All right. Let's talk about when you first met Mr. Coghill. Do you see Mr. Coghill in the courtroom today?
20	A.	Yes.
21	Q.	And where is he?
22	A.	He's in between the two gentlemen to my left.
23	Q.	Okay. And when did you first meet Mr. Coghill?
24	A.	I met him at DMS in a training class, in, I would say, November of '99.

PIMA COUNTY SUPERIOR COURT

1 Q. And what were you guys doing there?
2 A. We were trying to get, we got hired to work at a
3 call center to take cell phone orders for Nextel cellular
4 phones.
5 Q. And did guys become friends outside of work at some
6 point?
7 A. Yeah.
8 Q. How long did that take?
9 A. Um, about, probably about a week or so into the
10 training.
11 Q. Did you guys have some interests in common that lead
12 you to have some kind of a relationship outside of work?
13 A. I told him I could get him some --
14 Q. Let's --
15 MR. EUCHNER: Ask the witness wait.
16 BY MR. JENSVOLD:
17 Q. Did you guys have computer interests in common?
18 A. Yeah.
19 Q. Did, at some point, did you move in with
20 Mr. Coghill?
21 A. Yes.
22 Q. Do you remember when that was?
23 A. The very first time, I'm going to have to say,
24 October of '01.
25 Q. And do you remember, why do you remember it was

1 October of '01?
2   A.   Because I had gotten out of prison at the end,
3 September 29th I had gotten out of prison, and I was staying
4 in the town of Safford for about a week or so. And then I had
5 just came back into Phoenix and I got back in contact with
6 him, you know, called him to see how he was doing or whatever.
7 And then I ended up going over there and I ended up staying
8 over there.
9   Q.   Where is there?
10   A.   Over at his parents.
11   Q.   And where is that?
12   A.   On Moon Valley Drive, in Phoenix.
13   Q.   In Phoenix?
14   A.   Yes.
15   Q.   Where specifically were you and Mr. Coghill
16 sleeping?
17   A.   Motor home. Motor home.
18   Q.   Where was the motor home parked?
19   A.   Next to the house.
20   Q.   And did Mr. Coghill have a computer installed in the
21 motor home in October of '01?
22   A.   Yeah.
23   Q.   And did you use that computer?
24   A.   Yeah.
25   Q.   Did it have internet access?

1 A. As far as I remember, yeah. Maybe not at first,
2 because I think he had to run the cable like from the house to
3 the, I think he had a cable running from outside his bedroom
4 window in the house to the motor home. But I don't think, I
5 don't know, I'm not certain if he had it immediately when I
6 first got there or not.
7 Q. But at some point he did?
8 A. Yeah, shortly after.
9 Q. How long do you think you were living there when you
10 started living there in October of '01? In other words, for
11 how long did you live there the first time?
12 A. Um, probably until, only until like, December of '01
13 or like January of '02, because there was a period during that
14 time where I was homeless.
15 Q. Okay. Do you remember the specific day that you
16 stopped living there?
17 A. No, I do not. No.
18 Q. And how long were you homeless, if you remember?
19 A. I would say for a couple of weeks, because it was,
20 January of '02, because I had just found a job and I was
21 staying in like in a, in an abandoned apartment or whatever,
22 you know, an apartment complex they have like for utilities, I
23 found one that was unlocked, so I used to sleep in there. And
24 I would wake up at 7:00 in the morning and go to work. And I
25 did that until I got my first check, and then I ended up I --

MR. SKITZKI: Objection, this is nonresponsive.

THE COURT: Sustained.

All right.

THE WITNESS: All right.

BY MR. JENSVOLD:

Q. So how long do you think you were in this abandoned apartment?

A. A week or two.

Q. And then you say you got a job?

A. Uh-huh.

Q. Is that "yes"?

A. Yes.

Q. Where did you get a --

A. Synergy Solutions, a place in Phoenix.

Q. What were you doing there?

A. Tele sales work.

Q. Where did you move, then, after you stopped living in the abandoned apartment?

A. I ended up moving back in with Jim. And then he was giving me rides to work and stuff. I remember that.

Q. Then when do you think that started?

A. Um, probably maybe February or March of '02. And I pretty much, I stayed with him until about August of '02 straight on.

Q. Okay. So from February or March of '02 through

1 August of '02, you were living consistently with Mr. Coghill?
2   A. Right.
3   Q. At the motor home?
4   A. Yeah.
5   Q. What happened in August of '02, where did you go?
6   A. I ended up getting into a townhouse with a lady who
7 already had it.
8   Q. Okay. And where was that?
9   A. It was off of like Bell Road and 29th Street, in
10 Phoenix.
11   Q. Okay. How long were you at the townhouse?
12   A. I was only there, like, for like about two months,
13 until about November.
14   Q. Until November of '02?
15   A. Yes, of '02.
16   Q. Where did you live starting in November of '02?
17   A. I moved back and stayed back with Jim again.
18   Q. And then how long were you with Jim that time?
19   A. Until about January when my grandfather passed away.
20 I ended up moving to my grandfather's house after he passed
21 away.
22   Q. January of '03?
23   A. January '03, yes.
24   Q. Do you remember the day he died?
25   A. The 23rd of '03.

PIMA COUNTY SUPERIOR COURT

1   Q.   Do you remember telling Detective Moretz when you
2 interviewed with him, it was the 20th?
3   A.   Yeah, you were right.
4   Q.   Do you remember saying that?
5   A.   Yes, because it was a week before my cousin's
6 birthday, so that's on the 27th, so yes, it was the 20th. I
7 stand corrected.
8   Q.   Where did you go after your grandfather died?
9   A.   I went over to his place and stayed over there with
10 my aunt.
11   Q.   Okay. And how long were you there?
12   A.   Um, probably almost a month.
13   Q.   Then where were you living after that?
14   A.   After that I was just staying with some friends kind
15 of here and there. And then I ended up back with my friend,
16 Shannon. I ended up, I ended up going and living with my
17 friend Shannon.
18   Q.   And where was that?
19   A.   It was in Phoenix, off of like 44th Street and
20 Indian School.
21   Q.   How long were you living with Shannon?
22   A.   Two or three months.
23   Q.   And at some point did you come to live in Tucson
24 with Mr. Coghill?
25   A.   Yeah.

PIMA COUNTY SUPERIOR COURT

1 Q. Okay. How did that happen?
2 A. Well, he came up to -- I talked to him on the phone
3 and I explained to him that I couldn't find work or nothing.
4 And he said he might be able to find me some work down there.
5 So he came up and we ended up going down there.
6 Q. Okay.
7 A. And it, I went down there with him in order to find
8 a job, and find some work for myself.
9 Q. How long were you in Tucson before you called the
10 Sheriff's Department?
11 A. Um, it was at least a week, maybe a day or two after
12 a week.
13 Q. If it was April 1st of 2003, when you called the
14 police --
15 A. Uh-huh.
16 Q. -- do you remember which specific day it was that
17 you came down here?
18 A. I couldn't tell you off the top of my head, no.
19 Q. Do you remember which day of the week it was?
20 A. No.
21 Q. Do you remember stating at a previous hearing about
22 three years ago, you thought it might have been a Thursday or
23 Friday?
24 A. I vaguely remember something like that. I remember
25 saying something like that in court.

PIMA COUNTY SUPERIOR COURT

1   Q. Do you have any particular memory of it being a
2 Thursday or Friday as you stand here today?
3   A. No.
4   Q. Were you in Tucson celebrating Jim's birthday on
5 March 9th of 2003, or a couple of days before that?
6   A. Not on the 9th, no, I wasn't down there yet.
7   Q. Did Mr. Coghill come and pick you up sometime in
8 early March of 2003 from Phoenix, brought you down to Tucson,
9 and then took you back up about a week later?
10   A. No, it wasn't a previous Tucson trip. That was,
11 that was the only one, the only time I have been there.
12   Q. And have you ever been to Tucson before that?
13   A. Um, let me see. Hold on. No. Because I hadn't, I
14 hadn't gone to the prison down here yet, so, no, I hadn't.
15 That was my first time.
16   Q. And you never visited Tucson socially?
17   A. No.
18   Q. Buddies down here or anything?
19   A. No. I am from Phoenix. Sorry.
20   Q. You weren't attending the University of Arizona?
21   A. No, I was not.
22   Q. All right. So let me see if we can get these dates
23 somewhat straight based on what you said. Your testimony was
24 that you think it was October of '01 when you moved in with
25 Jim the very first time?

PIMA COUNTY SUPERIOR COURT

1 A. Yes.
2 Q. "JC" is for Jim Coghill. (Indicating)
3 A. Okay.
4 Q. How long did you say you were there?
5 A. From August until --
6 Q. I'm sorry. Starting in October.
7 A. Oh, October, I'm sorry. Until either November or
8 December. Probably December.
9 Q. Okay. And then the second time you think you lived
10 with him was when?
11 A. Shortly after I found a job in '02.
12 Q. So which month in '02 do you think that was?
13 A. I'm going to have to say either February or March.
14 Q. Okay. And I believe you said earlier that you
15 stayed there until August of '02, straight through?
16 A. Uh-huh.
17 Q. Is that a "yes"?
18 A. Yes. Yeah, I was there the whole summer.
19 Q. And then when was the third time that you lived at
20 the motor home?
21 A. The third time of '02, I would say from about
22 November of '02 to January of '03.
23 Q. Okay. And did you live with him at all between the
24 time that you left to go with your grandfather on January 20th
25 of '03, and when you came down here to Tucson sometime in

PIMA COUNTY SUPERIOR COURT

1 March of '03?

2 A. No, I never lived with him after that.

3 Q. Do you know when Mr. Coghill moved to Tucson?

4 A. I think it was about a month before he came and got
5 me, cause he had been down here about a month, I think, to get
6 himself established.

7 Q. Were you communicating with Mr. Coghill over e-mail
8 while he was in Tucson and you were still up in Phoenix?

9 A. Either e-mail or phone, I'm not sure. I don't think
10 we really exchanged too many e-mails that I'm aware of.

11 Q. Did he know your e-mail address back then?

12 A. Probably, yeah.

13 Q. Back then, what was your e-mail address back than?

14 A. I think it was like sequoiajade@hotmail.com or
15 something like that.

16 Q. Do you remember giving that e-mail address to the
17 detectives in April, April 1st of '03 when you talked to them?

18 A. Yeah, I do.

19 Q. And did you know Mr. Coghill's e-mail address at
20 that point, when you were in Phoenix and he was in Tucson?

21 A. Yeah.

22 Q. Okay. And then let's talk about what happened when
23 you came down to Tucson. When you guys got down to Tucson,
24 what kind of place were you living in?

25 A. I was living in his motor home in an RV park, off of

PIMA COUNTY SUPERIOR COURT

1 Benson Highway, down by the airport.
2   Q. And what was the first thing that you did when you
3 got down here, if you remember?
4   A. I don't remember.
5   Q. Did you spend some time on the computer while you
6 were down here in Tucson?
7   A. Oh, yeah.
8   Q. Was there, was there a computer inside the motor
9 home?
10   A. Correct. Yes.
11   Q. Do you know if it was the same computer that was in
12 the motor home back in Phoenix?
13   A. I couldn't tell you. I had no idea.
14   Q. Did you have your own computer that you were using
15 at that time?
16   A. No, not at that time, no.
17   Q. Were you using the website or program KaZaA when you
18 were in Tucson?
19   A. Yes.
20   Q. Were you using it to download music?
21   A. Yes.
22   Q. And can you tell the jury, if you remember, some of
23 the artists that you were downloading off of KaZaA at that
24 time?
25   A. Evanescense, Twizted.

PIMA COUNTY SUPERIOR COURT

1	Q.	How do you spell Twizted, by the way?
2	A.	T-W-I-Z-T-E-D.
3	Q.	It has nothing to do with Twisted Sister the drag
4	group?	
5	A.	No. No. They're a pop group.
6	Q.	Who else?
7	A.	Evanescence, probably Insane Clown Posse. Like,
8	probably like, like that genre of hip hop, but probably more	
9	leaning towards like evil kind of stuff.	
10	Q.	What about Dr. Octogan?
11	A.	Dr. Octogan, yes, I remember that one.
12	Q.	What about Q Strange?
13	A.	Yes, I remember that one, too.
14	Q.	And you were listening to those?
15	A.	Yes. Yeah, no, no, not his style of music at all.
16	Q.	That's Mr. Coghill?
17	A.	Yes.
18	Q.	Is that what you're talking about?
19	A.	Yeah. Mr. Coghill doesn't listen to music like
20	that, no.	
21	Q.	Was there a group called Rare Bird that you were
22	also downloading at that point?	
23	A.	Yeah, I downloaded the Rare Bird. That's actually a
24	group from the 70's or 60's that a friend of mine turned me on	
25	to.	

PIMA COUNTY SUPERIOR COURT

1 Q. Were there any other groups that you remember
2 downloading while you were in Tucson?
3 A. Not off the top of my head I cannot remember.
4 Q. Did you burn any movies to CD while you were in
5 Tucson, that you remember?
6 A. Not that I can recall. What kind of movies do you
7 mean?
8 Q. I'm just asking in general.
9 A. Just movies in general?
10 Q. Yeah.
11 A. No. Not that I'm aware of, no.
12 Q. Okay. Did you burn, let's be more specific. Did
13 you burn How The Grinch Stole Christmas to CD?
14 A. No, I never burned that disk.
15 Q. The Jim Carey version, I'll be specific.
16 A. No. I never, I never, no, I don't think I ever even
17 saw that movie until a few years ago.
18 Q. Have you ever seen the movie Pie?
19 A. I think I was going to, but I don't think I ever got
20 the chance to watch it.
21 Q. Did you burn that to CD while you were in Tucson?
22 A. No.
23 Q. Did you burn Total Recall to CD while you were in
24 Tucson?
25 A. No.

PIMA COUNTY SUPERIOR COURT

```
 1      Q.   How about Terminator?
 2      A.   No.
 3      Q.   How about Patch Adams?
 4      A.   No.
 5      Q.   Um, did you, have you ever made business cards for
 6  yourself in a business that you were going to create?
 7      A.   No.
 8      Q.   Did you download any operating software for this
 9  computer while you were in Tucson?
10      A.   Like Windows, you mean?
11      Q.   Or anything like that.
12      A.   No, not that I'm aware of.
13      Q.   Did you download any CD ram software for burning
14  CDs?
15      A.   Not that I'm aware of, no.
16      Q.   What programs on the computer while you were in
17  Tucson were installed on the computer that allowed you to burn
18  CDs?
19      A.   The only one that I can think of, well, I'm not sure
20  if, at that same time, I know for a fact that Nero was on
21  there.  And I know he used to use Roxio Easy CD Creator, but I
22  don't know if that was on the computer at the time.
23      Q.   Have you seen the forensic reports that Detective
24  Englander created in this case?
25      A.   I've heard about them.  I don't think I've really
```

PIMA COUNTY SUPERIOR COURT

```
 1  looked into them too much. I think I might have scanned over
 2  them, but I don't think I've ever really read them, no.
 3       Q.   Do you remember seeing, at least glancing at some of
 4  them, including the KaZaA logs at the last hearing about three
 5  years ago?
 6       A.   Well, yeah. I do actually, yeah, I saw that
 7  recently somewhere. Yeah, I do remember seeing the KaZaA
 8  logs.
 9       Q.   Okay. What did you bring with you from Phoenix to
10  Tucson when you came down here?
11       A.   Um, clothes, personal hygiene stuff, a CD case with
12  CDs of my own.
13       Q.   What kind of CDs did you have in that case?
14       A.   Music.
15       Q.   Were they music CDs that you had burned yourself, or
16  were they like commercial CDs, or both?
17       A.   Both.
18       Q.   Did you have any movies?
19       A.   No.
20       Q.   On DVD?
21       A.   No, not that I'm aware of. No, I did not own any
22  DVDs at the time, no.
23       Q.   All right. Let's talk about the other issues about
24  why we are here. Have you ever seen any images of children
25  engaging in sexual activity on Mr. Coghill's computer while
```

PIMA COUNTY SUPERIOR COURT

1 you were in Phoenix?
2   A.   Yeah.
3   Q.   Do you know, do you remember when, the first time
4 that you saw them?
5   A.   It had to have been like in the year '02. It was in
6 the year '02. I don't remember when. Probably during the
7 whole, the stretch I stayed during the summer perhaps.
8   Q.   But you're not positive when it happened?
9   A.   No, I'm not positive, no.
10   Q.   How did you come about seeing it, do you remember
11 that?
12   A.   I was asleep. The computer is pretty much where I
13 slept. It's a motor home, so it's kind of small and condensed
14 and that in there. And there was, say, a, like a little couch
15 deal. And basically right across the little walk way, it's
16 only like this far (indicating), there's a computer right
17 there.
18   And when I woke up, I seen him looking at it on the
19 computer. Or kind of glanced, and I noticed he was looking at
20 something and it didn't look like anything he should have been
21 looking at, you know what I mean?
22   Q.   And how many times do you think you saw Mr. Coghill
23 watching similar videos?
24   A.   Probably about three or four times, but I didn't
25 even, I don't think I ever even made my presence -- I think I

PIMA COUNTY SUPERIOR COURT

may have, I may have made my presence known that I was aware once, but a lot of times I just would roll back over and go to sleep and just like, whatever.

Q. Did, at some point, did you ever talk to Mr. Coghill about why he was watching those videos?

A. Yeah.

Q. And did he ever tell you why?

A. Um --

Q. That's a one word answer, yes or no.

A. Yes.

Q. Were some of his responses -- did they include, it turns me on?

A. Yes.

Q. Did he also say to you at some point that he's a sick and twisted individual?

A. Yes.

Q. Did you know that he shouldn't be allowed to watch those kinds of videos?

A. Yeah.

Q. Why didn't you ever call the police before April 1st of 2003?

A. Because I looked at it like this, the dude was helping me out. I never had to pay rent or nothing. He never bugged me about nothing. He just wanted me to do better for myself I think; you know, so I just, I kind of had a blind,

PIMA COUNTY SUPERIOR COURT

like, I kind of turned a blind -- you know, I was like, I kind of, I tried to overlook it and tried to pretend like he didn't have any of that. And, you know what I mean? I tried to fool myself into thinking that none of that stuff was even there, you know what I mean? Cause I didn't want to ruin the friendship with the guy, you know?

Q. Okay. Did Mr. Coghill, did he have an interest in Buddhist, for a lack of a better word, theologians or philosophers?

A. Absolutely.

Q. Who were some of those, if you remember?

A. Joseph Campbell, Alan Watts. That's the dude I can think of off the top of my head.

Q. Did you download any audio files from Joseph Campbell or Alan Watts while you were in Tucson?

A. No, I didn't download any of those.

Q. And if you had had, I mean, not to go into this, but you had had some conversations with Mr. Coghill about his Buddhist beliefs at some point during your relationship?

A. I had taken an interest in it myself, yes.

Q. And who would you say was more knowledgeable about it, you or Mr. Coghill?

A. Probably Mr. Coghill, yeah.

Q. Okay. Let's go to what happened on, let's start with March 31st of 2003, the day before you called the police.

PIMA COUNTY SUPERIOR COURT

A. Okay.

Q. What happened that day, as far as you remember?

A. He went to work. I took his go-ped out. I don't think I was supposed to take his go-ped out as far as I took it. I took it all the way pretty much to where we are at in this area now, and I got hit by a car when I was on it. And as a result, it destroyed his go-ped, and, you know.

Q. Okay. After you got hit by the car, what happened?

A. I got, I went to the hospital because my leg was pretty messed up and then somebody called the ambulance, and then they took me to Kino Hospital or something.

Q. Did the police respond?

A. No, I don't remember ever seeing the police.

Q. Do you remember seeing a police report or anything like that?

A. Wait a second, yes, yes, they did. I take that back, because they gave me a ticket for jaywalking or something, yeah.

Q. Can you describe for the jury what this go-ped looks like?

A. A go-ped is, it's a motor, it looks like a skateboard. The bottom looked like a skateboard, but it also looks like a scooter that you'll see like a kid go on. But it has like a lawnmower engine so you can start it up and you can go a lot faster.

PIMA COUNTY SUPERIOR COURT

1 Q. Did you have discussions with Mr. Coghill about you
2 being able to use this go-ped prior to March 31st of '03?
3 A. Oh, yeah, yeah. He said I could use it as long as I
4 stayed within a certain, like, vicinity. He didn't want me
5 going too far.
6 Q. Were you using it to try to find jobs down there?
7 A. Yeah.
8 Q. And, but he never gave you permission to come all
9 the way downtown?
10 A. Oh, no, no. I did that on my own, unfortunately. I
11 shouldn't have done it probably.
12 Q. All right. So what was the condition of the go-ped
13 after you got in the accident?
14 A. The go-ped was inoperable. I don't think it was
15 going to work. It looked like it got hit by a car.
16 Q. Did you take it with you to Kino Hospital?
17 A. Yeah. I wasn't going to leave it. It wasn't mine.
18 Q. What happened to you at Kino Hospital?
19 A. They didn't do much.
20 Q. What were your injuries?
21 A. I had a leg injury, ankle injury. They gave me,
22 they didn't really do nothing. Looked at it and said there
23 was nothing broken. They gave me a couple of prescriptions
24 and they sent me on my way.
25 Q. Okay.

PIMA COUNTY SUPERIOR COURT

1 A. That's all they did.
2 Q. How did you get from Kino Hospital back to the motor
3 home?
4 A. Well, I met a guy in front of the hospital who gave
5 me a ride about halfway down to the motor home from Kino, and
6 then I walked the rest of the way.
7 Q. How far was that?
8 A. Probably a good mile.
9 Q. All right. And then when you got back to the motor
10 home, was Mr. Coghill there?
11 A. No, he wasn't home yet.
12 Q. What happened when he got home?
13 A. He got home and I explained to him what happened.
14 And he was kind of, you know, pretty, you know, he was pretty
15 upset about the situation, but he was also concerned, you
16 know, glad I was okay, too, I think. So, I don't know, there
17 might have been a little animosity in the air there
18 afterwards.
19 Q. Okay. Did you guys have a discussion about that
20 that night, about what happened to the go-ped and all of that
21 stuff?
22 A. Yeah.
23 Q. Do you remember giving Mr. Coghill any information
24 about the police reports?
25 A. Not that I'm aware of, I don't think.

PIMA COUNTY SUPERIOR COURT

Q. Do you remember him writing anything down about it?

A. In regards to the go-ped?

Q. In regard to the police report that you had after being involved in the accident.

A. I don't remember.

Q. Did you ever call the police back, or did you ever have any reason to do that?

A. No, I never did; no.

Q. Did you ever have a court hearing that you had to go to afterwards?

A. No, nothing like that.

Q. Okay. So that night, what happened after you had the discussion about the go-ped and all of what happened that day?

A. That night, I don't think much happened. I think he went to bed and I went to bed. And there was, he wanted me to get my own -- I had a job interview the next day at the place that he worked at, and he said that it was my responsibility to find a way back from it. Or I could have sworn he told me, back than, I could have sworn he told me it was my responsibility to get a ride there, to my interview, and that was the go-ped which was destroyed now.

Q. Okay.

A. So, there was a discussion about that that night.

Q. How far away was the place that you were going to

```
 1  work from the motor home?
 2      A.  Probably a little over a mile.  I'm not sure.  It's,
 3  all right.  The motor home is on -- the motor home was at like
 4  Alvernon and Benson, and then this place is by the airport on
 5  Valencia.  I don't know if that's a mile or two miles, or --
 6      Q.  So, the plan was for you to have an interview there
 7  the next morning?
 8      A.  Um-hum.
 9      Q.  Yes?
10      A.  Yes.  Sorry.
11      Q.  Do you remember what time that interview was going
12  to be?
13      A.  I believe 9:00 a.m., or 9:30 a.m.
14      Q.  Okay.  And what happened the next morning?
15      A.  The next morning we got into an argument about the
16  shirt that I was going to wear.  I had a big, large shirt that
17  probably had some wrinkles in it and it didn't look like it
18  was going to be an appropriate shirt to wear, and he expressed
19  his concerns about it, and gave me a different shirt to wear.
20          And we were arguing with each other and nitpicking,
21  and it got to the point where he was fed up, and he said to
22  just pack all your stuff up and I'm just going to take you
23  back up to Phoenix and just forget about what we're trying to
24  do down here.
25      Q.  This shirt, did it fit you properly, the T-shirt
```

PIMA COUNTY SUPERIOR COURT

that you had on?

A. It was about a three-X shirt, so I would say, no, it was quite large on me, actually.

Q. Was that an appropriate shirt, in your opinion, to wear to this interview?

A. Maybe then, but now, no. No, not at all.

Q. But you thought it was okay back then?

A. Yeah, but I was a lot younger and less mature.

Q. Okay. So what happened after you guys got into this argument?

A. I left the motor home. I went, I just walked off to like blow off steam, you know. And than I started thinking that he was just going to, like you said, just drop me back off in Phoenix and that was going to be it. And I started feeling like anger towards him, you know what I mean? So I decided that I let him get away with what I knew for too long, so I decided that I needed to do the right thing.

Q. And what did you do?

A. I called the, I went to the pay phone at the Circle K, and I sat there for like 10 minutes and I thought about doing it, and I thought about doing it, and finally I called the 9-1-1 or something, I got them down there and I talked to them.

Q. Okay. Did some Sheriff Deputies come to the Circle K where you were, and talk to you?

A. Yeah, I think two of them did.

Q. After they talked to you, did you basically tell them what happened?

A. Yes.

Q. And did you tell them specifically about where to look for these particular files?

A. Uh-huh.

Q. Is that a "yes"?

A. Yes. Sorry.

Q. And what happened after you finished talking with theses two deputies?

A. They told me to kind of like hang around in the area, but not to go back or whatever. And then they went and they like, they went, they went over there.

Q. Okay. You didn't see them?

A. No, I did actually. I actually went over to the fence and I was looking and I watched them approach him and everything.

Q. You didn't go into the motor home when they were in there, did you?

A. No. No, I stayed away.

Q. So what did you do while they were at Mr. Coghill's?

A. Well, they said to like meet me back, they said to just wait here at the Circle K or whatever. That's what they told me, we'll be back. So you can just wait here at the

PIMA COUNTY SUPERIOR COURT

1 Circle K, kind of thing.
2   So after I went over there and I saw that, I just
3 went back to the Circle K and they probably came back about a
4 half hour later or so, and said that I needed to go and answer
5 questions.
6   Q.   Okay. And did you go at some point and do a sit
7 down interview with a detective?
8   A.   Yes.
9   Q.   And where was that?
10   A.   It was, it was at the Sheriff's station that has,
11 like, the multi floors.
12   Q.   How far away was that from where you were?
13   A.   A couple of miles.
14   Q.   Okay. And when you had this sit down interview with
15 the detective, were there a couple of different detectives
16 there?
17   A.   There was two of them.
18   Q.   And did another detective show up later?
19   A.   I don't remember.
20   Q.   Okay. So after you're done with the detectives,
21 what happened to you after that?
22   A.   Um, they set me up with some victim's rights people
23 or whatever, and they met me at the Greyhound Station and they
24 brought me some Eegees, and they said, here's a bus ticket for
25 you to go home, and said, thanks for your help, we'll be in

PIMA COUNTY SUPERIOR COURT

1 touch kind of thing.
2   Q. All right. While you were in Tucson, did you burn
3 any what you thought were child pornography files to a CD?
4   A. Yeah, there was one disk I did because it was on the
5 hard drive, and I told him I didn't want to have that shit on
6 the hard drive where I had my files.
7   Q. Okay. So when did that happen, if you remember, in
8 relation to the first day that you were down here?
9   A. Um, probably about halfway through.
10   Q. Okay. Do you remember the specific day?
11   A. Couldn't tell you.
12   Q. Okay. What did you do with that CD?
13   A. I asked him what he wanted me to write on it. He
14 said, write the word --
15   MR. SKITZKI: Objection, hearsay.
16   THE COURT: Overruled.
17   THE WITNESS: He asked me -- I asked him what to
18 write on it and he asked me to write the word "dirty" on it,
19 so I did.
20 BY MR. JENSVOLD:
21   Q. And what did you do with that CD?
22   A. Gave it to him.
23   Q. Do you know what he did with it?
24   A. No.
25   Q. And so what did you do after you took that CD out of

the drive?

A. Um, I think I put another blank CD in and probably burned stuff that I had, that I wanted to burn.

Q. And what was that?

A. Just music.

Q. What kind of a CD drive was it? Was it installed in the tower, was it external?

A. External.

Q. Were there any other external devices hooked up to the computer?

A. There was a scanner and there was a printer.

Q. Do you remember seeing a zip drive or anything like that?

A. Yes, there was a zip drive, too.

Q. Do you remember what the label was for the CD drive that was external? Was it, what letter designates it when you pull up the window to see it?

A. It was either E or F, one of the two, or G. Could have been G for all I know; E, F, or G.

Q. You don't remember specifically?

A. No, not specifically, no, sorry.

Q. How many CDs were there that were next to the computer in the motor home?

A. Oh, I don't know. A lot. I would say over a hundred.

Q. Okay. Do you know how many different spindles there were?

A. I would say four or five.

Q. Were any of those CDs on the spindles yours?

A. I think I had a small, I had a small spindle with me in a small CD case. That was it, that was mine.

Q. What about the ones that were standing near the computer, were those yours?

A. Don't remember. Don't remember what they were.

Q. How many bags did you have with you when you were down there, do you know?

A. Just the one, I think. I think I just had one.

Q. Would you recognize your own handwriting if you saw it?

A. Absolutely.

Q. All right. Mr. Coghill, I want to show you a number of different exhibits.

A. I'm Mr. Franks.

Q. What did I call you?

A. You called me Mr. Coghill.

Q. I'm sorry. All right.

Mr. Franks, let's start with State's Exhibit 16-A; do you recognize that?

A. Yeah.

Q. What is it?

PIMA COUNTY SUPERIOR COURT

1   A.   That's the word "dirty." That's the one I labeled
2 that you just brought up a minute ago.
3   Q.   Is that your handwriting?
4   A.   Yeah. That's my handwriting; really quick, jotted.
5 sloppy, handwriting.
6   Q.   I'm going to show you some other, let's see, State's
7 Exhibit number, well, great--16-B. Hold on one second.
8   With the counsels' permission, I'm going to flip one
9 of these CDs around so the label can be seen. Fingerprints
10 don't matter at this point.
11   All right. State's Exhibit 16-B. Do you recognize
12 either of these two CDs?
13   A.   Look like a lot of the CDs that were in there.
14   Q.   Okay. And did you write the words that are on the
15 outside of either of these CDs? The letters that are on the
16 outside of either one of these two CDs?
17   A.   No. Nope on that one.
18   Q.   Sorry. Wait until I ask you a question.
19   A.   Okay.
20   Q.   State's 16-C, have you seen these two before?
21   A.   They look familiar.
22   Q.   Did you write these two letters on either one of
23 these CDs?
24   A.   No, sir.
25   Q.   Same question for 16-D.

PIMA COUNTY SUPERIOR COURT

1	A.	No, sir.
2	Q.	Same question for 16-E?
3	A.	No.
4	Q.	16-F?
5	A.	No.
6	Q.	16-G?
7	A.	No.
8	Q.	16-H?
9	A.	No.
10	Q.	16-I?
11	A.	Nope.
12	Q.	16-J?
13	A.	No.
14	Q.	16-K?
15	A.	No, sir. Nope.
16	Q.	16-L?
17	A.	No.
18	Q.	Do you know who wrote the writing on the outside of
19	any of these CDs?	
20	A.	Yeah, I do.
21	Q.	Did you see the person write it?
22	A.	No, I can't say that I did.
23	Q.	Okay. So you can't say for sure who actually, you
24	didn't see the person writing on the CDs?	
25	A.	I can't say that I saw the person writing on any of

PIMA COUNTY SUPERIOR COURT

1 these CDs at all, honestly. I recognize the handwriting, but
2 I can't be for sure that I -- I didn't see anybody write them.
3   Q. Prior to April 1st of 2003, were you familiar with
4 Mr. Coghill's handwriting?
5   A. It was never, nothing I ever thought about, no.
6   Q. Okay. All right. Let's see. This is State's
7 Exhibit 16-Q. Do you recognize the writing on that CD?
8   A. That's my writing.
9   Q. How about 16-P?
10   A. Not my writing.
11   Q. 16-O?
12   A. Nope.
13   Q. 16-M?
14   A. No.
15   Q. 16-N?
16   A. No.
17   Q. Okay. So out of all the CDs I have shown you, the
18 only exhibits that you say are your handwriting are 16-A and
19 16-Q?
20   A. Correct.
21   Q. All right. Mr. Franks, at some point after April
22 1st of 2003, did you fill out a handwriting sample?
23   A. Yes.
24   Q. How did that come about? How were you, I mean, who
25 contacted you, and how was that whole thing set up?

PIMA COUNTY SUPERIOR COURT

1 A. I was actually in Maricopa County Jail, and they
2 said I had a visitor. And so of course I went to go see who
3 it was. And it was a gentleman who had me do a bunch of
4 handwriting samples.
5 Q. And did you fill that out?
6 A. Of course, I had to.
7 Q. And did you use your normal handwriting as far as
8 you know when you filled that out?
9 A. Yeah.
10 Q. I am going to open, with the counsels' permission,
11 State's Exhibit 25-B.
12   MR. SKITZKI: That's fine.
13 BY MR. JENSVOLD:
14 Q. Okay. Mr. Franks, take a look at the document
15 that's inside the outer envelope marked 25-B and C, and see if
16 you recognize it.
17 A. Yes, I recognize it.
18 Q. What is it?
19 A. It's the first paper that he gave me when he started
20 the handwriting analysis.
21 Q. Flip through there and see if you recognize the
22 other documents that are attached.
23 A. Yes, I recognize these.
24 Q. Okay. Is all of that your handwriting, except for
25 the signatures of somebody else at the bottom?

```
 1    A.   Yeah.  Yeah, even these here, when he had me write
 2  with my left hand and all of that, yup, that's all, yeah.
 3         MR. JENSVOLD:  Your Honor, the State would move for
 4  the admission of State's Exhibits 25-B, 16-A and 16-Q.
 5         MR. SKITZKI:  No objection.
 6         THE COURT:  State's 16-A, 16-Q and State's 16-B are
 7  admitted.
 8  BY MR. JENSVOLD:
 9    Q.   Mr. Coghill, what was your sleeping schedule like
10  when you were down at -- I did it again.
11    A.   That's fine.
12    Q.   Mr. Franks, I'm sorry.  I'm just going to call you
13  Jake.
14    A.   That's fine.
15    Q.   Jake, when you were down in Tucson, what was your
16  sleeping schedule like?
17    A.   Probably stay up all night and sleep all day kind of
18  schedule.  Not a very responsible schedule in society's terms.
19    Q.   And you weren't working during that week?
20    A.   No.
21    Q.   Did you know any of Mr. Coghill's neighbors in
22  Tucson?
23    A.   Just one.
24    Q.   Who was that?
25    A.   Probably, I'm probably wrong, but I think it was
```

PIMA COUNTY SUPERIOR COURT

```
 1  Bill Hoppe.
 2       Q.   How do you know him?
 3       A.   Well, it was a guy that he's worked with several
 4  times in the aviation industry, and I guess it's just been a
 5  friend of his for years.  And he happened to get a place, his,
 6  his lot or whatever was like right next door to this guy.
 7       Q.   And so did you see him while you were in Tucson?
 8       A.   Yeah, we went over there once; had a brisket.
 9       Q.   And did you celebrate Mr. Coghill's birthday or, in
10  the early first week of March with Mr. Hoppe?
11       A.   No, I wasn't there for that.
12            MR. JENSVOLD:  I think that's all I have.
13       Thank you.
14            THE COURT:  Cross-examination?
15
16                       CROSS-EXAMINATION
17  BY MR. SKITZKI:
18       Q.   Good morning, Mr. Franks.
19       A.   Good morning.
20       Q.   I guess before we start asking you some questions, I
21  want to go over a couple of things.  You were convicted in
22  Maricopa County Superior Court in CR-2006-124912 back on June
23  19th, 2006, correct?
24       A.   Yes.
25            MR. JENSVOLD:  Objection; cumulative.
```

PIMA COUNTY SUPERIOR COURT

1 THE COURT: Overruled.
2 BY MR. SKITZKI:
3 Q. And, Mr. Franks, you were convicted of CR-2003-
4 02195 in Maricopa County Superior Court back on December 2nd,
5 2003?
6 A. Yes.
7 Q. Mr. Franks, you were convicted of CR-2003-015892 in
8 Maricopa County Superior Court on December 2nd, 2003 as well?
9 A. Yes.
10 Q. You were also convicted of CR-2002-006002 in
11 Maricopa County Superior Court on April 17th, 2002?
12 A. Yes.
13 Q. And now, finally, you were convicted of CR-1999-0
14 01550 in Maricopa County Superior Court, I guess, in early,
15 would that be early 2000?
16 A. That's correct.
17 Q. Now, you and Jim Coghill have been friends on and
18 off since approximately 1999, correct?
19 A. Yes.
20 Q. And that friendship came about because you and
21 Mr. Coghill were working at the same call center?
22 A. Yeah.
23 Q. During the time that you have been friends with
24 Mr. Coghill, it would be fair to state that he has, he has on
25 occasions assisted you in obtaining employment?

```
 1    A.   Yeah.
 2    Q.   More than once?
 3    A.   He has, yes.
 4    Q.   He's gotten you jobs.
 5    A.   He has, yes.
 6    Q.   And you have already told us when Mr. Jensvold was
 7  asking you questions, that on more than one occasion
 8  Mr. Coghill has given you a place to stay.
 9    A.   Yes.
10    Q.   And he gave you a place to stay when you didn't have
11  anywhere else to go?
12    A.   Yes.
13    Q.   He gave you a place to stay when you, up until that
14  point in time on occasion, you were homeless.
15    A.   Yeah.
16    Q.   You had no roof over your head.
17    A.   That is true.
18    Q.   All the times that Mr. Coghill let you stay with
19  him, he never charged you rent.
20    A.   No.
21    Q.   The times that Mr. Coghill let you stay with him
22  were, in part, to get you back on your feet?
23    A.   Yes.
24    Q.   He would let you stay because, I think you told us
25  originally that he wanted to help you better yourself.
```

PIMA COUNTY SUPERIOR COURT

1   A. Right.
2   Q. He never asked for anything from you.
3   A. No.
4   Q. He never asked for any money from you for rent.
5   A. Right.
6   Q. He never asked for any money from you for anything
7   when you, when you eventually got work and you were staying
8   with him.
9   A. That's true.
10 Q. He would feed you?
11 A. Yeah. I would feed myself, too, you know, but--
12 Q. But he would provide, he would put food in the
13 refrigerator?
14 A. He did. Yeah, he helped me.
15 Q. And he didn't take any position that you couldn't
16 touch that food. What he had, he shared with you?
17 A. Right.
18 Q. He allowed you free reign of, because it was the
19 motor home that you were living with him in on the occasions
20 that you were living with him?
21 A. Correct.
22 Q. So you could come and go as you please?
23 A. Yeah.
24 Q. You could use the computer?
25 A. Yeah.

PIMA COUNTY SUPERIOR COURT

```
 1     Q.    You could watch TV?
 2     A.    Um-hum
 3     Q.    You could bathe?
 4     A.    Um-hum.
 5     Q.    Do whatever, it was your house?
 6     A.    Yeah.
 7     Q.    You have some proficiency and some experience with
 8  computers.
 9     A.    Yes.
10     Q.    You, I think that you mentioned in some prior
11  interview that somebody stuck you in front of a computer when
12  you were seven, and you basically taught yourself over the
13  years?
14     A.    Correct.
15     Q.    It's your testimony here today, that as of April
16  1st, 2003, you had only been in Tucson for a little more than
17  a week?
18     A.    Right.
19     Q.    You never came, or Mr. Coghill never came up to
20  Phoenix to pick you up and bring you down in early March of
21  2003 for his birthday?
22     A.    I didn't go down to Tucson.
23     Q.    First time you came down to Tucson?
24     A.    Last week of March of '03.
25     Q.    Okay.  Since 1999, separate and apart from Mr.
```

PIMA COUNTY SUPERIOR COURT

1 Coghill, how many other different places have you lived?
2 A. Um, quite a few.
3 Q. And on many of those occasions that you lived in
4 different places, the folks that you stayed with kicked you
5 out, is that fair to say?
6 A. Sometimes, yes.
7 Q. So, you know, you have worn out your welcome in more
8 than one household before you got to Jim Coghill, correct?
9 A. Sometimes, yes.
10 Q. In January of 2003, your grandfather died?
11 A. Yes.
12 Q. At that time after your grandfather died, you moved
13 into his house with your aunt, correct?
14 A. Uh-huh, yes.
15 Q. Your aunt, within about a month, kicked you out of
16 your grandfather's house, correct?
17 A. Yes.
18 Q. Your aunt in the process of kicking you out of your
19 grandfather's house, took your clothes and lit them on fire in
20 the front yard?
21 A. No, she put them in the fireplace.
22 Q. Sorry.
23 A. But, yeah, she did that.
24 Q. But you did have, so it would be fair to say that
25 you had a falling out with your aunt?

PIMA COUNTY SUPERIOR COURT

```
 1    A.   Yeah.
 2    Q.   So by the time you got back to staying with
 3  Mr. Coghill in late March of 2003, you had a couple of duffle
 4  bags of cloths and your spindle of disks, is that about right?
 5    A.   Yeah.
 6         MR. SKITZKI:  If I may approach the witness?
 7         THE COURT:  Yes.
 8  BY MR. SKITZKI:
 9    Q.   So, Mr. Franks, back in, I guess, 2003, your e-mail
10  address was, it was sequoiajade, is that all one word?
11    A.   Uh-huh; yes.
12    Q.   And that's at hotmail, and that's that "@" symbol,
13  correct?
14    A.   Yes.
15    Q.   And it's hotmail.com?
16    A.   Yes.
17    Q.   And when you -- you talked to, at some point in
18  time, to the police about this child pornography that you
19  reported that Mr. Coghill had, do you remember that?
20    A.   Yeah.
21    Q.   And one of the things that you talked to them about
22  was, they were asking you the specifics of what this stuff
23  was?
24    A.   Yes.
25    Q.   You told them that there was stuff that was labeled,
```

1 I think you said it was R@ygold?
2   A. Yes.
3   Q. And you described to them what R@ygold, how that
4 would be written, is that correct?
5   A. Yes.
6   Q. And when we're talking about R@ygold, are we saying
7 R-A-Y-G-O-L-D?
8   A. No.
9   Q. Could you please write on that board up there what
10 we are talking about by way of R@ygold.
11   A. Well, the A was actually the @ symbol, so it was
12 like, R@ygold. Like that (indicating).
13   Q. Okay. And you pronounced it Raygold, though, fair
14 to say?
15   A. It looks like Raygold to me.
16   Q. So that @ symbol sort of looks like an a, so we just
17 pronounce it like an 'a."
18   A. Okay.
19   Q. That's what you're telling us?
20   A. Yes.
21   Q. Okay.
22   A. That's the way I looked at it.
23   Q. You had -- when you spoke with the police, you told
24 them about four, five folks who would, I guess, vouch or
25 substantiate the statements that you had made about Mr.

PIMA COUNTY SUPERIOR COURT

1 Coghill and the child pornography, correct?
2   A. Yeah.
3   Q. And you gave the police the names of those four or
4 five people, isn't that true?
5   A. Uh-huh. Yes.
6   Q. That's a "yes"?
7   A. Yes.
8   Q. Okay. You told the police, I guess, when you had
9 that interview with them -- and that was April 1st, 2003,
10 correct?
11   A. Yes.
12   Q. You told them in part that, you know, what had been
13 going on in your life, that everyone was getting sick of you.
14 Do you remember telling them that?
15   A. I think so, yes.
16   Q. But Mr. Coghill kept giving you chances, is that
17 correct?
18   A. Yes.
19   Q. When you were there that last week in March, it was
20 Mr. Coghill that arranged for the job interview for you with
21 his employer?
22   A. Yes.
23   Q. You indicated to the police when you spoke with them
24 back on April 1st, 2003, that you believed when you walked out
25 of that motor home after having that argument with Mr. Coghill

PIMA COUNTY SUPERIOR COURT

1 in the morning, that you believed that your friendship with
2 him was going to be over forever, correct?
3   A.   Seemed like it at the time, yes.
4   Q.   You were angry about that?
5   A.   I was.
6   Q.   And you told the police that the reason why, you
7 know, you called, was that you were pissed at Mr. Coghill.
8   A.   Yeah.
9   Q.   Do you remember, during the period of time that you
10 were friends with Mr. Coghill, telling him that he should
11 never make you angry?
12   A.   I don't remember that.
13   Q.   Do you remember telling a Sheriff's Deputy that you
14 had told Mr. Coghill early on in your friendship that he
15 should never make you angry?
16   A.   I don't recall that, no.
17   Q.   When you, during the time that you've known
18 Mr. Coghill, even on those occasions when you weren't living
19 with him, there would be occasions that you would come over to
20 visit him on weekends, isn't that true?
21   A.   Yeah, we would visit.
22   Q.   So you would hang out there. Would you spend the
23 night, you know, even though you weren't living with him, but
24 you might spend the night over, you know, one or two days of
25 the weekend?

         A.   Yeah. I have, yeah.
         Q.   And again, on those occasions, you would have had access to the computer, correct?
         A.   Yes.
         Q.   And at the time, well, at all the times that you lived with Mr. Coghill, would it be fair to state that you were pretty much a night owl?
         A.   Yeah.
         Q.   So you would, you would be up late at night and oftentimes sleep during the day?
         A.   Yes.
         Q.   When you would be up late at night, oftentimes you would be on the computer, would that be fair to say?
         A.   Yes.
         Q.   You would be surfing the net, or downloading things?
         A.   Perhaps, yes.
         Q.   Because one of the things that you did enjoy doing would be downloading, downloading music onto the computer, correct?
         A.   I still do to this day.
         Q.   And in part, when you would download music onto the computer, sometimes you would take that music and then you would burn that on to CD?
         A.   Yes.
         Q.   Now you said that, let's talk about at around April

```
 1   1st of 2003.  When you were staying with Mr. Coghill in that
 2   motor home here in Tucson, there were hundreds of disks in
 3   that motor home, correct?
 4        A.   Yeah.
 5        Q.   You said that some of those disks that might have
 6   been around the computer may have belonged to you, correct?
 7        A.   The ones around the computer, I don't remember what
 8   they were or what.  It's been a couple of years I think.
 9        Q.   In any event, that day, April 1st, at some point in
10   time, the Sheriff's Deputies, before they put you on the bus
11   back up to Phoenix --
12        A.   Hum-um.
13        Q.   -- they took you back to Mr. Coghill's house because
14   you needed to get your property, isn't that true?
15        A.   Right.  Yeah.
16        Q.   The Sheriff's Deputies let you back into
17   Mr. Coghill's motor home?
18        A.   Um-hum.
19        Q.   That's a "yes"?
20        A.   Yes.  Yes, they did.
21        Q.   When you went back into the motor home, you got your
22   clothes?
23        A.   Uh-huh.
24        Q.   That's a "yes"?
25        A.   Yes.
```

PIMA COUNTY SUPERIOR COURT

Q. Were you, when you left that morning to go to the Circle K, or to walk out and cool down, and then you ultimately made the phone call, did you think that you were leaving that morning?

A. Yeah. Yes, sir, I did

Q. Had you already packed your things?

A. I don't think, I don't think I had my things packed up, or I was only there, so I didn't really unpack anything to begin with, you know what I mean. I didn't really unpack anything. I think I was just living out of the bag.

Q. So you got back in after you called the police, when the Deputies took you back, you got your bag and your, you went through the place to make sure that you didn't have any stuff laying around, would that be fair to state?

A. They didn't let me do much when I was in there. They said, get your stuff and get out of there, like fast. They didn't give me time to look around, really. They just said, get your shit and go.

Q. But you got your spindle and your CD case with your disks?

A. Yes.

Q. You took that with you?

A. Yes.

Q. They let you take it?

A. Yes, they did.

PIMA COUNTY SUPERIOR COURT

1 Q. Did they look at it?
2 A. I don't think they did.
3 Q. Did they have you go through any of the other
4 spindles and disks to see if you were going to say that any of
5 that stuff was yours?
6 A. No.
7 Q. Did you ask them for the time to go through the
8 spindles to see if there was anything of yours mixed in there?
9 A. No, because I didn't think they would have gave me
10 the time. They didn't seem to want to be doing too much more
11 on the whole situation. They wanted to move on. You know,
12 they weren't, they were kind of in a hurry, it seemed like to
13 me.
14 Q. You told the detectives that interviewed you, well,
15 actually, you told us when we interviewed you, that the disks
16 with the child pornography were on the bottom of the spindles.
17 A. I believe so, yes.
18 Q. I think back in 2003 when there was a prior court
19 hearing, you had been working around that time as a loan
20 specialist. Do you remember that?
21 A. You got your dates wrong, '06, you mean.
22 Q. 2006, you were you working as a loan specialist, is
23 that correct?
24 A. Not for very long.
25 Q. Did you get terminated, fired from that job?

PIMA COUNTY SUPERIOR COURT

    A. Yeah, because they found that I had a criminal history that I neglected to mention.
    Q. So you filed, you had to fill out a job application for that loan specialist position, is that correct?
    A. Um-hum.
    Q. Is that correct?
    A. Yes.
    Q. That you put your work background, and I take it that on that job application there was a question that asked about any kind of felony history, correct?
    A. Yes.
    Q. I take it you didn't put anything on that job application about your felony history?
    A. I did not.
    Q. So in the process of filling out that job application, you lied?
    A. I did. Yes. I did, yes.
    Q. Would it be fair to state that you have lied on other job applications?
    A. Not anymore, no.
    Q. Well, not anymore, but how about prior to recently now that you have decided to be truthful and honest on a job application?
        MR. JENSVOLD: Objection, cumulative.
        THE COURT: Sustained. Maybe you can rephrase your

```
 1  question, but not sustained on cumulative, sustained on
 2  sarcastic.
 3  BY MR. SKITZKI:
 4      Q.  I apologize, Mr. Franks.
 5      A.  That's okay.
 6      Q.  Can you give us an estimate as to how many job
 7  applications you have lied on?
 8      A.  I would say two.  That one and one other, that's it.
 9      Q.  When you had your interview with the detectives back
10  on April 1, 2003. midway through that interview, do you
11  remember a Detective Englander coming in?
12      A.  Yes.  Sounds familiar.
13      Q.  At that point when Detective Englander came into the
14  interview in the midway period, he indicated to you that he
15  had spoken with Mr. Coghill.
16      A.  That's correct.
17      Q.  At the time that he indicated to you that he had
18  spoken with Mr. Coghill, he told you that Mr. Coghill
19  basically denied ownership or knowledge of the child
20  pornography.
21      A.  Yes.
22      Q.  And then he said, he basically said, you know, now
23  we've got this issue about, you know, whose child pornography
24  it is basically.
25      A.  Okay.
```

1	Q.	Do you remember him saying things to that effect?
2	A.	Yes. Yes, I do actually.
3	Q.	You were aware at the time that you were doing this interview with the detectives from the Sheriff's Department, that child pornography is illegal?
6	A.	Yes.
7	Q.	That it's a crime to possess child pornography?
8	A.	Yes.
9	Q.	That it carries with it some significant penalties?
10	A.	Absolutely.
11	Q.	At that point in time, then you told Detective Englander that you very likely had probably handled or touched those child pornography disks.
14	A.	Yes.
15	Q.	And you have told us here today, that you agree that you personally burned a disk that contained child pornography?
17	A.	Yes, because I was instructed to.
18	Q.	So what you are telling us is that you burned a disk containing child pornography, yes or no?
20	A.	That's correct.
21	Q.	What year was it that you did the writing sample from the jail?
23	A.	Um, probably -- good question.
24	Q.	Is it on the, is it on the samples there that you have in front of you?

PIMA COUNTY SUPERIOR COURT

1   And could you tell us what that exhibit is marked?
2   MR. JENSVOLD: It's 25-B.
3   THE COURT: It's probably on the back.
4   MR. SKITZKI: I think it was on the back; that's the
5 problem.
6   THE WITNESS: Oh, yeah, it was; shit, yeah, 25-B.
7 BY MR. SKITZKI:
8   Q. So you are looking at 25-B. Does it have a date on
9 it?
10   A. Yeah, it does, actually. October 15, 2003.
11   Q. So October 15, 2003, Detective Englander comes out
12 to visit you at the jail up at Maricopa County.
13   A. No, it wasn't him.
14   Q. It was some other detective?
15   A. No, it was a handwriting specialist guy.
16   Q. Does he tell you what he is there for?
17   A. Yes. Yes, he does.
18   Q. What is your understanding as to what the purpose is
19 of you filling out that paper?
20   A. Yeah, he wants to make sure that I didn't write all
21 those disks, or, you know, what was written, you know what I
22 mean; whose handwriting is on those disks.
23   Q. So when you're filling out that paper, you know that
24 the purpose that somebody is going to be looking at that, is
25 to see if they can match your writing that you're going to

PIMA COUNTY SUPERIOR COURT

1 give them to the writing on the disks, is that right?
2   A.   Right.
3   Q.   Do you remember telling one of the uniformed
4 Sheriff's Deputies that you had been in Tucson for a month
5 before you had made that call on April 1st, 2003?
6   A.   No. I don't remember that Deputy.
7   MR. SKITZKI: I don't have anything further.
8   Thank you, Mr. Franks.
9   THE WITNESS: You're welcome.
10   THE COURT: Any Redirect?
11
12   REDIRECT EXAMINATION
13 BY MR. JENSVOLD:
14   Q.   Mr. Coghill, do you have an interest in child
15 pornography?
16   MR. SKITZKI: Objection; Mr. Franks.
17 BY MR. JENSVOLD:
18   Q.   Jake, do you have an interest in child pornography?
19   A.   No.
20   Q.   If you had one adjective to choose, what would you
21 use in describing it?
22   A.   One adjective, despicable.
23   Q.   Do you remember telling the Detectives you found it
24 repulsive?
25   A.   Repulsive, disgusting, grotesque.

PIMA COUNTY SUPERIOR COURT

Q. Okay. Did you ever while you were on the computer at Mr. Coghill's motor home in Phoenix or in Tucson, download any images from the internet, images of child pornography?

A. No, I did not.

Q. What were the, as far as you know, what were the disks that Mr. Coghill had transferred the child pornography images to, what were they labeled?

A. As far as I know, they were all labeled K-P, standing for kiddy porn.

Q. Did he tell you that?

A. Yeah, I don't know when, I don't remember when, but it was, it was made obvious. So --

Q. Jake, did you fake your handwriting sample?

A. No.

Q. Jake, did you tell the two Deputies that came to the Circle K when you first called 9-1-1, did you tell them that you had been in Tucson for about a week?

A. For about a week, yes.

Q. Did you tell Detective Englander later on in that formal interview that you thought you had been in Tucson for a week to 10 days?

A. A week to 10 days, yes. That's the correct time frame. This month thing, I don't know. I'm sorry.

Q. Oh, did you have your belongings with you when you went to the formal interview with the Detectives at the

1 Sheriff's Department?
2   A. No, my belongings were still in the motor home.
3   Q. So did you go back and get them after your
4 interview?
5   A. Yes.
6   Q. Is that when it happened?
7   A. Yes. I told them to take me to get my stuff, let me
8 get my stuff if I wasn't going to stay there anymore.
9   Q. Do you remember specifically when any of the
10 deputies or detectives had looked through your CDs while this
11 happened?
12   A. I no idea what happened, because I wasn't in there.
13 As far as I know, Mr. Coghill went to Phoenix to get his
14 go-ped fixed, so it sounds like they were just in there by
15 themselves or something.
16   I'm sorry, I don't mean to speculate.
17   Q. I don't want to ask you to speculate. I just want
18 to ask you if you know, whether any --
19   A. I don't know. I do not know if they went through my
20 stuff or not.
21   Q. You have got to let me finish. You don't know
22 whether they looked through your stuff while you were with the
23 Detectives at the Sheriff's Department headquarters?
24   A. Don't know.
25   Q. How did you find out what the, what some of these

PIMA COUNTY SUPERIOR COURT

child porn files were labeled with the R@ygold that you talked about with Mr. Skitzki?

A. Because sometimes I would find disks in the spindles that didn't have labels or whatever. Or like, some, I don't know, I mean, am I allowed to look through these? Or --

Q. You can if you want to.

A. I'd rather not. But there is some of them in there that didn't say R-P, they might have said something else, and I would bring it up, and I would say that the file titles were kind of like describing what was going on in the movie, in regards to the child stuff.

Q. Okay. Do you also remember telling Detective Moretz during your interview on April 1st, 2003, that you had been on the computer and you inadvertently clicked on something and it was entitled something similar to R@ygold?

A. Yes. Yes, it did, and it came up, and I was like, oh, my God, and I clicked it off.

Q. Did you have any child pornography images in your spindle of CDs?

A. No, sir.

Q. Those people that you had spoken about with Mr. Skitzki that you might have mentioned some of these activities with Mr. Coghill about, did those people, did you tell them about Mr. Coghill watching child pornography?

A. Yeah, I believe I did.

PIMA COUNTY SUPERIOR COURT

1 Q. Who were some of those people, if you remember?
2 A. Well, the McClellans, I told them. They were
3 friends of mine who I also kind of had Jim kind of like over
4 there sometimes. He was kind of friends with them as well.
5 Q. Did you tell them before April 1st, 2003?
6 A. Huh-uh. Wait. Yes. Yes. I take that back, I did,
7 yeah.
8 Q. Was it before you moved to Tucson?
9 A. Yes. Yeah. Yes, it was.
10 Q. Jake, I want to show you just a few pages of what's
11 been marked as State's Exhibit 12-D. Do you recognize what
12 this is? Have you seen it before?
13 A. I didn't see this part, but the other part that you
14 just pulled up a second ago, the KaZaA logs are all the ones I
15 seen. No, I have never seen all this.
16 Q. I am referring you to page 13 --
17 A. Okay.
18 Q. --to be more specific. There is, this is the KaZaA
19 log. It will be identified later through Mr. Englander but,
20 that this is the KaZaA log from Mr. Coghill's computer. There
21 is -- I have the wrong exhibit. Hold on a second.
22   12-C. Sorry.
23   Okay. Do you recognize this? Have you seen any of
24 this before?
25 A. Yeah, I think I have a copy of that. Yeah.

PIMA COUNTY SUPERIOR COURT

1	Q.	Okay. Does it--
2	A.	Yeah.
3	Q.	This is State's Exhibit 12-C. It's marked KaZaA at

the top, it has the KaZaA label?

4. A. Um-hum.

1 Q. Okay. Does it--
2 A. Yeah.
3 Q. This is State's Exhibit 12-C. It's marked KaZaA at
4 the top, it has the KaZaA label?
5 A. Um-hum.
6 Q. Is that "yes"?
7 A. Yes. Yes, I have seen that, or at least that part
8 of it.
9 Q. On page 13 there is some indications about a
10 download Accelerator Plus 6.1.exe. Did you download that on
11 KaZaA while you were with Mr. Coghill?
12 A. I believe so.
13 Q. You think you did?
14 A. Yeah.
15 Q. Why?
16 A. Why? Because it allegedly makes your downloads
17 faster.
18 Q. Okay. It says it was on March 4th. Were you there
19 on March 4th?
20 A. I wasn't there on March 4th though.
21 Q. Did you download Space Invaders?
22 A. Is that like a game?
23 Q. I can't answer your question.
24 A. Space Invaders, not that I'm aware of, no.
25 Q. On page number one, there is an indication that

PIMA COUNTY SUPERIOR COURT

1 there is Evanescence, Fallen, on March 26th. Did you do that?
2   A.   That one, yeah.
3   Q.   There is this group you mentioned earlier, Twizted,
4 on March 26th. Did you do that?
5   A.   Yeah. Yeah, that is me.
6   Q.   Was KaZaA already set up and running when you came
7 down to Tucson?
8   A.   I'm pretty sure it was. A KaZaA light.
9   Q.   Or were you able, as soon as you got on the
10 computer, were you able to --
11   A.   There was already a computer, there was already the
12 program installed on the machine, yes.
13   Q.   Did you have to install KaZaA on the machine?
14   A.   No, it was already on there.
15   Q.   I don't want to go through all of these, but there
16 are some more on page 27, record number 125 says, Evanescence,
17 Silver Rain?
18   A.   Yeah.
19   Q.   Did you download that?
20   A.   Yeah. Yeah. Yup. Yup. Yeah.
21   Q.   Were you really into Evanescence at the time that
22 you were down there?
23   A.   Yeah. Yeah. I could safely say that.
24   Q.   And this is page 41. There is an indication, record
25 number 183 is Q Strange. Did you download that?

PIMA COUNTY SUPERIOR COURT

```
 1      A.   Yeah.  Yeah.  Those are me.  I did that.
 2           MR. JENSVOLD:  I think that's all I have.
 3           THE WITNESS:  Okay.
 4           MR. JENSVOLD:  Thank you.
 5           THE WITNESS:  You're welcome.
 6           THE COURT:  Do any members of the jury have
 7  questions for Mr. Franks?  All right.  Go ahead and put it
 8  down on a piece of paper, if you haven't already, and the
 9  bailiff will pick it up from you.
10           A JUROR:  I'm not too clear if it's a question for
11  Mr. Franks or for someone to answer.  It's a technical
12  question regarding --
13           THE COURT:  Why don't you write it down and then
14  we'll figure it out.
15           (Whereupon there was a conference at the bench among
16  the Court and counsel, on the record, as follows:)
17           (The Court and counsel review the jury question.)
18           THE COURT:  Can you help me decipher that?
19           MR. JENSVOLD:  What's this word?
20           MR. SKITZKI:  "From"?  I don't know.
21           THE COURT:  Mr. Bagwell, can you help us out, I'm
22  having trouble reading your handwriting.  I'm sorry, sir.  I
23  don't know if you remember what that word is right there?
24           JUROR:  Not from this distance.
25           MR. JENSVOLD:  It looks like "from."
```

PIMA COUNTY SUPERIOR COURT

                JUROR: Yes, "from."

                MR. JENSVOLD: I think basically Detective Englander will establish that it was from the computer later.

                (Whereupon proceedings continued in open court, on the record, as follows:)

                THE COURT: I think that this question is going to be answered through a different witness that will have more knowledge about that.

                Do any other members of the jury have questions?

                Okay. We'll come get it from you.

                If you want to approach.

                (Whereupon the Court and counsel confer at the bench, out of the hearing of the jurors, as follows:)

                (The Court and counsel review the jury question.)

                THE COURT: That was submitted to my bailiff this morning. It's not a -- I'll make copies of it for you all so you can address it when the time is appropriate, but I think they are just wondering what the law means.

                That's two. Is this one of the, is that one of the questions? You brought that up to me?

                THE BAILIFF: It's what she handed me.

                THE COURT: Okay. Here's three.

                (The Court and counsel review the jury question.)

                THE COURT: Any objection to two?

                MR. SKITZKI: No.

PIMA COUNTY SUPERIOR COURT

```
 1            THE COURT:  Three?
 2            MR. JENSVOLD:  No.
 3            THE COURT:  Here's four.
 4            (The Court and counsel review the jury question.)
 5            MR. SKITZKI:  No objection.
 6            MR. JENSVOLD:  No.
 7            THE COURT:  Here's five.
 8            (The Court and counsel review the jury question.)
 9            MR. JENSVOLD:  I don't think he's the appropriate
10   witness to answer that.
11            THE COURT:  Do you agree?
12            MR. SKITZKI:  Yeah, I agree.
13            THE COURT:  All right.
14            (Whereupon proceedings continued in open court, on
15   the record, as follows:)
16            THE COURT:  All right, folks, some of these
17   questions are going to have to be answered by a later witness.
18   So if your question isn't answered, remember the instructions
19   that I gave you earlier.
20            Mr. Franks, what type of device did you have to
21   listen to music on?
22            THE WITNESS:  A MP3 program that was installed on
23   the computer.  It wasn't an Ipod or nothing like that.  It was
24   just the MP3 program software that was on the computer.
25   That's what I would listen to it off of.
```

1	THE COURT: Did you have a device of your own that
2	you could independently listen to music on?
3	THE WITNESS: No, I didn't at the time. No.
4	THE COURT: You had testified earlier that the file
5	on the hard drive was pornographic and that you wanted it off
6	the hard drive. Who did the computer belong to?
7	THE WITNESS: It belonged to Mr. Coghill.
8	THE COURT: Did Mr. Coghill tell you that he,
9	meaning Mr. Coghill, was sick and twisted?
10	THE DEFENDANT: Yes.
11	THE COURT: Do either counsel have any follow-up
12	questions on the jury's questions.
13	MR. JENSVOLD: No, Your Honor.
14	MR. SKITZKI: No.
15	THE COURT: Any additional questions from our jury?
16	(No response.)
17	THE COURT: Okay.
18	May Mr. Franks be excused?
19	MR. JENSVOLD: Yes.
20	MR. SKITZKI: Yes.
21	THE COURT: You are excused, Mr. Franks. Thank you
22	for your time. Watch your step going down.
23	THE WITNESS: Thank you, Your Honor.
24	(Whereupon the witness was excused.)
25	THE COURT: We're going to go ahead and take our

PIMA COUNTY SUPERIOR COURT

lunch recess at this time, folks. If you want to be back in the jury room by 1:20. Remember the admonition. Keep your juror badges on. And we'll see you about 1:20-ish.

JUROR: Can we leave stuff right here, or take it to the jury room?

THE COURT: If you want to put your notes back into your notebook just so you can keep it all together, but if you have personal items, why don't you go ahead and take those.

(11:54 a.m. Whereupon the jury is excused and leaves the courtroom, and proceedings continue in their absence, as follows:)

THE COURT: All right. Okay.

The record will show the absence of the jury, the presence of all counsel and Mr. Coghill.

We're going to go off the record, but one of the jurors had submitted to my bailiff, I guess it's a three by five card with some questions on it. So, I'm going to copy it for both counsel, and I'm going to go ahead and mark it, what, six for the record. I think it's questions that have to be addressed in closing argument about what the law is.

So, any objection to handling it that way?

MR. JENSVOLD: That's fine.

MR. SKITZKI: No, that's fine.

THE COURT: Anything that we need to take up?

MR. JENSVOLD: No, I think we can figure it out

PIMA COUNTY SUPERIOR COURT

1 before we come back.
2   THE COURT: All right. We'll see you all back at
3 1:20.
4   (12:00 noon. Whereupon proceedings were recessed.)
5   (Whereupon proceedings resumed, as follows:)
6   THE COURT: Show we're back on the record.
7   Show the absence of the jury.
8   Show the presence of all counsel and Mr. Coghill.
9   I think we are waiting on one juror.
10   Is there anything that we need to take up before we
11 bring them back in?
12   MR. JENSVOLD: Do you want to take up the Willits
13 instruction now, or --
14   MR. EUCHNER: Also I just want to make sure, I think
15 Mr. Jensvold wants to introduce some of Mr. Coghill's prior
16 trial testimony. We just want, I think we discussed that we
17 just do it through --
18   MR. JENSVOLD: That will be tomorrow, but yeah.
19   MR. EUCHNER: -- but it will be through Mr.
20 Englander; just with some questions and how did he respond and
21 that kind of thing.
22   THE COURT: Okay.
23   MR. EUCHNER: And as far as the Willits instruction,
24 we have heard some of the testimony now from Jacob Franks,
25 that he was allowed to take CDs from the motor home that he

had burned himself. And what we will hear tomorrow based on what Mr. Englander gave us in our interview with him, is that he would never have let him take CDs out, but he's not aware of anything happening along those lines.

There's multiple officers that are here, some of whom we don't know who they are. So our position is that an unknown officer allowed Mr. Franks in to take his CDs. Because Mr. Englander did say that he would have let him take CDs that were commercially made, but anything that he burned himself, he would want to keep as evidence.

And the reason why we think that that's relevant to the case, is obviously those CDs would have burn dates. Those CDs would have files on them. And without knowing what the files are, what the burn dates are, it's possible we would have been able to connect that. Well, I think it's actually definite we would have been able to connect it to Mr. Coghill's hard drives.

The question is how would we have been able to connect it to the hard drives; what dates would it have shown us? Is it reasonable to say that we might have found some March 4th burn dates on those CDs that connected to this hard drive in this case?

So, for that reason we think a <u>Willits</u> instruction to the jury is appropriate.

THE COURT: All right. I don't know if you want to

respond now, or wait until all the evidence is in where I can make a more meaningful -- I'm not going to rule until I hear everything.

MR. JENSVOLD: I think I can argue now, because even assuming everything that Mr. Euchner says is correct, I still don't think it meets the prejudice prong. I mean, look at <u>State versus Perez</u>, which is 141 Arizona 459, Arizona Supreme Court case from 1984. There was a videotape from a convenience store that the police had plenty of time to access and failed to secure it. It's just speculation as to whether that videotape would inculpate or exculpate the defendant in that case.

And there is no evidence that the defense is going to be able to present to show that they would have been prejudiced by whatever was on Mr. Coghill's -- Mr. Franks' CDs that he had with him, and was presumably allowed to take with him. Unless they can demonstrate that there is something specific that would have exculpated Mr. Coghill, I don't think they've met the prejudice prong and, therefore, the <u>Willits</u> instruction is not, should not be given.

THE COURT: All right. Well, I am not prepared to even, like, I appreciate you bringing it to my attention. I'll be able to read the <u>Perez</u> case and I'll go back and read <u>Willits</u>. But what I would prefer to do, is hear all the evidence that's going to come in on that topic, and then I can

PIMA COUNTY SUPERIOR COURT

1 let you all know once that has, once I have everything.
2   MR. EUCHNER: And, Your Honor, it is definitely
3 premature to rule, because Mr. Englander needs to testify
4 first --
5   THE COURT: Right.
6   MR. EUCHNER: --in order to lay that foundation for
7 our claim. But it just, it doesn't have to, anything that
8 creates the third party culpability claim here is exculpatory
9 as well to Mr. Coghill. So, that, because it would implicate
10 Mr. Franks, the Willits instruction would be appropriate. And
11 if the Court requests, we could do further briefing overnight.
12   THE COURT: You know, I don't know that that's
13 necessary. I'm pretty familiar with Willits and the cases
14 that come after Willits. I mean, I just prefer you can argue
15 what your respective positions are.
16   If you want to file something, I'm not going to stop
17 you from doing that. But, I know you get busy in trial, and I
18 am not going to order you to file pleadings while you're in
19 the middle of trial.
20   So, okay. We can just take it up after
21 Mr. Englander testifies.
22   Christina is going to get the jury to see if they
23 are all present and accounted for.
24   THE BAILIFF: Jury is entering.
25   (1:25 p.m. Jury now present.)

         THE COURT: All right.
         The record will show the presence of the jury, the presence of all counsel, and Mr. Coghill.
         MR. JENSVOLD: Your Honor, the State would call Deputy Judd.

                           JACE JUDD,
having been first duly sworn, was examined and testified, as follows:

                      DIRECT EXAMINATION
BY MR. JENSVOLD:
    Q.   Deputy, would you please introduce yourself to the jury.
    A.   My name is Jace Judd.
    Q.   And it's pretty apparent, but can you tell us who you work for.
    A.   I work for the Pima County Sheriff Department.
    Q.   How long have you been there?
    A.   Since 1995.
    Q.   What's your current assignment?
    A.   As of today, I work the Rincon Patrol District.
    Q.   Prior to that, where have you worked?
    A.   The San Xavier Patrol District.
    Q.   In 2003, April 1st to be specific, which district

PIMA COUNTY SUPERIOR COURT

1 did you patrol?
2   A. The San Xavier district.
3   Q. What are the boundaries of that district?
4   A. Well, I'll give you a rough estimate. The north
5 side is roughly Ajo, to the south to, I believe parts of
6 Mexico, or close to it. East is, I believe, Kolb Road, and
7 west is getting close to the town of Ajo, so it's quite large.
8   Q. Where is the Sheriff's Department Headquarters?
9   A. 1750 East Benson Highway.
10   Q. Is that within the San Xavier District?
11   A. It is.
12   Q. And is the area east of that on Benson Highway also
13 within that same district?
14   A. It is.
15   Q. And all of that is within Pima County?
16   A. Yes.
17   Q. On April 1st of 2003, were you on duty?
18   A. I was.
19   Q. Did you respond to a call somewhere around 7:00 in
20 the morning?
21   A. Yes, I did.
22   Q. And do you remember what specific time it was that
23 you were called?
24   A. It was approximately 7:30 in the morning.
25   Q. And what was the nature of the call to which you

PIMA COUNTY SUPERIOR COURT

```
 1  were responding?
 2      A.   If I remember correctly, it was dispatched to me as
 3  a suspicious activity.
 4      Q.   Where did you go?
 5      A.   I initially responded to Benson Highway and Country
 6  Club, and at that intersection there is a Circle K.
 7      Q.   Did you meet with someone there?
 8      A.   Yes.
 9      Q.   Who was it?
10      A.   Mr. Jacob Franks.
11      Q.   And what was Mr. Franks' demeanor like when you
12  first began to speak to him?
13      A.   He was not overly upset or nervous or agitated, but
14  he wasn't calm either.
15      Q.   Without going into all the specifics about what
16  Mr. Franks told you, did he give you information about
17  somebody else?
18      A.   Yes, he did.
19      Q.   And who was the other person?
20      A.   James Coghill.
21      Q.   And did you later meet with Mr. Coghill?
22      A.   I did.
23      Q.   And where was that?
24      A.   3356 East Benson Highway.
25      Q.   And what was the location like?  Or just describe
```

PIMA COUNTY SUPERIOR COURT

1   it, I'm sorry.
2   A.   I believe it's called The Apollo RV Park or trailer
3   park. It's on Benson Highway. It's a relatively small
4   property. Maybe a couple of acres, and it's where you can
5   park a small trailer or a motor home.
6   Q.   How long were you with Mr. Franks back at the Circle
7   K?
8   A.   An estimation would be maybe 15 to 20 minutes.
9   Q.   And was there somebody else there with you besides
10   yourself from the Sheriff's Department?
11   A.   Yes, Deputy Schupbach.
12   Q.   And so just, did Mr. Coghill tell you things to look
13   for within Mr. Coghill's motor home?
14   THE COURT: Do you mean Mr. Franks?
15   MR. JENSVOLD: Yeah, it's one of these days.
16   THE COURT: I'm sorry, I didn't mean to interrupt.
17   THE WITNESS: I didn't want to either.
18   MR. JENSVOLD: You're not the first person to do
19   that to me, to correct me, that is.
20   BY MR. JENSVOLD:
21   Q.   Did Mr. Franks give you information about what was
22   in Mr. Coghills' motor home?
23   A.   Yes.
24   Q.   And, specifically, did he tell you about some CDs
25   and what to look for on top of the CDs that was written on

PIMA COUNTY SUPERIOR COURT

1 there?
2 A. Yes.
3 Q. Did Mr. Cog-- I almost did it again. Did Mr. Franks
4 tell you how long he had been in Tucson?
5 A. No.
6 Q. Did he tell you -- so you didn't write that down in
7 your report?
8 A. No.
9 Q. Were you speaking with Deputy Schupbach at the same
10 time with Mr. Franks, or was there a time when Deputy
11 Schupbach was speaking with Mr. Franks without you there?
12 A. Yes. Deputy Schupbach, although it was my call,
13 Deputy Schupbach arrived and began speaking with Mr. Franks
14 prior to my arrival.
15 Q. Okay. So after you left Mr. Franks, did you or
16 Deputy Schupbach give him any instructions as to what to do
17 when you left?
18 A. I did.
19 Q. What did you tell him?
20 A. Due to the nature of the information that Mr. Franks
21 gave me, I felt it may be necessary to speak with him again.
22 He did not have a cell phone or a home telephone number that I
23 could use, so I gave him my pager number and told him to page
24 me in one hour so that I could re-contact him and speak with
25 him again if I needed.

PIMA COUNTY SUPERIOR COURT

1 Q. Okay. So you left the Circle K and you went to
2 Mr. Coghill's RV?
3 A. Correct.
4 Q. And what did you see when you first got there?
5 A. His motor home, or are you asking for --
6 Q. Was anybody outside the motor home?
7 A. No, not that I remember.
8 Q. So what did you do?
9 A. I knocked on his door.
10 Q. And what happened?
11 A. Mr. Coghill, or a gentleman later identified as
12 Mr. Coghill answered the door.
13 Q. And what did you tell Mr. Coghill?
14 A. I said: Hello. Can I talk to you inside your motor
15 home.
16 Q. And he agreed?
17 A. Yes, he did.
18 Q. And so did you go in?
19 A. I did.
20 Q. And then what happened?
21 A. I began speaking with him about Jacob Franks and
22 their relationship.
23 Q. And did you immediately tell him what Mr. Franks had
24 told you about what was inside the RV?
25 A. No.

PIMA COUNTY SUPERIOR COURT

1 Q. Okay. So you just, what did Mr. Coghill have to say
2 about your, about his relationship with Mr. Franks?
3 A. He said that Mr. Franks had lived with him for
4 approximately two months.
5 Q. Did you ever follow-up with Mr. Coghill about
6 anything specific about when he arrived in Tucson?
7 A. When Mr. Franks arrived in Tucson?
8 Q. When Mr. Coghill -- I'm sorry, Mr. Coghill told you
9 that he, Mr. Coghill, had been in Tucson for two months?
10 A. No, he said that he had been roommates with Jacob
11 Franks for about two months. That was my understanding of our
12 conversation anyway.
13 Q. That's what Mr. Coghill told you?
14 A. Correct.
15 Q. Did Mr. Coghill tell you how, let me see if I can
16 phrase this correctly. Did Mr. Coghill say that Mr. Franks
17 had been with him the entire time that he had been in Tucson?
18 A. The entire time who had been in Tucson?
19 Q. That Mr. Coghill had been in Tucson.
20 A. No.
21 Q. Did Mr. Coghill say that the two were here the
22 entire time that they were in Tucson together, or was there
23 any --
24 A. No. And he simply said that he had been, that they
25 had been roommates for two months, and I did not really go

PIMA COUNTY SUPERIOR COURT

into detail as to whether or not it was in Tucson or some other location.

Q. Did you ever clarify with Mr. Coghill as to what day he arrived in Tucson?

A. No.

Q. And I guess, can you describe for the jury your role as a sort of first responding officer versus what a Detective does later in an investigation.

A. As a first responder, when I respond to an incident, be it an emergency or something less benign, I will gather information, take immediate action if necessary. If there is substantial follow-up work to be completed, I will call the appropriate Detective unit so that they can continue the investigation.

I am responsible for answering calls, emergency calls for service, so I do not have the luxury of devoting time to a lengthy investigation. For instance, a call of this nature in the morning, I will have to respond to several more calls during the day.

Q. Do you typically, as a first responding officer, tape record your interviews with the people that are involved?

A. Typically, no.

Q. Why not?

A. Various reasons. Quite honestly, a lot of the calls that I go to are mundane calls that, quite frankly, aren't worthy of recording. I talk to maybe two dozen people a day. I would have to devote a substantial amount of time just categorizing my calls or the conversations that I record, much less doing actual police work.

Q. So to your knowledge, do Detectives tape record their interviews with investigations after you have responded?

A. Typically they do, yes.

Q. Okay. So you talked to Mr. Coghill about his relationship with Mr. Franks, and he tells you that they have been there for two months, is that correct?

A. Correct.

Q. Then where does the conversation go from there?

A. I informed Mr. Coghill that there had been allegations regarding materials in his motor home.

Q. Was there anything in between those two periods of time that you remember?

A. No.

Q. Do you remember asking Mr. Coghill or hearing Deputy Schupbach ask Mr. Coghill about where Jacob Franks' stuff was in the motor home?

A. I don't recall her asking that.

Q. Were there any conversations that Deputy Schupbach had with Mr. Coghill that you might not have heard?

A. There could have been a period of time where Deputy Schupbach was alone with Mr. Coghill.

PIMA COUNTY SUPERIOR COURT

Q. Okay. What were you doing during that period of time, if you remember?

A. If I remember correctly, I had stepped outside his motor home to make a telephone call.

Q. Okay. So when you informed Mr. Coghill of what Mr. Franks had told you, what was his response?

MR. JENSVOLD: Actually, may we approach?

THE COURT: Yes.

(Whereupon the Court and counsel confer at the bench, out of the hearing of the jurors, as follows:)

MR. JENSVOLD: I didn't want to step into a mistrial. You know what I am talking about here, don't you?

MR. SKITZKI: You just want to date him.

MR. JENSVOLD: There is one issue here, however, is that the line here (indicating).

MR. SKITZKI: Yeah.

MR. JENSVOLD: Do you have an objection to that?

MR. SKITZKI: This one, yeah. I have an objection to that. I don't have an objection about the K-P question. I have a objection to his, to the line where Mr. Coghill purportedly says that one stack is pornography.

MR. JENSVOLD: Okay. So I believe that's relevant, and it doesn't cross the line that we've been discussing, because the stack to which he's referring to, according to what the Deputy would say, is the stack specifically that had

PIMA COUNTY SUPERIOR COURT

the disk labeled K-P, which, to be fair, Mr. Coghill as soon as he says that, says to the Deputy, that's not mine, that must be Jake's. But he does identify the stack as pornography.

THE COURT: I am going to let him ask about it being pornography, but, I mean, you know what my prior ruling is. So, any additional record you want to make about that? I mean, I think it's relevant. It goes to knowledge.

MR. SKITZKI: No objection.

THE COURT: All right.

(Whereupon proceedings continued in open court, on the record, as follows:)

BY MR. JENSVOLD:

Q. Okay. Deputy, I want to hand you a copy of State's Exhibit 4, and see if you recognize that?

A. Yes.

Q. And what is that?

A. This is a copy of my narrative, my police report.

Q. Was that the narrative for this case?

A. It is.

Q. And I want to be just specific about these questions. Did you ask Mr. Coghill about the contents of the CDs that were found around the computer?

A. Yes, I did.

Q. And did he tell you that there was one stack that

```
 1  was X files?
 2      A.  Yes.
 3      Q.  Did he tell you there was another stack that was the
 4  Star Trek Trilogy?
 5      A.  He did.
 6      Q.  Did he also identify one stack as being pornography?
 7          MR. SKITZKI:  Objection, relevance.
 8          THE COURT:  Overruled.
 9          THE WITNESS:  Yes.
10          A JUROR:  I'm sorry?
11          THE WITNESS:  Yes.
12  BY MR. JENSVOLD:
13      Q.  And then did you look at that stack that Mr. Coghill
14  had identified?
15      A.  Yes, I did.
16      Q.  What did you see?
17      A.  I saw at least one disk with the initials K-P on it.
18      Q.  And did Mr. Coghill say anything to you about the
19  person that owned that CD, or was responsible for it?
20      A.  Yes.
21      Q.  Okay.  I guess.  I'll just be specific.  Did you
22  quote Mr. Coghill as saying:  I don't know, some of those
23  aren't mine.  Some of them are Jacob's, and he must have
24  written K-P on them?
25      A.  Yes.
```

PIMA COUNTY SUPERIOR COURT

1 Q. And at some point, did you go through the rest of
2 the motor home with Mr. Coghill; he pointed out certain things
3 that were his within the motor home?
4 A. Yes.
5 Q. And was the living space or the bedroom space of the
6 motor home, was that Mr. Coghill's?
7 A. I would assume so. I really don't know other than
8 it seemed that his property was there inside the sleeping
9 quarters.
10 Q. He identified some of the property back there as
11 his?
12 A. Correct.
13 Q. Deputy, you have seen some photographs that I showed
14 you earlier. I just want to ask you a series of questions
15 about all of them and then I will show them to the jury,
16 hopefully.
17   Do you recognize all of the photographs? They have
18 been identified as State's Exhibit 2 all the way in order
19 through 2-S.
20 A. Do you want me to look through all of them?
21 Q. Just look through all of them and I will just ask
22 you a series of questions at the end.
23   Do you recognize the contents, or what's been
24 depicted in all these photographs?
25 A. Yes.

1   Q.   Okay. Do they appear to represent what you saw at
2 the time on April 1st of 2003?
3   A.   Yes, with some variation, as far as the great detail
4 as to the back of the computer.
5   Q.   Okay.
6   A.   Things of that nature. Maybe what was in a printer
7 tray and what was written on that. I didn't look that close.
8 But, yes, they do appear to represent the interior of
9 Mr. Coghills' motor home.
10   Q.   Okay. I will take out those that you have expressed
11 some doubt about whether you saw the specific views of the
12 photographs. With the exception of these, can you state that
13 you saw what was depicted in those photographs and it appeared
14 to be the same as what you saw at the time?
15   A.   Certainly, yes.
16   MR. JENSVOLD: Your Honor, the State would move for
17 the admission of 2 through 2-S, with the exception of 2-J, O,
18 R, Q, and S.
19   MR. SKITZKI: No objection.
20   THE COURT: State's 2 through 2, I'm sorry?
21   MR. JENSVOLD: 2 through 2-I, and then, 2-K through
22 2-M, and also 2-P.
23   THE COURT: All right. So 2 through 2-I, State's
24 2-K through 2-M, and State's 2-P are all admitted.
25   MR. JENSVOLD: Can everybody see that, or should I

```
 1  move it closer?
 2  BY MR. JENSVOLD:
 3      Q.   All right.  Deputy Judd, this is State's Exhibit 2.
 4  Can you just describe what it is?
 5      A.   That appears to be the motor home that Mr. Coghill
 6  was living in.
 7      Q.   And 2-A?
 8      A.   That would be the rear view.
 9      Q.   2-B?
10      A.   That would be the driver's side of the same motor
11  home.
12      Q.   2-C?
13      A.   Can you back that off just a little?
14      Q.   Yeah.
15      A.   Thank you.  That appears to be the entrance to the
16  motor home.
17      Q.   2-D?
18      A.   I am at an angle.  May I get a better view?
19           THE COURT:  You sure can.
20           THE WITNESS:  That appears to be the view once you
21  have entered the motor home, looking back to the sleeping
22  quarters.
23  BY MR. JENSVOLD:
24      Q.   2-E?
25      A.   That appears to be standing in or near the sleeping
```

1 quarters looking toward the living area, if you will, and the
2 driver's seat.
3   Q. 2-F?
4   A. That's the same area, the portion of the kitchen and
5 the living quarters.
6   Q. 2-G?
7   A. That looks like the small nightstand in the bedroom.
8   Q. 2-H?
9   A. Again, the bed and a nightstand counter area in the
10 bedroom.
11   Q. 2-I?
12   A. That appears to be the bedroom.
13   Q. 2-K?
14   A. That appears to be the living area in the motor
15 home.
16   Q. And were these CDs as they are seen here in the
17 photograph, do they appear to be in the same placement as when
18 you saw them, or do you know for sure?
19   A. That was six years ago. I, I hope so.
20   Q. And you did not take these photographs, is that
21 correct?
22   A. I did not.
23   Q. And this is State's 2-L?
24   A. That looks like the living area, or maybe the
25 computer room.

PIMA COUNTY SUPERIOR COURT

1	Q.	2-M?
2	A.	That appears to be the living area.
3	Q.	2-N?
4	A.	That looks like the driver's seat to the motor home.
5	Q.	And 2-P?
6	A.	That appears to be the computer area in the living quarters.
8	Q.	All right. Thank you.

Now, Deputy, there has been some discussion at different times in this case about what was the top disk and what was its label, the one that we talked about before with the K-P. Do you remember whether the very top disk on that stack was labeled K-P?

A. I don't remember if it was the top disk or under the top disk.

Q. Do you ever recall seeing a disk that was labeled "dirty" on that stack of CDs?

A. Not that I recall.

Q. Did you handle the CD's?

A. I may have.

Q. Okay.

A. I don't remember whether I did or didn't.

Q. Did you use gloves when you handled them, if you remember?

A. I don't remember wearing gloves. I almost always

have a pair of latex gloves in one of my pockets for emergencies or touching something that I shouldn't leave prints on.

Q. But you don't remember specifically whether you handled them or not?

A. I do not.

Q. Do you know if Mr. Coghill handled them in your presence?

A. I can't remember.

Q. And you weren't responsible for taking the fingerprints or processing them, or anything like that?

A. No.

Q. Okay. When you were -- did you leave the investigation in somebody else's hands, basically, when you left?

A. Yes, I did.

Q. Who was that?

A. Specifically, I would say Sergeant Pesqueira, who was a Sergeant of a Detective unit.

Q. Was there a specific Detective present when you left the motor home?

A. There were a few, and I can't remember exactly who they were.

Q. Okay. What was your next role in the investigation after you left the motor home?

1   A. I left and went back to the Circle K at Benson
2   Highway and Country Club and recontacted Jacob Franks.
3   Q. Had somebody, had he contacted you first, meaning
4   Mr. Franks?
5   A. I don't believe so. I believe he recontacted the
6   Sheriff's Department communications.
7   Q. And how long was it from the time that you left
8   Mr. Franks at the Circle K to the time that you went back, if
9   you remember?
10 A. I don't remember that.
11 Q. More than an hour, more than two hours?
12 A. I would say at least an hour.
13 Q. And was he there when you went back?
14 A. Yes. Let me back up. I made contact with him
15 there. I don't remember if I had to wait, or if he was
16 waiting on me.
17 Q. But you ran into him at some point?
18 A. I certainly did.
19 Q. At the same place that you left him before?
20 A. Correct.
21 Q. Where did you take him?
22 A. I took him to the Sheriff's Department
23 Administration building located at 1750 East Benson Highway.
24 Q. Did you have any conversations with Mr. Franks on
25 the ride over that you remember?

PIMA COUNTY SUPERIOR COURT

1   A.   Not that I noted.
2   Q.   And was that basically the end of your involvement
3   in this case after you left Mr. Franks at the Sheriff's
4   Department?
5   A.   As far as I remember. I think so.
6   Q.   You don't remember going back and participating in
7   the search warrant or anything like that?
8   A.   Oh no, as far as that day and going back, and
9   participating, I did not.
10   MR. JENSVOLD: That's all I have. Thank you.
11   THE COURT: Cross-Examination?
12
13   CROSS-EXAMINATION
14   BY MR. SKITZKI:
15   Q.   Deputy Judd, you get a call around 7:00 and you go
16   out to that Circle K at Benson Highway and Country Club?
17   A.   Correct.
18   Q.   When you arrive, the civilian that you need to talk
19   to, or at least you see Deputy Schupbach talking to a
20   civilian?
21   A.   Correct.
22   Q.   And so then you come over there and join the
23   conversation?
24   A.   I do.
25   Q.   Do you find out that the person, the civilian is an

PIMA COUNTY SUPERIOR COURT

1 individual by the name of Jacob Franks?
2   A.   Yes.
3   Q.   Can you describe Mr. Franks' appearance when you
4 came into contact with him?
5   A.   No. His physical appearance?
6   Q.   His physical appearance.
7   A.   Such as dress, haircut, things of that nature?
8   Q.   Was he clean, disheveled or anything like that, do
9 you recall?
10   A.   I don't recall.
11   Q.   In any event, you have a conversation with him, with
12 Deputy Schupbach there, and he starts giving you information
13 about some child pornography that is at the motor home where
14 he was living with Mr. James Coghill, correct?
15   A.   Correct.
16   Q.   He gives you specific information, tells you where
17 you can find the alleged pornography inside the motor home, is
18 that correct?
19   A.   He gives a general area, yes.
20   Q.   Can you -- he indicates it's sort of by the computer
21 itself in some stack of disks basically?
22   A.   Yes.
23   Q.   Eventually after you and Deputy Schupbach finished
24 with Mr. Franks initially at the Circle K, you give him some
25 information, so that I guess he can contact your pager, is

PIMA COUNTY SUPERIOR COURT

1 that what you gave him?
2   A.   We must have had pagers back then, because my report
3 says I gave him my pager number to contact me.
4   Q.   And you, you were aware that he didn't have a
5 telephone, a cell phone himself?
6   A.   Correct.
7   Q.   So after that, after you make those arrangements so
8 that he can get back in contact with you since there is no way
9 for you to directly contact him by telephone or anything of
10 that nature, you and Deputy Schupbach go over to the RV park?
11   A.   Yes.
12   Q.   You find the motor home that Mr. Franks had
13 described to you, and you knock on the door?
14   A.   Correct.
15   Q.   Mr. Coghill answers?
16   A.   Yes.
17   Q.   Do you see Mr. Coghill here in the courtroom?
18   A.   I do.
19   Q.   Can you tell us where he is?
20   A.   He is seated at the defense in a dark suit, the
21 defense table, well, and there is three of you, so, so I will
22 name him as the middle gentleman.
23   Q.   And you encounter him and you ask if you could speak
24 with him?
25   A.   Yes.

1	Q.	Does he agree to speak to you?
2	A.	He does.
3	Q.	Do you, does he invite you into the motor home, or do you ask if you can come in?
5	A.	No, I asked if I could speak to him in his motor home.
7	Q.	He said that would be fine?
8	A.	He said "yes".
9	Q.	And, he brought you into the house?
10	A.	He invited us in.
11	Q.	Then you sat down and began to converse with him?
12	A.	Did not sit down.
13	Q.	You were standing up when you were talking to him?
14	A.	Correct.
15	Q.	The entire time that you were dealing with him on April 1st, 2003, was he cooperative with you?
17	A.	Yes.
18	Q.	Did he answer the questions that you asked him?
19	A.	He did.
20	Q.	Did the responses that he gave, were they appropriate to the questions that were asked?
22	A.	Can you be more specific?
23	Q.	Well, I mean, if you asked him something, was the answer, you know, sort of responsive to the question, or was it not responsive?

PIMA COUNTY SUPERIOR COURT

1   A.   His answers were relevant to my question.

2   Q.   I'm going to show you what you've already identified as, State's Exhibit 2-L. And if you need to see --

4   A.   Your Honor --

5   THE COURT: Please.

6 BY MR. SKITZKI:

7   Q.   Come down and see it more clearly. That depicts -- I guess the computer that was in that motor home? Am I blocking anyone's view?

10   A.   What was your question, sir?

11   Q.   This would be the monitor to the, this is basically the computer area that was in that motor home, correct?

13   A.   Yes.

14   Q.   And I guess these things that I am pointing at with my pen to the left of the monitor, those appear to be stacks of disks?

17   A.   They appear so, yes.

18   Q.   Like this blue stack, that would be a lot of disks we are talking about, is that fair to state?

20   A.   To me it's a lot of disks, yes.

21   Q.   In the course of your being in that motor home on that day, I mean, there were in excess of hundreds of disks, is that fair to state?

24   A.   I can not testify to the number of disks.

25   Q.   But there were a lot?

1	A. As I look at this photo, to me, that's a lot.
2	Q. Do you recall amongst these various stacks of disks
3	where it was that you encountered that first disk that was
4	labeled K-P?
5	A. No.
6	Q. Do you recall if it was near the top of the stack
7	wherever it came from, or was it something that you, you know,
8	you pulled through a stack and, you know, went 10 or 15 in
9	before you found it?
10	A. I don't recall.
11	Q. In any event, when you found a K-P disk, you asked
12	Mr. Coghill -- and you can sit down --
13	A. Thank you.
14	Q. -- Deputy. You asked Mr. Coghill what K-P stood
15	for?
16	A. If I can refer to this report?
17	Q. Absolutely.
18	A. I want to -- yes, I asked what K-P stood for.
19	Q. And, in fact, in your report you actually write
20	down, I guess it's verbatim, what he responded to you because
21	you put it in quotation marks, is that correct?
22	A. Correct.
23	Q. And he said, I quote: I don't know. Some of those
24	aren't mine. Some of them are Jacobs', and he must have
25	written K-P on them. End quotes.

PIMA COUNTY SUPERIOR COURT

1   That's exactly what he told you?
2   A.   Yes.
3   Q.   In the course of your being in that motor home that
4 day, you also became aware that, or you asked Mr. Coghill if
5 he had any photo albums, is that correct?
6   A.   No. I asked if he had any photographs in his
7 possession.
8   Q.   You asked him if he had photographs, and he showed
9 you some photo albums that he had?
10   A.   He did.
11   Q.   You looked through those photo albums?
12   A.   Yes, I did.
13   Q.   You found no depictions of child pornography in
14 those photo albums, correct?
15   A.   Correct.
16   Q.   You basically at the conclusion of your encounter,
17 the time that you spent with Mr. Coghill, you asked him if he
18 would be willing to speak with Detectives from the Sheriff's
19 Department concerning the allegations about the child
20 pornography, is that correct?
21   A.   Yes, I did.
22   Q.   And he told you, Mr. Coghill told you that he would
23 be, he would be fine with speaking with the Detectives, is
24 that correct?
25   A.   Yes, he did.

PIMA COUNTY SUPERIOR COURT

         Q.   You knew that day when you spent time with
Mr. Franks at the Circle K, that he had been arguing with
Mr. Coghill earlier?
         A.   That's a statement. Could you ask a question?
         Q.   Sure. Were you aware that Mr. Franks had had a
previous argument or disagreement with Mr. Coghill before you
came into contact with him?
         A.   I don't recall that information.
              MR. SKITZKI: I don't have any other questions.
              THE COURT: Any Redirect?
              MR. JENSVOLD: No, thank you.
              THE COURT: Do any members of the jury have any
questions for Deputy Judd?
              Go ahead and write them down for us.
              And counsel want to approach.
              A JUROR: Can I have 2-F, please?
              THE COURT: Mr. Skitzki, could you bring 2-F up with
you, if you still have it still, sir.
              Thanks.
              (Whereupon the Court and counsel confer at the
bench, out of the hearing of the jurors, as follows:)
              (The Court and counsel review the jury question.)
              THE COURT: Any objections to seven?
              MR. SKITZKI: Not to the first part, and not to the
second part. You can tell him not to say anything about -- I

PIMA COUNTY SUPERIOR COURT

think it's family photos.

MR. JENSVOLD: They are family photos, not, not child pornography.

MR. SKITZKI: Yeah.

THE COURT: I am the one that gets to ask the questions, so --

MR. SKITZKI: The problem with that is there, it's normal photographs but there are photographs of a male penis in there that --

THE COURT: How about if we ask Mr. Englander? Did he look at the photo album?

MR. JENSVOLD: Yeah.

THE COURT: Let's have him address that question then, and then I don't need to touch the answer.

Okay. So what's with the question.

MR. JENSVOLD: It's all irrelevant except for one, I guess.

THE COURT: All right. All right. I will ask him that. Okay.

MR. JENSVOLD: If he knows.

THE COURT: Okay. So, no objection to nine?

MR. JENSVOLD: No.

(Whereupon proceedings continued in open court, on the record, as follows:)

THE COURT: Deputy Judd, the first question is photo

            1   2-J--F, shows what appears to be a second computer or monitor
            2   in a bedroom. How many computers were in the motor home?
            3   THE WITNESS: I only see one computer there.
            4   THE COURT: Do you recall how many computers you saw
            5   when you were in the motor home that day?
            6   THE WITNESS: No. Is the question did I see a
            7   computer in the bedroom?
            8   THE COURT: No, the question is how many computers
            9   were in the motor home.
           10   THE WITNESS: That I saw, one.
           11   THE COURT: Did Mr. Coghill grant you permission to
           12   enter his home?
           13   THE WITNESS: He did.
           14   THE COURT: To search his home?
           15   THE WITNESS: I didn't ask to search the home.
           16   THE COURT: All right. Did he grant you permission
           17   to search or review or collect the CDs that were at issue?
           18   THE WITNESS: No, and I did not ask. Again, I did
           19   not ask to search and view the CDs or take possession of them.
           20   THE COURT: All right.
           21   Did you yourself, or do you have knowledge about
           22   whether or not anybody else got a search warrant later for
           23   that RV?
           24   THE WITNESS: Yes, to my knowledge a search warrant
           25   was served.

PIMA COUNTY SUPERIOR COURT

1   THE COURT: To the best of your knowledge, was
2 Mr. Coghill's RV hooked up to internet or did it have wireless
3 connection when you were there?
4   THE WITNESS: I am not sure if he had internet
5 access, and if he did, what type it was.
6   THE COURT: All right.
7   Any additional questions from our jury?
8   Okay. There is one, Christina.
9   All right, Counsel, do you want to approach?
10   (Whereupon the Court and counsel confer at the
11 bench, out of the hearing of the jurors, as follows:)
12   (The Court and counsel review the jury question.)
13   MR. JENSVOLD: That's fine. No objection.
14   THE COURT: Okay.
15   (Whereupon proceedings continued in open court, on
16 the record, as follows:
17   THE COURT: Deputy Judd, was the method of your
18 response to Jacob Franks' allegations of James Coghill typical
19 of correct police protocol?
20   THE WITNESS: Yes.
21   THE COURT: Any additional questions?
22   THE DEPUTY: Your Honor, there is one additional
23 question.
24   THE COURT: Counsel, want to approach?
25   (Whereupon the Court and counsel confer at the

PIMA COUNTY SUPERIOR COURT

        bench, out of the hearing of the jurors, as follows:)
                (The Court and counsel review the jury question.)
                THE COURT: Any objections to 11, if he knows?
                MR. JENSVOLD: I don't know.
                MR. SKITZKI: I don't care.
                MR. JENSVOLD: The next witness will answer that question, but --
                (Whereupon proceedings continued in open court, on the record, as follows:)
                THE COURT: Deputy Judd, do you know what the time frame was between your first response and when the search warrant was served?
                THE WITNESS: No, I don't.
                THE COURT: Thank you.
                Anymore questions from the jury?
                (No response.)
                THE COURT: Do either counsel have follow-up questions based on the jury's questions?
                MR. JENSVOLD: No.
                MR. SKITZKI: No.
                THE COURT: May Deputy Judd be excused?
                MR. JENSVOLD: Yes.
                MR. SKITZKI: Yes.
                THE COURT: Thank you, sir. You're excused. Go ahead and step down, but watch your step.

PIMA COUNTY SUPERIOR COURT

                    (Whereupon the witness was excused.)

                    MR. JENSVOLD: The State will call Deputy Schupbach.

                    A VOICE: Your Honor, there's an issue with a bloody nose.

                    A JUROR: I have a bloody nose.

                    THE COURT: We're going to go ahead and go off the record and take a short recess. Go ahead, Mr. Winkenwerder. If all the rest of you want to stand up, and we'll take a break. We'll see you back in 10 minutes.

                    If you all want to go ahead and head back to the jury room. I think there is a matter that the lawyers want to take up real quick, so we can use your time more efficiently when we bring you guys back.

                    Thank you, guys.

                    (Whereupon the jury was excused and left the courtroom, and proceedings continue in their absence, as follows:)

                    THE COURT: All right. The record will show the absence of the jury.

                    For the record, in case it wasn't clear, Mr. Winkenwerder, I don't know what his juror number is, had a bloody nose so we immediately excused the jury. Now they're all gone. But all counsel and Mr. Coghill are still here.

                    MR. SKITZKI: Judge, at this time the defense would move for a mistrial with respect to the testimony elicited

PIMA COUNTY SUPERIOR COURT

from Deputy Judd about the child pornography. What it does, I understand that the context in which it came in, but when put in that context with Mr. Coghill indicating that he didn't know what the K-P was for, but yet the statement attributed to him, that it was a stack of pornography, what we have gotten into is exactly what the Court of Appeals did not want us to get into, which was the issues of the adult pornography.

Because that's, depending upon how the jury would accept that evidence, we now have a situation where the jury has some inference or some belief possibly about child pornography and Mr. Coghill's relationship with child pornography, or with adult pornography, I am sorry.

THE COURT: Mr. Jensvold?

MR. JENSVOLD: Well, Your Honor, I guess I don't see it that way, obviously, or I wouldn't have asked it. But I don't think it's any different than the disks that are labeled K-P or porn movies.

And I believe if our stipulation is going to, if we are going to come to a stipulation about, in particular JE3-QQ, is titled Porn, and there is evidently some child pornography on there. I think it's very analogous to the fact that there may have been child pornography on this particular spindle, but the jury doesn't know anything about adult pornography. They know there is things that are titled Porn or have some indications of pornography. They are going to find out, they are only going to know about the presence of child pornography.

THE COURT: Anything else, Mr. Skitzki?

MR. SKITZKI: Judge, but, I mean, the fact of the matter is that the case is about child pornography. The question posed to, or initially to Mr. Coghill, he indicates pornography, then he's asked about what the K-P is, and he consistently denies knowledge or connection to child pornography.

So, therefore, for the jury to accept what Mr. Coghill had to say, it clearly makes it pornography. And now we have him tied to pornography which was the whole subject of the case going up to the Court of Appeals.

THE COURT: Well, I think the whole subject of the case going up to the Court of Appeals is the jury finding out that in addition to child pornography being in the home that there was also adult pornography. I mean, if the whole issue in this case is his knowledge, clearly I would have precluded the statement if what Mr. Coghill said was, oh, that's just some adult porno, or adult porn, but he makes a general statement about what it is. And I don't think any of us are in a position to know at this point what he meant. He just said that it was pornography. He was right, there was pornography there.

So I do think that it's relevant to his knowledge as

to what was on that spindle. I don't think it violates, I don't think it violates the Court of Appeals ruling. I certainly don't believe it is prejudicial to Mr. Coghill at this point, when he denies knowing that there's disks on there with child pornography on it. I mean, it goes to his knowledge about what is on that disk. He told the deputy what he thought was on that disk, or spindle, I'm sorry.

MR. SKITZKI: But I think that, indeed, is the problem, Judge, is that he's denying the child pornography. He says it's pornography, therefore, it's either that, adult pornography or child pornography. He's not saying it's child pornography. He's claiming knowledge of pornography.

So now we've got the jury chooses to accept what Mr. Coghill allegedly said to the Deputy, and not accept or accept everything in toto. Then it would be he denies knowledge of child pornography, but tells the Deputy that on that disk is pornography which, de facto, would fall back to adult pornography.

THE COURT: And I can't parcel out what he meant when he made that statement. What I have in front of me is, I don't think it's one or the other, it could be both. And to the extent that it could be both, and there's actually pornography on there, and this jury is not hearing about adult pornography, I don't think that we're violating the ruling by the Court of Appeals. So, your motion for mistrial is denied.

```
 1              Do you want to check on Mr. Winkenwerder and see how
 2   he's doing, Ms. Cook.
 3              We're off the record.
 4              (Whereupon proceedings were recessed.)
 5              (Whereupon proceedings resumed, as follows:)
 6              THE BAILIFF:  The jury is entering.
 7              THE COURT:  All right.  Show we're back on the
 8   record.
 9              The record will show the presence of our jury,
10   Mr. Coghill, counsel.
11              Mr. Jensvold, if you would care to call your next
12   witness.
13              MR. JENSVOLD:  Deputy Schupbach.
14
15                        BRENDA SCHUPBACH,
16   having been first duly sworn, was examined and testified, as
17   follows:
18
19                        DIRECT EXAMINATION
20   BY MR. JENSVOLD:
21       Q.    Deputy, would you please introduce yourself to the
22   jury.
23       A.    I am Deputy Brenda Schupbach.  I am employed by the
24   Pima County Sheriff's Office for the last 10 and a half years.
25   I have worked patrol the entire time.
```

PIMA COUNTY SUPERIOR COURT

1   Q.   And which area of town were you patrolling back on
2   April 1st of 2003?
3   A.   I was working the San Xavier District, out on the
4   south side of town.
5   Q.   Did you respond to a call somewhere around 7:00 in
6   the morning?
7   A.   Yes.
8   Q.   Where was that?
9   A.   It was a call, I was to meet, I was a backup
10 officer. I was supposed to meet the reportee at the Circle K
11 at Benson Highway and Country Club.
12 Q.   And did you go there?
13 A.   Yes, I did.
14 Q.   And were you the first Deputy to arrive?
15 A.   Yes, I was.
16 Q.   And who was there?
17 A.   I was supposed to meet, I was dispatched to an
18 anonymous male who wanted to report a friend of his for being
19 in possession of some child pornography, so I didn't have a
20 name.
21   I arrived at the Circle K. And when I pulled up in
22 my patrol car, a gentleman walked towards me, and indicated
23 that he's the one who had called me. And he was later
24 identified as Mr. Franks, Jacob Franks.
25 Q.   What was Mr. Franks' demeanor when you first started

PIMA COUNTY SUPERIOR COURT

1 talking to him?
2 　　A.　He seemed angry. Irritated.
3 　　Q.　Did he tell you why he was angry or irritated?
4 　　A.　In talking to him, he told me that he was supposed
5 to go for a job interview that day, and that his friend who he
6 had been living with, Mr. Coghill, was supposed to give him a
7 ride to that job interview. But instead, Mr. Coghill told him
8 to pack up his belongings, that Mr. Coghill was going to take
9 Mr. Franks back to Phoenix that day.
10 　　Q.　And did he go on to tell you that there was child
11 pornography within the motor home?
12 　　A.　Yes, he did.
13 　　Q.　And did he tell you specifically where to find it?
14 　　A.　He told me it was going to be burned onto some
15 compact disks, and that the compact disks were located by the
16 computer in the RV, and that the disks were marked with the
17 initials K-P.
18 　　Q.　Did Mr. Franks tell you how long he had been in
19 Tucson?
20 　　A.　Mr. Franks told me he had lived with Mr. Coghill for
21 one week in Tucson.
22 　　Q.　Did he ever tell you anything different than that?
23 　　A.　No. He said he had known Mr. Coghill for a few
24 years, but that he had only lived with Mr. Coghill in Tucson
25 for one week.

PIMA COUNTY SUPERIOR COURT

Q. Did he ever tell you that he had been there for a month in Tucson?

A. No.

Q. Okay. Then where did you go after you spoke with Mr. Franks?

A. I waited with Mr. Franks until the responsible officer, Deputy Judd, responded. Both of us were going to go to the recreational vehicle. And so, as soon as we got done talking to Mr. Franks, we, we realized we wanted talk to him again probably after we contacted Mr. Coghill. So we gave Deputy Judd's pager number to Mr. Franks and told him to call us in an hour. And he said he would do that. And we went to the recreational vehicle park to make contact with Mr. Coghill. So, probably talked to Mr. Franks maybe 15 minutes or so. I don't know the exact time.

Q. Okay. And then when you went to the RV park, what did you see when you first arrived?

A. Well, we weren't sure what space it was, and so Mr. Franks gave us a description and we found the home, and Mr. Coghill was outside raking.

Q. And did you talk to Mr. Coghill?

A. Yes, we did.

Q. Did you and Deputy Judd arrive at the exact same time?

A. Yes. One of us followed the other one, so we

PIMA COUNTY SUPERIOR COURT

1 arrived at the same time.

2 Q. And you distinctly remember Mr. Coghill being
3 outside raking when you arrived?

4 A. Yes.

5 Q. And so, what did you and Deputy Judd do when you saw
6 Mr. Coghill?

7 A. We made sure it was the right house and that he was
8 Mr. Coghill. We talked to him a little bit of small talk
9 outside. Something about a motorized scooter had been wrecked
10 and we talked about that, and then we asked him if we could
11 talk to him inside his RV, and he invited us in.

12 Q. At that point had you told Mr. Coghill anything
13 about what Mr. Franks had said about the alleged child
14 pornography?

15 A. I don't believe we talked specifics about that.
16 It's a small recreational vehicle park. Trailers are very
17 close together. We didn't want the neighbors to hear the
18 personal stuff we were going to ask him. I believe we asked
19 him everything about the allegations inside the recreational
20 vehicle.

21 Q. When you got inside, did you ask Mr. Coghill about
22 where Mr. Franks' belongings were?

23 A. That did come up. By then Mr. Coghill knew that we
24 were there because of Mr. Franks. He was, there was a pile of
25 clothes in a chair by the door, and Mr. Coghill indicated that

PIMA COUNTY SUPERIOR COURT

was Mr. Franks' property. If Mr. Franks was going to go back to the recreational vehicle to get to his property, because of the allegations that were made, we thought a Deputy should go with him so there would be no problems. And so I asked, is this all of Mr. Franks' property? He said, yes. And he was, he being Mr. Coghill, was concerned about how he was going to get that property back to Mr. Franks.

Q. Okay. Now, I just want to be specific. Did you ask that question of Mr. Coghill exactly the same way that you have just phrased it?

A. Is this Mr. Franks' property?

Q. Okay. And the way you had just asked it was, is this all of Mr. Franks' property?

A. Yes. Is this -- I don't know if I said exactly all. But my intent of the question was, is this Mr. Franks' property? He didn't have anything with him at the Circle K. I didn't know how much property he had. He had indicated that Mr. Coghill told him to pack up his stuff, that he was going to go back to Phoenix.

Q. In your report, is it correct that you documented that you asked Mr. Coghill, was this all of Mr. Franks' belongings?

A. Was it my initial report? Can I refer to my initial report?

Q. Yes. Let me show you what's been marked as State's

PIMA COUNTY SUPERIOR COURT

```
 1  Exhibit 5.  If you want to turn to the second page, I think
 2  it's in that long, the longest paragraph in the middle.
 3      A.   Yes.  I did ask him if that was all of Mr. Franks'
 4  belongings, or if he had anymore, and he indicated that that
 5  was all of Jake's belongings.
 6      Q.   And then, after that, did Deputy Judd ask him about
 7  some of the CDs?
 8      A.   Yes.
 9      Q.   Okay.  And then did Deputy Judd ask Mr. Coghill what
10  the K-P stood for?
11      A.   Yes, he did.
12      Q.   And Mr. Coghill's response was that he did not know?
13      A.   He said he did not know.
14      Q.   And he believed, according to your report, he
15  believed that Jacob's CD, that that was Jacob's CD, the one
16  with K-P?
17      A.   Yes.  And then there was one that said photographs
18  on the bottom of that disk.  And Mr. Coghill indicated that he
19  might have put some of his photographs on the empty space of
20  that disk.
21      Q.   On the disk that was on the bottom of the spindle?
22      A.   No, the same disk, the disk was marked, I believe,
23  K-P, and then had "photographs" also written on it.
24      Q.   Okay.  That's what you remember seeing?
25      A.   Let me -- excuse me.  Yes.  At the bottom of that
```

PIMA COUNTY SUPERIOR COURT

disk was the word "photographs." Mr. Coghill stated he may have put some of his photographs on the empty space of that disk. And he believed that was on the disk, yes.

Q. So what you remember is that he wasn't talking about the spindle itself, but that particular disk?

A. That particular disk.

Q. Did you see either Deputy Judd or Mr. Coghill handle any of those CDs as they were talking about them?

A. I remember I was, it's a very small area in the recreational vehicle, and there was like three adults trying to be in the space of two. I do remember they were talking about the stacks of spindles and what was on the stacks, like this is science fiction, this is Star Wars, and there were some that they discussed with the marking of K-P.

I believe, I believe that there was a compact disk that was being handled. I remember Deputy Judd had some gloves on just in case he had to handle some things. But I can't remember who was handling it at that time when the subject came up.

Q. Do you remember anything like Deputy Judd taking a whole bunch of CDs off that spindle and then putting them back on, anything like that?

A. I just remember the discussion about all the compact -- there were a lot of CDs there, several spindles, and they were talking about the different spindles, and I was

PIMA COUNTY SUPERIOR COURT

1 behind both of them at the time.
2   Q.   Okay. So I guess, to be specific with my question,
3 do you remember anything, either Deputy Judd or Mr. Coghill
4 pulling a bunch of CDs off of any particular spindle?
5   A.   Not a bunch. It was so long ago I just really can't
6 remember exactly if one was handled. I believe one was
7 handled, or one was pointed out or talked about.
8   Q.   You think Deputy Judd had gloves on?
9   A.   I think I remember he had gloves on.
10   Q.   You didn't document anything in your report about
11 the handling of CDs?
12   A.   No, I didn't. No.
13   Q.   Did you ask Mr. Coghill how long he had been in
14 Tucson?
15   A.   No. I don't believe I asked him how long he had
16 been in Tucson.
17   Q.   Did you hear him make any statements to Deputy Judd
18 about how long he had been in Tucson?
19   A.   Not that was in my notes or on my report.
20   Q.   Deputy Judd had testified that there was at least a
21 brief period of time where you were speaking with Mr. Coghill
22 and he was outside. Do you remember that?
23   A.   This is before we went in, we were talking about the
24 motor scooter that had been wrecked, I'm not sure. I know I
25 had talked to Mr. Coghill. I know we went outside after we

```
 1  were done and we were waiting for Detectives to arrive.
 2      Q.   Was there any time that you remember that Deputy
 3  Judd was talking to Mr. Coghill when you were somewhere else
 4  where you were out of ear shot of the conversation?
 5      A.   I don't recall that, no.
 6           MR. JENSVOLD:   I think that's all I have.
 7           Thank you.
 8           THE COURT:   Cross-Examination.
 9
10                      CROSS-EXAMINATION
11  BY MR. SKITZKI:
12      Q.   Deputy Schupbach, you responded to the Circle K at
13  Benson Highway and encountered Mr. Franks, correct?
14      A.   Yes.
15      Q.   You arrived there before Deputy Judd?
16      A.   Yes.
17      Q.   Not very much before him.  You just talked to
18  Mr. Franks a little bit, and then Deputy Judd arrives?
19      A.   Yes.
20      Q.   Mr. Franks, when you first encountered him and he
21  starts talking to you about Mr. Coghill, he's angry, correct?
22      A.   Yes.
23      Q.   He's upset?
24      A.   Yes.
25      Q.   And he's talking about, I guess he's not getting a
```

PIMA COUNTY SUPERIOR COURT

1 ride to some job interview, is that what he's talking about?
2 A. Yes. That's part of why he was mad he said.
3 Q. So he told you that he was mad at Mr. Coghill and
4 that was sort of what prompted him to call?
5 A. Well, he indicated that he was angry, and he did
6 make a statement to me, that he was just mad enough now that
7 he wanted to report this, this being the child pornography.
8 Q. So you and Deputy Judd have a conversation with
9 Mr. Franks at the Circle K, and he gives some specifics about
10 where the disks containing the child pornography can be found
11 within the motor home?
12 A. Yes.
13 Q. After you and Deputy Judd have completed your
14 conversation with Mr. Franks, you and Deputy Judd then, in
15 separate cars, proceed over to the motor home park?
16 A. Yes.
17 Q. You arrive at the motor home park basically at the
18 same time?
19 A. Yes.
20 Q. One car's following the other?
21 A. Yes.
22 Q. You both get out at the same time, out of your
23 vehicles?
24 A. Yes.
25 Q. You encounter Mr. Coghill raking outside of his

PIMA COUNTY SUPERIOR COURT

motor home.

A. Yes.

Q. And you come up and identify yourself and make sure that he's Mr. Coghill, the person that you're looking for?

A. Yes.

Q. And then there is some small talk, but nothing about the allegations of the child pornography that happened outside?

A. That's correct.

Q. You then get, suggest to Mr. Coghill or somehow that everybody go inside the motor home to have a further discussion.

A. Yes. Deputy Judd and I asked if we could come inside, we were going to discuss some things that, like I said, it's a small mobile home park and people could hear. And --

Q. You don't want to talk about that stuff --

A. Exactly.

Q. --within the ear shot of everyone else.

A. Exactly.

Q. Mr. Coghill is cooperative and friendly with you when you first arrived?

A. Yes.

Q. He, in fact, has no problem going inside his motor home with you and Deputy Judd?

PIMA COUNTY SUPERIOR COURT

1   A.   That's correct.
2   Q.   When the three of you were inside there, do you guys
3 sit down or were you standing?
4   A.   We are standing.
5   Q.   When you get inside the motor home, it's pretty
6 small so can you already see the computer area when you enter
7 the motor home?
8   A.   As soon as you walk up the steps into the
9 recreational vehicle, it's like, a couch for a living room, a
10 kitchen, there is a desk to your right that has a computer,
11 and there's spindles of compact disks around the computer
12 area. Past the computer would be the driver's and passenger
13 seat for the vehicle.
14   Q.   So you noticed, when you first came in there, a
15 large number of disks by this computer?
16   A.   Yes.
17   Q.   And they are stacked on top of each other in these
18 spindles?
19   A.   I don't know if that's what they're called, but
20 they're like pieces of wood or plastic that you just put the
21 holes of the CD on the spindles. I don't know, I think that's
22 what they're called.
23   Q.   And some of these are stacked pretty high?
24   A.   Yes.
25   Q.   In the course of your being in there, that's when,

1 you know, one of those disks at some point in time get shown
2 to Mr. Coghill, or discussed with Mr. Coghill, and it's got
3 K-P written on it?
4   A. Yes.
5   Q. And Mr. Coghill, in the course of when you and
6 Deputy Judd were speaking with him, indicated that some of the
7 burned CD's were not his and belonged to Mr. Franks?
8   A. Yes, he did mention that after, after we had asked
9 him about Mr. Franks' property.
10   Q. He also indicated that he did not know what the K-P
11 stood for on the disk with K-P?
12   A. That's what he said, yes.
13   Q. When you left Mr. Coghill's motor home, did you take
14 Mr. Franks' property with you?
15   A. I don't recall taking Mr. Franks' property with me.
16 I believe we left it there because we talked to the Detectives
17 and they indicated that there was going to be a search
18 warrant.
19   Mr. Franks wasn't with us. Deputy Judd, I think
20 later, went and picked up Mr. Franks to take him to the
21 Sheriff's office for an interview.
22   Q. So your purpose in not taking that property, is you
23 didn't want to disturb anything that could possibly be
24 evidence?
25   A. Yes.

PIMA COUNTY SUPERIOR COURT

1 Q. Did you actually go through the pile of clothes to
2 see if there was anything in the pile or underneath the pile?
3 A. I don't recall going though the pile itself. I just
4 remember seeing it in the chair.
5 Q. So in that pile on the chair, did you notice, you
6 know, personal hygiene items?
7 A. In my report I just recall seeing clothes. I didn't
8 mention anything else, and I cannot recall now if there is
9 anything else.
10 Q. So for all you know, since you didn't go through the
11 pile, there could have been a bag under there, or toothpaste,
12 things like that, you just don't know.
13 A. I don't know.
14 Q. And you didn't want to touch anything because it was
15 your belief that there possibly would be a search warrant;
16 somebody would be searching the entirety of that motor home?
17 A. Yes. And I really had no reason to go through
18 Mr. Franks' property at that time.
19 Q. Was the only time that you had contact with
20 Mr. Franks on April 1st, 2003, was that when you initially
21 responded to that call at Circle K?
22 A. Yes.
23   MR. SKITZKI: I don't have any other questions.
24   THE COURT: Any Redirect?
25   MR. JENSVOLD: No, Your Honor.

PIMA COUNTY SUPERIOR COURT

THE COURT: Any members of our jury have any questions for Deputy Schupbach?

All right. One question.

Counsel want to approach.

Wait.

(Whereupon the Court and counsel confer at the bench, out of the hearing of the jurors, as follows:)

(The Court and counsel review the jury question.)

MR. JENSVOLD: I think Englander can testify, or Knuth. One of them can testify about when the search warrant started, hopefully.

She can't. I don't think she can answer it.

THE COURT: I don't know, sir.

MR. JENSVOLD: Well, I don't think she can, know what time they started the search warrant. And I don't think this is the right witness for the first one. I think Englander can handle that.

MR. SKITZKI: I object. Englander can answer the first one. As to the second one, I don't have a problem with that. I don't have any objection to that.

MR. JENSVOLD: No.

THE COURT: All right. So I'm going to ask question two, on juror submitted question form 12. And no objection to 13?

MR. SKITZKI: Correct.

PIMA COUNTY SUPERIOR COURT

1	THE COURT: All right.
2	(Whereupon proceedings continued in open court, on
3	the record, as follows:)
4	THE COURT: Deputy, do you know the time frame
5	between when you first responded to the RV and when the search
6	warrant was served?
7	THE WITNESS: I don't know how long it took to get
8	the search warrant. I know that we were probably at
9	Mr. Coghills' recreational vehicle for about an hour, because
10	we told Mr. Franks to call us in an hour after we left him,
11	and we were still with Mr. Coghill when Mr. Franks called. We
12	had to call the Detectives. It took them about 20 minutes to
13	get out to the mobile home park. And I don't know how long it
14	took them to get the paperwork and contact the judge, to get
15	the search warrant.
16	Once I provided the Detectives with the information
17	they needed for the warrant, I departed back to my patrol
18	duties that day.
19	THE COURT: Okay. What was the demeanor of
20	Mr. Coghill?
21	THE WITNESS: He was cooperative with us. He never
22	seemed angry when I was there.
23	THE COURT: All right. How far away was the closest
24	RV to Mr. Coghill's?
25	THE WITNESS: It's a very small drive. You pull in

PIMA COUNTY SUPERIOR COURT

off of Benson Highway. There is probably 12 spaces. Each space doesn't really have a yard beside it. I would say space enough for one RV between him and a neighbor. He didn't have a neighbor that I recall directly beside him, but it's a small park and RVs don't have very thick walls. Having one, I know that. So, I would say there was an empty space on the side of him.

THE COURT: Okay.

Were you concerned that Mr. Coghill might throw away any evidence?

THE WITNESS: As I recall, Mr. Coghill stayed with Deputy Judd and myself, so he wouldn't have the opportunity to throw anything before the Detectives arrived.

THE COURT: Any additional questions from the jury?

(No response.)

THE COURT: Any follow-up questions from either lawyer?

MR. JENSVOLD: No, Your Honor.

MR. SKITZKI: I have one.

THE COURT: Sure.

BY MR. SKITZKI:

Q. And, Deputy, the procedure was, after you got there, and based upon what the alligations were, you knew that somebody was going to try to get a search warrant to search Mr. Coghill's motor home, correct?

PIMA COUNTY SUPERIOR COURT

1   A.   I believe there was enough reasonable suspicion to
2   warrant a search warrant, so that's why we called the
3   Detectives.
4   Q.   You and Deputy Judd remained at the scene until the
5   Detectives arrived because that's standard procedure, because
6   you want to make sure that Mr. Coghill, at that point,
7   wouldn't have the opportunity to try to get rid of anything?
8   A.   Correct.
9   MR. SKITZKI: All right. I don't have anything
10   else.
11   Thank you.
12   THE COURT: All right. May this Deputy be excused?
13   MR. JENSVOLD: Yes.
14   THE COURT: Thank you, Deputy. You're excused.
15   Watch your step going down.
16   (Whereupon the witness was excused.)
17   THE COURT: Mr. Jensvold.
18   MR. JENSVOLD: The State calls, I think, Detective
19   Knuth.
20   THE COURT: Sir, if you will step forward, please,
21   we'll have the clerk swear you in.
22
23   WILLIAM KNUTH,
24   having been first duly sworn, was examined and testified, as
25   follows:

PIMA COUNTY SUPERIOR COURT

1   THE COURT: Watch your step going up, the floor
2 slants.
3   DIRECT EXAMINATION
4 BY MR. JENSVOLD:
5   Q. Would you please introduce yourself to the jury.
6   A. My name is Deputy William Knuth. I'm a deputy at
7 the Pima County Sheriff's Office.
8   Q. How long have you been with the Sheriff's
9 Department?
10   A. 10 years.
11   Q. And what was your position back in April of 2003?
12   A. I was a Detective assigned to the Crimes Against
13 Children Unit.
14   Q. And as part of being in that unit, do you respond to
15 cases involving potential possession of child pornography?
16   A. That would be correct.
17   Q. And did you respond to a call sometime during the
18 morning of April 1st of 2003?
19   A. Yes.
20   Q. What was your specific role?
21   A. Initially, I just sat in, which is kind of customary
22 on an interview with another individual involved in this case;
23 with Detective Moretz. Once I completed that, I went to the
24 incident location and assisted in the service of a warrant.
25   Q. And what was the warrant for?

PIMA COUNTY SUPERIOR COURT

```
 1    A.    It was a warrant to search the residence.
 2    Q.    What was the residence?  What kind of residence?
 3    A.    It was a travel trailer, is how I would describe it.
 4    Q.    And where was it?
 5    A.    Benson Highway, 3365 East Benson Highway, I believe
 6 it was.
 7    Q.    Who was the owner of the residence?
 8    A.    James Coghill.
 9    Q.    And do you know what time the search warrant
10 started?
11    A.    I cannot say definitely what time it was started,
12 the service of the warrant.
13    Q.    Do you know what time you got there to assist in the
14 search of the residence?
15    A.    Not, not exactly.  I know it was the morning hours,
16 so I don't know that my report even stated my arrival time.
17    Q.    You assisted Detective Moretz with the interview of
18 Jacob Franks?
19    A.    I didn't really assist.  I just sat in.  It's kind
20 of common practice with us to have a second Detective sit in
21 on an interview.
22    Q.    Who was leading the interview?
23    A.    Detective Moretz.
24    Q.    And did Detective Englander show up during the later
25 portions of that interview?
```

PIMA COUNTY SUPERIOR COURT

1 A. Not that I am aware of. I recall meeting him at the
2 search location.
3 Q. Okay. Deputy, I want to show you, if you can take a
4 look at all of these photographs, and then I will ask you some
5 questions at the end.
6 A. Okay.
7 Q. If you will look at those first.
8 THE COURT: Mr. Jensvold, while he's doing that, do
9 you want to take that item off the screen.
10 MR. JENSVOLD: Sorry.
11 THE COURT: That's okay.
12 BY MR. JENSVOLD:
13 Q. Okay. These photographs which, let's see, include
14 State's 2-J, 2-O, 2-Q, R and S, and then T, all the way
15 through 2-PP, do you recognize all of those photographs, or
16 are there any in there that you don't recognize?
17 A. I don't immediately recognize a lot of the computer
18 hardware type photographs, because I didn't really work with
19 that portion of the trailer.
20 Q. Okay.
21 A. But more of my involvement was with media, or, you
22 know, the disks and those kinds of things. So, the actual
23 computer hardware I really had no involvement with.
24 Q. Did you collect a cable bill?
25 A. Yes.

PIMA COUNTY SUPERIOR COURT

1   Q.   Or receipt at some point?
2   A.   Yes.
3   Q.   And, is that indicated in photograph 2-MN?
4   A.   Yes.
5   Q.   And I want to show you what's been marked as State's
6   Exhibit 31. And it's been previously opened. I just want to
7   show it to you. Do you recognize that?
8   A.   Yes.
9   Q.   Okay. And what is it?
10   A.   It's a Cox bill bearing the name of Jim Coghill, at
11   3356 East Benson Highway, number seven.
12   Q.   What was the date?
13   A.   This, it has a date, has a 2-27-03 date on it, I
14   see.
15   Q.   Do you see any other dates on there?
16   A.   Oh, here, this one, it has a Cox representative
17   signature dated 2-27-03.
18   Q.   And Mr. Coghill signed it as well?
19   A.   Yes.
20   MR. JENSVOLD: The State would move for the
21   admission of State's Exhibit 31.
22   MR. SKITZKI: No objection.
23   THE COURT: State's 31 is admitted.
24   BY MR. JENSVOLD:
25   Q.   Let's take out the photographs that you don't

PIMA COUNTY SUPERIOR COURT

1 recognize. Do you recognize 2-O?
2   A. I do not.
3   Q. Okay. Do you recognize 2-BB and the subsequent
4 photographs?
5   A. I do not.
6   Q. Okay. So we've got, okay, take a look at that stack
7 again, and make sure you recognize all of those.
8   A. I do recognize all of these from being in the
9 trailer. The majority of them were not collected by me. I
10 just merely remember seeing them there.
11   Q. And did you participate in the, I guess, the
12 itemization of these CDs later?
13   A. Yes, I believe I did.
14   Q. And is that some of what's reflected in these
15 photographs?
16   A. Yes.
17   MR. JENSVOLD: Your Honor, the State would then move
18 for the admission of, let's see, 2, 2-T through 2-AA, and then
19 2-LL, through 2-PP.
20   THE COURT: Any objection?
21   MR. SKITZKI: May I look at those again one last
22 time?
23   Then I have no objection, Judge.
24   THE COURT: All right. 2-T through 2-AA are
25 admitted, and 2-LL through 2-PP are admitted.

PIMA COUNTY SUPERIOR COURT

BY MR. JENSVOLD:

Q. All right. Other than what you have already talked about, did you participate in any other aspects of the investigation?

A. No.

Q. Okay. Deputy, I just want to show these photographs that we have just admitted and just have you describe them briefly, if you could.

A. It's, I will refer to it as spindles of a number of compact disks.

Q. And this is State's Exhibit 2-T. There is a gloved hand with some writing on a paper bag, what is that?

A. That's the processor identifying items seized during a warrant. The bag being photographed would be the bag that would ultimately hold that item that's being photographed.

Q. Did you -- or who else was with you when you were looking at these disks in the motor home?

A. To my recollection, I had the back half of the trailer and Detective Englander was in the front.

Q. But did you see the CDs?

A. I did see them, yes.

Q. This is 2-U. What does that show?

A. Once, again, excuse me, the photograph process when we are collecting evidence.

Q. 2-V?

1   A.   I believe that this was a photo of the packaged
2 evidence prior to possibly opening it to sort, or to further
3 label, I'm thinking. I don't specifically recall.
4   Q.   And then 2-W?
5   A.   That tells me that I was correct; that we went ahead
6 and opened that piece of evidence, and for whatever reason we
7 are going to sort of categorize or something.
8   Q.   2-X?
9   A.   Again, labeling a evidence item.
10   Q.   2-Y?
11   A.   Again, documentation of the item number and what the
12 item is prior to packaging.
13   Q.   And Z, is that basically the same thing?
14   A.   Same process.
15   Q.   Different item?
16   A.   Different item, same process.
17   Q.   I think the same questions go for a lot of these;
18 this is 2-AA?
19   A.   Correct, another item.
20   Q.   2-LL?
21   A.   That's another item being prepared for packaging.
22   Q.   And in this group of photographs, is that being
23 photographed in the motor home itself?
24   A.   Yes. I believe it is. Looks like it.
25   Q.   And this is 2-MM. We talked about that already.

PIMA COUNTY SUPERIOR COURT

```
 1      A.   Yes, that's the cable bill.
 2      Q.   Is that the same bill that you just referred to
 3 earlier?
 4      A.   Yes, it is.
 5      Q.   And 2-NN?
 6      A.   Some sort of categorizing process, I believe.
 7      Q.   And 2-OO?
 8      A.   I would imagine that was the same time, the same
 9 process we would have gone through.
10      Q.   And 2-PP?
11      A.   Also the sorting, or categorizing, or what have you.
12      Q.   And these photographs, were they taken back to the
13 Sheriff's Department?
14      A.   Yes.
15           MR. JENSVOLD:  I believe that's all I have.
16           Thank you.
17           THE COURT:  Cross-Examination?
18
19                       CROSS-EXAMINATION
20 BY MR. SKITZKI:
21      Q.   Deputy, the photographs, the last couple that we saw
22 where they were at the Sheriff's station, with the disks
23 spread out all over the tables, was that the way that you
24 encountered them at the motor home?
25      A.   I -- probably not.  I mean, I can't say for sure.  I
```

PIMA COUNTY SUPERIOR COURT

```
 1  recall most of the CD's were being in those spindles.
 2      Q.  And then I think there was one photograph that
 3  looked like there were CD's or disks like in some kind of book
 4  or something like that?
 5      A.  It was a case holder, or CD holder.
 6      Q.  CD holder kind of thing?
 7      A.  Yeah.
 8      Q.  But the majority of the disks were on spindles, sort
 9  of stacked on top of one another?
10      A.  That's what I recall.
11      Q.  Ultimately, I guess, were the number of disks that
12  were taken in the service of the search warrant, would that
13  have numbered in the hundreds?
14      A.  It would be a guess, but I would say it must have.
15      Q.  It's a lot?
16      A.  Yeah, it was a lot.
17      Q.  And besides your participation in the search warrant
18  and the, and the recordation of the items that were taken, you
19  participated, or I guess you sat in on the interview that
20  Detective Moretz did with a person by the name of Jacob
21  Franks?
22      A.  Correct.
23      Q.  It was Deputy or Detective Moretz, though, who was
24  directing the interview and asking the questions, is that fair
25  to say?
```

         A.   Yes. And I documented nothing about the interview
in my report, so I really don't recall it, to be perfectly
honest.
         Q.   Did you participate in any other interviews with any
other individuals in this case?
         A.   No, I didn't.
         Q.   And at the end of the day, the case Detective on
this case was Detective Englander?
         A.   Correct.
         MR. SKITZKI: I don't have anything else.
         THE COURT: Any Redirect?
         MR. JENSVOLD: No, Your Honor.
         THE COURT: Any questions from our jury?
         All right.
         Counsel want to approach, I am sorry.
         (Whereupon the Court and counsel confer at the
bench, out of the hearing of the jurors, as follows:)
         (The Court and counsel review the jury question.)
         MR. JENSVOLD: He can't answer that.
         MR. SKITZKI: Right.
         THE COURT: Which one?
         MR. JENSVOLD: The bottom one.
         THE COURT: You're on question 16 from the jury?
         MR. JENSVOLD: I am not sure who is going to know
the top one. If you give him the bill, maybe it says, I don't

PIMA COUNTY SUPERIOR COURT

1 know. I don't care.
2 THE COURT: All right. So are we not asking the
3 final question on 16.
4 MR. JENSVOLD: Right.
5 THE COURT: But no objection to any of the others on
6 14, 15 or 16?
7 MR. JENSVOLD: No.
8 MR. SKITZKI: No.
9 THE COURT: All right. Thanks.
10 (Whereupon proceedings continued in open court, on
11 the record, as follows:)
12 THE COURT: Deputy, what was your experience at the
13 time of the incident?
14 THE WITNESS: At that time I had just over four
15 years of patrol experience, and I believe about three to four
16 months experience in criminal investigations.
17 THE COURT: I am going to hand you what's admitted
18 as State's 31 because you may need it. What was the inclusive
19 date of the Cox cable service?
20 THE WITNESS: I hope it says that very thing,
21 because I won't know if it doesn't.
22 THE COURT: And you all are going to have State's 31
23 back there to take a look at as well.
24 While you're looking for that, the other question
25 is, does the bill include internet or just cable TV service,

```
 1  or both?
 2          THE WITNESS:  It has, it's talking about computer
 3  information and an IP address, so that would tell me that it
 4  does serve a computer.  It lists basic service.  There is also
 5  a modem service mentioned.
 6          THE COURT:  All right.
 7          Okay.  And you can't find an inclusive date on
 8  there?
 9          THE WITNESS:  The only date that I see on this bill
10  in two places is 2-7-03.
11          THE COURT:  Can I have the envelope back, too?
12          Do you photograph items such as the spindles, where
13  they were found in the motor home?
14          THE WITNESS:  Yes.
15          THE COURT:  And where was the case that had the CD's
16  in it located?
17          THE WITNESS:  I did not collect that myself.  I
18  couldn't tell you honestly where it was.  If I saw that
19  photograph again, I might be able to tell you, but I'm not
20  sure.
21          THE COURT:  Okay.  Do you want to take a look at it,
22  if I can find it?
23          THE WITNESS:  We can try.  I recall the trailer
24  somewhat, so maybe.
25          THE COURT:  All right.  I'm going to show you what
```

PIMA COUNTY SUPERIOR COURT

has been admitted as 2-LL. State's 2-LL. Is that where you found it, or is that just showing what was in it?

THE WITNESS: It probablly was located in this general area; I will say that. It wasn't necessarily in thisn very position.

Detective Englander recovered this item, so, I can say by looking at the photo that, that to the best of my recollection, there was like, I guess what I call a computer work station just inside the door, and this looks like that area to me by looking at the photo.

THE COURT: Anymore questions from the jury?

Okay. You guys want to come on up? Counsel.

(Whereupon the Court and counsel confer at the bench, out of the hearing of the jurors, as follows:)

(The Court and counsel review the jury question.)

THE COURT: Any objections to 17?

MR. SKITZKI: No.

MR. JENSVOLD: No.

(Whereupon proceedings continued in open court, on the record, as follows:)

THE COURT: Where was Mr. Coghill during the search warrant?

THE WITNESS: I would assume that he was at the Sheriff's Administration Building being interviewed by another Detective. But that's, once again, an assumption. He wasn't

PIMA COUNTY SUPERIOR COURT

```
 1  there.
 2          THE COURT:  Any other questions from the jury?
 3          No?
 4          Any follow-up questions from counsel?
 5  BY MR. SKITZKI:
 6      Q.  Deputy, do you know where Mr. Coghill was
 7  interviewed, or if he was around?
 8      A.  I had nothing to do with his interview, so I
 9  couldn't say.
10          MR. SKITZKI:  No objection.
11          THE COURT:  May the Deputy be excused?
12          MR. JENSVOLD:  Yes.
13          THE COURT:  Deputy, thanks so much for your time.
14  Watch your step going down.
15          (Whereupon the witness was excused.)
16          THE COURT:  Folks, we are going to take our regular
17  afternoon recess.  We didn't break when you all broke, so
18  we're going to start up again at, well, why don't we just
19  start up again at 3:30.  So make sure you're in the jury room
20  no later than 3:30, okay.
21          So remember the admonition, and we'll see you back
22  in a few.
23          (Whereupon the jury is excused and leaves the
24  courtroom, and proceedings continue in their absence, as
25  follows:)
```

PIMA COUNTY SUPERIOR COURT

1   THE COURT: All right. Let the record show the
2 absence of the jury, the presence of all counsel and
3 Mr. Coghill.
4   Anything we can take up before we have a brief
5 recess?
6   No? All right.
7   We'll see you guys back at about 3:30.
8   Oh, and we are off the record.
9   (Whereupon proceedings were recessed.)
10   (Whereupon proceedings reconvened.)
11   THE COURT: We are back on the record.
12   The record will show the absence of the jury, the
13 presence of both counsel, and -- I'm sorry, all counsel, and
14 Mr. Coghill.
15   State's 2-I, I think somebody noticed that there
16 was, in that photograph there was a title that is potentially
17 pornographic on the video depicted in that photograph. It was
18 far enough away from the jury that they couldn't have possibly
19 read it, but, in any event, the State has photo shopeed 2-I to
20 delete that title.
21   Has the defense seen the new proposed 2-I?
22   MR. EUCHNER: Yes, Your Honor. There are actually
23 two options, and I think that the one the Court has in the
24 right hand was the first one to go with, better one that we
25 suggested that we go with, the photo shopped version. There

PIMA COUNTY SUPERIOR COURT

1 was a cropped version as well.
2   THE COURT: All right.
3   Mr. Jensvold.
4   MR. JENSVOLD: That's fine with the State.
5   THE COURT: So what I'm going to do is, I'm going to
6 make the photo shopped version the new 2-I, so the jury won't
7 have any questions. And the original photograph I'm going to
8 make 2-I-1.
9   All right?
10   THE CLERK: And that is not to go back to the jury?
11   THE COURT: And that is not to go back to the jury.
12 2-I-1 will not go back to the jury.
13   And can we get the jury.
14   (Bailiff complies.)
15   THE BAILIFF: Jury is entering.
16   (Jurors again present.)
17   (3:35 p.m. Whereupon proceedings resume, as
18 follows:)
19   THE COURT: The record will show the presence of the
20 jury, the presence of all counsel, Mr. Coghill.
21   Mr. Jensvold, do you have your next witness here?
22   MR. JENSVOLD: Yes. The State calls Mr. Brian
23 McGraw.
24   ****
25   ****

PIMA COUNTY SUPERIOR COURT

```
 1              BRIAN MARK MCGRAW,
 2  having been first duly sworn, was examined and testified, as
 3  follows:
 4
 5                   DIRECT EXAMINATION
 6  BY MR. JENSVOLD:
 7       Q.   Mr. McGraw, will you please introduce yourself to
 8  the jury.
 9       A.   My name is Brian Mark McGraw.  I am a Forensics
10  Technician with the Pima County Sheriff's Department.
11       Q.   And how long have you been in your current position?
12       A.   I have been working for the Sheriff's Department for
13  14 years and five months.
14       Q.   And have you done anything else besides Forensic
15  Technician?
16       A.   My current job; no, that's all I've been doing.
17       Q.   What do you do as far as what are your range of
18  duties?
19       A.   Okay.  Well, I'm a civilian employee with the Pima
20  County Sheriff's Office.  I provide technical support service
21  for law enforcement.  My basic duties are to respond to crime
22  and accident scenes and to photograph those scenes for
23  documentation purposes.
24            I also photograph victims, suspects, autopsies,
25  search warrants, items of evidence that are to be collected.
```

PIMA COUNTY SUPERIOR COURT

I also process crime scenes, accident scenes, items of evidence for latent prints by using various powders and/or chemicals. I preserve that latent print that I develop by either photographing it, scanning it on a flatbed scanner, or the most common method, lifting it with a strip of tape and placing that onto a latent lift card.

I search crime scenes and items of evidence for suspected bodily fluids by using various tools and/or chemicals. I also assist in the collection and preservation of DNA evidence at crime scenes, and on items of evidence.

These basic duties I've explained to you are all at the request of a sworn law enforcement official.

Q. And is fingerprint powder something that you use in processing fingerprints?

A. Yes, it is.

Q. In your experience, does that powder have any effect on electronic media?

A. Yes, it does.

Q. What does it do to CDs specifically?

A. Well, as I am dusting a CD -- when I'm dusting a CD and I'm going to examine -- when I lift a latent print off of CDs, a CD, the strip of tape that I use sometimes will damage the metal of the CD, the metal writable part of the CD.

Q. Does the powder itself have any effect on the media of the CD?

1   A.   No, to the best of my knowledge.
2   Q.   All right. Mr. McGraw, did you respond to a
3 incident on April 1st of 2003?
4   A.   Yes.
5   Q.   And what was the nature of the, what were you called
6 to do at this particular scene?
7   A.   I was called to photograph the execution of a search
8 warrant on a mobile home.
9   Q.   Where, what was the address?
10   A.   The address was 3566 East Benson Highway, space
11 number seven.
12   Q.   And did you take photographs there?
13   A.   Yes, I did.
14   Q.   Did you take photographs of the exterior as well as
15 the inside of the motor home?
16   A.   Yes, I did.
17   Q.   And then did you take photographs as evidence was
18 being collected?
19   A.   Yes, I did.
20   Q.   Did you witness all of the evidence being collected?
21   A.   Yes, I did.
22   Q.   Do you remember if all of the evidence that was
23 collected was photographed as it was found?
24   A.   I don't remember.
25   Q.   And -- okay. Do you remember anything specific

```
 1   about the CDs that were photographed, if they were manipulated
 2   in any way?
 3        A.   No.
 4        Q.   No, you don't remember?
 5        A.   No, I don't remember.
 6        Q.   I have had you look at just a small sample of the
 7   total photographs that we have already admitted.  State's
 8   Exhibits 2-J, O, Q through S, and then looks like BB through
 9   2-KK.  Have you looked at all of these?
10        A.   Yes, I did.
11        Q.   Did you take all of these?
12        A.   These appear to be the photographs that I've taken.
13        Q.   And do the photographs appear to represent the scene
14   as you photographed it?
15        A.   Yes.
16             MR. JENSVOLD:  Your Honor, the State would move for
17   the admission of the previously mentioned exhibits.
18             MR. EUCHNER:  Can I see them again?  These are --
19             No objection, Your Honor.
20             THE COURT:  All right.  State's 2-J, 2-O, 2-Q
21   through S, State's 2-BB through KK, are all admitted.
22   BY MR. JENSVOLD:
23        Q.   And other than what's in the photographs, do you
24   have any specific knowledge about the contents of the items
25   that were photographed?
```

PIMA COUNTY SUPERIOR COURT

1   A. No.

2   Q. And I'm just going to show these one by one to the
3 jury without any comment, if that's okay.

4   (Exhibits displayed for the jury.)

5   MR. JENSVOLD: This is 2-J. 2-O. 2-Q. 2-R. 2-S.
6 2-BB. 2-CC. 2-DD. 2-EE. 2-FF. 2-GG. HH. II. JJ. KK.
7 BY MR. JENSVOLD:

8   Q. Mr. McGraw, besides taking the photographs on April
9 1st of 2003, did you have any other involvement in the
10 investigation on that day?

11   A. Not on that day.

12   Q. Did you also take the photographs back at the
13 Sheriff's Department?

14   A. I took photographs of an item of evidence that I
15 processed.

16   Q. And then did you have some later involvement
17 regarding processing some items for fingerprints later?

18   A. Yes.

19   Q. What day was that?

20   A. Actually that was spread out over three days. One
21 day was on September 23rd of 2003. Another day was September
22 30th of 2003. And the last final day was October 20th of
23 2003.

24   Q. Okay. On September 23rd of 2003, what did you do
25 regarding attempts to process items for fingerprints?

PIMA COUNTY SUPERIOR COURT

         A.   I, routinely I photograph the package of the item of
evidence before I open the package up. It's a sealed package.
And then I remove the item of evidence from the package and I
take more photographs of an item of evidence.
         This item of evidence was marked as JE-3, which was
a spindle of compact disks, and then I processed those for
latent fingerprints.
         Q.   What happened as you were processing the items
within that spindle for fingerprints?
         A.   First I processed the spindle itself. I got
fingerprints off of that. And as I started processing the
CDs, the metal on the CDs started to peel. The middle part of
the CD that the information is recorded on started to peel.
         So I stopped processing for prints, and I called
Detective Englander, and asked him if he had made copies of
the CDs. I wanted to make sure he made copies of them before
I destroyed them.
         Q.   And what did he say?
         A.   He said, yes, he did make copies. So I continued to
process the CDs for latent prints.
         Q.   And then you continued on processing for
fingerprints September 30th and October 20th?
         A.   Yes.
         Q.   And you were not responsible for the identification
of the fingerprints, is that correct?

1   A.   No.
2   Q.   Somebody else did that?
3   A.   Yes.
4   MR. JENSVOLD: And I think that's all I have.
5   Thank you.
6   THE COURT: Cross-Examination?
7   MR. EUCHNER: Thank you, Your Honor.

                    CROSS-EXAMINATION
BY MR. EUCHNER:
    Q.   Hi, Mr. McGraw.
    A.   Hello.
    Q.   So on April 1st, 2003, you didn't do any fingerprint lifting, no latent lifting?
    A.   No.
    Q.   And on September 23rd, and September 30th, and October 20th of 2003, did you do any additional photographing?
    A.   Just on September 23rd, I took photographs of the CDs.
    Q.   Are you referring to the damaged CDs?
    A.   Yes. Yeah, prior to damage.
    Q.   And through -- how many CDs would you say you dusted in total?
    A.   Approximately a hundred and 15.
    Q.   And were those all from the JE-3 spindle?

1   A. Yes.
2   Q. And you got some prints on some CDs?
3   A. Yes.
4   Q. And some CDs you got no prints?
5   A. Right.
6   Q. And you got some prints off the spindle?
7   A. Yes, I did.
8   Q. And from there, you turned those prints in to
9 Detective Englander?
10   A. No, from there I turned those prints in to the
11 Latent Print Examiner.
12   Q. For them to be processed, to be examined by a Latent
13 Print Examiner?
14   A. Yes.
15   MR. EUCHNER: Nothing further.
16   THE COURT: Any Redirect?
17   MR. JENSVOLD: No.
18   THE COURT: Any questions from our jury?
19   (Whereupon the Court and counsel confer at the
20 bench, out of the hearing of the jurors, as follows:)
21   (The Court and counsel review the jury question.)
22   MR. EUCHNER: The back and hook-up.
23   THE COURT: No objection to 18?
24   MR. JENSVOLD: No objection.
25   MR. EUCHNER: This might be the time to read the

PIMA COUNTY SUPERIOR COURT

```
 1   stipulation as well.
 2          MR. JENSVOLD:  That's fine.
 3          THE COURT:  All right.
 4          (Whereupon proceedings continued in open court, on
 5   the record, as follows:)
 6          THE COURT:  All right.
 7          Mr. McGraw, what is the purpose of photographing the
 8   back and hook-ups of the computer?
 9          THE WITNESS:  The purpose of photographing the back
10   and hook-ups of the computer is so that when the Detective
11   needs to re-hook up that computer for his analysis or whatever
12   he has to do, he knows the order to plug all the plugs back
13   into the ports, et cetera.
14          THE COURT:  Any additional questions?
15          All right.
16          (Whereupon the Court and counsel confer at the
17   bench, out of the hearing of the jurors, as follows:)
18          (The Court and counsel review the jury question.)
19          MR. JENSVOLD:  I don't think he knows.  There's a
20   later witness.
21          THE COURT:  All right.  Okay.
22          (Whereupon proceedings continued in open court, on
23   the record, as follows:)
24          THE COURT:  We can't ask 19 right now.  That will
25   probably be answered through a later witness.
```

PIMA COUNTY SUPERIOR COURT

1   Anymore questions?
2   One more.
3   (Whereupon the Court and counsel confer at the
4 bench, out of the hearing of the jurors, as follows:)
5   (The Court and counsel review the jury question.)
6   MR. EUCHNER: If he can --
7   MR. JENSVOLD: Well --
8   MR. EUCHNER: It's a later witness.
9   THE COURT: Any objections to 20?
10   MR. EUCHNER: Yes, a later witness.
11   THE COURT: Pardon me?
12   MR. EUCHNER: A later witness.
13   THE COURT: For both of them?
14   MR. EUCHNER: He can answer this one, if he knows.
15   The second one is a later witness.
16   (Whereupon proceedings continued in open court, on
17 the record, as follows:)
18   THE COURT: Where was the evidence package sealed?
19   THE WITNESS: The evidence package sealed? I would
20 have to look at the photographs. But usually there is a flap
21 on the evidence package that the seal, usually it's a brown
22 bag or a white envelope. The top of the bag would be folded
23 over and there would be a tape placed over it, and then
24 initials. Same goes with a white envelope as well.
25   THE COURT: All right.

PIMA COUNTY SUPERIOR COURT

            And in case the question was the location where the actual evidence item was sealed, do you know the location? Not the bag itself, but the actual location where the bag was sealed.

            THE WITNESS: Oh, okay. That I don't know.

            THE COURT: Okay.

            Anymore questions? Any follow-up questions by counsel?

            MR. JENSVOLD: No, Your Honor.

            MR. EUCHNER: No, Your Honor.

            THE COURT: All right.

            May Mr. McGraw be excused?

            MR. JENSVOLD: Yes.

            MR. EUCHNER: Yes.

            THE COURT: You're excused, sir. Thank you for your time. Watch your step going down.

            (Whereupon the witness was excused.)

            THE COURT: Mr. Jensvold.

            MR. JENSVOLD: Yes, sorry.

            THE COURT: Do counsel want me to read the stipulation at this point?

            MR. JENSVOLD: Yes.

            MR. EUCHNER: Yes.

            THE COURT: The entire stipulation?

            MR. EUCHNER: I think the entire stipulation is

fine.

THE COURT: Folks, if you remember when I told you at the preliminary instruction stage, a stipulation is where both attorneys agree that this is a fact, so you can find this as an actual fact in the case. This is not in dispute.

It is hereby stipulated by and between the undersigned attorneys:

One, all of the 15 files charged in the indictment depict exploitive exhibition or sexual conduct involving actual, not computer generated, minor children, under the age of 15 as defined by Arizona law, and as specifically described in the indictment.

Two, in addition to the 15 files charged in the indictment, approximately 20 CDs containing at least 200 child pornography files were found on the spindle labeled JE-3.

Three, police dusted all of the CDs for fingerprints and found prints belonging to James Coghill and Jacob Franks on some CDs. This includes both men's prints on CDs in the spindle JE-3. However, no fingerprints were found on any of the CDs containing child pornography.

And the stipulation will be going back with you to the jury room as well.

Mr. Jensvold.

MR. JENSVOLD: Your Honor, the State would call Detective John Mawhinney.

PIMA COUNTY SUPERIOR COURT

                        JOHN MAWHINNEY,
having been first duly sworn, was examined and testified, as
follows:

                        DIRECT EXAMINATION
BY MR. JENSVOLD:
    Q.   Would you please introduce yourself to the jury.
    A.   Hi. My name is Detective John Mawhinney. I'm a Detective with the Pima County Sheriff's Department.
    Q.   And how long have you been a Detective?
    A.   Nine years.
    Q.   And how long have you been with the Sheriff's Department in total?
    A.   17 years.
    Q.   And what unit are you assigned to as a Detective currently?
    A.   I'm assigned to the Crimes Against Children Unit.
    Q.   Do you have any specific duties within that unit as a Detective?
    A.   Yes, I do.
    Q.   What are those?
    A.   I am the Computer Forensics Examiner.
    Q.   What kind of training have you had to be able to conduct computer forensic examinations?
    A.   Numerous. I've attended both EnCase and Access Data

PIMA COUNTY SUPERIOR COURT

1 which are software programs that we utilize to do the
2 examinations, along with programs put on by the Department of
3 Justice, and numerous other companies that we use software
4 from.
5   Q. And you were not assigned to this case at the
6 beginning?
7   A. No, I was not.
8   Q. But you have conducted some, some examinations,
9 well, examinations may be going beyond what you did. You've
10 done some work on this case at my request?
11   A. Yes, I have.
12   Q. Okay. And you've had discussions with Jefford
13 Englander who used to be with the Sheriff's Department, who
14 was the lead Detective in this case?
15   A. Yes, I have.
16   Q. Have you also examined electronic copies of the hard
17 drives in this case?
18   A. Yes.
19   Q. Do you know how those copies were made?
20   A. How Jeff Englander made them?
21   Q. Yes.
22   A. They were made into what is called an EO-1 file,
23 which is a bit by bit copy in a particular format, put on to
24 CDs. And there was, I believe, nine or ten CDs involved.
25   Q. We're going to get into this later with the other

PIMA COUNTY SUPERIOR COURT

1 witnesses, but what is a hash value? An MD-5 hash value?
2 A. An MD-5 hash is an algorithm which is, I believe
3 it's 16 or 18 characters long, which, if you assign it to a
4 hard drive or to a file, identifies that file as being a
5 particular file. There would be no other file on the computer
6 or no other hard drive that would exactly match that
7 algorithm.
8 Q. And are there methods in software that you use when
9 you're conducting an examination to ensure that the copies
10 that you make of evidence that you have seized, that they are
11 identical copies?
12 A. Remain the same, yes.
13 Q. Have you had a chance to go back and verify the MD-5
14 hash values that Detective Englander generated through his
15 report with the copies that you looked at at the Sheriff's
16 Department?
17 A. No, I have not.
18 Q. In the things, in the EO-1 files that you have
19 viewed, have you identified two separate hard drives?
20 A. Yes.
21 Q. Okay. What are those numbers, if you remember?
22 A. JE-1-A, and JE-1-B.
23 Q. And have you, at my request, based on the copies
24 that you have looked at, not the originals, looked at when the
25 particular folders on JE-1-A were created?

PIMA COUNTY SUPERIOR COURT

1 A. Yes.
2 Q. In particular there is a, was there a folder that
3 was, well, okay. Let me just ask you which specific folder
4 did I ask you to look at as far as the creation date?
5 A. I cannot recollect the name of the folder.
6 Q. Okay. Detective, do you recall me asking you to
7 look at a folder that was marked "My Documents/porn"?
8 A. Yes.
9   MR. EUCHNER: Objection, Your Honor, leading the
10 witness.
11   THE COURT: Overruled.
12 BY MR. JENSVOLD:
13 Q. Okay. And did you check the final creation date
14 based on your copies of that folder?
15 A. Yes, I did.
16 Q. Do you recall what the date was?
17 A. My Documents/porn.
18 Q. Do you recall what the creation date was?
19 A. Oh, it was, not the exact date. I remember it was
20 in May, but I do not recollect the exact date.
21 Q. Well, we may have to call you back to verify that
22 information.
23   Did you meet with Detective Englander recently at
24 the Sheriff's Department to review some evidence in this case?
25 A. Yes. Yes, I did.

PIMA COUNTY SUPERIOR COURT

Q. Was looking at the creation date of that folder one of the things that you did?

A. I did not do any review at all. It was Jeff Englander who was doing the review.

Q. Okay. Were you with him when it happened?

A. I was in the room, correct.

Q. You weren't participating with him?

A. No, I was not.

Q. Okay. Then I think we'll have to get to that question at a later date then. Okay.

MR. EUCHNER: Your Honor, can we approach?

THE COURT: Sure, come on up.

(Whereupon the Court and counsel confer at the bench, out of the hearing of the jurors, as follows:)

MR. EUCHNER: There is no foundation for any of his testimony. I move that this entire line be stricken from the record, and the jury be instructed to disregard it. If he can lay it later, that's fine. But now it's sitting out there.

THE COURT: I don't understand what your objection is.

MR. EUCHNER: We have --my objection is we have a porn folder being talked about and it's sitting out there in the open and there's no foundation for any of it. There's no work. There's nothing other than what was recollected or not, and he has no recollection. This needs to be stricken.

            THE COURT: He has no recollection of the date. He has an absolute recollection of checking the hard drive to see when it was created, but he doesn't recall the date that it was created.

            And he was not lead. I will overrule the objection. He did recall the name of the folder; when Mr. Jensvold asked him the name of the folder then he went further. So, your objection is overruled and I am not going to strike any of the testimony.

            (Whereupon proceedings continued in open court, on the record, as follows:)

BY MR. JENSVOLD:

    Q. Okay. Detective Mawhinney, prior to any of this stuff we were talking about, did I ask you, and I guess, did I come over to the Sheriff's Department and look at some CDs that were part of this case?

    A. Yes, you did.

    Q. And as part of that, did you print some photographs from particular CDs?

    A. Yes, I did.

    Q. In particular, did you print photographs of a CD labeled JE3-MN?

    A. Yes, I did.

    Q. And was there also another one from JE3-NNN?

    A. I believe so.

1   Q. Let me hand you what's been marked first as State's
2   Exhibit 23, 23-A, B and C; see if you recognize those.
3   A. Yes, I do recognize them.
4   Q. Were those photographs printed directly from JE3-MN?
5   A. Yes, they were.
6   Q. And did you also take some photographs, or print
7   some photographs from the CD labeled JE3-NNN?
8   A. Yes.
9   Q. Look at State's Exhibits 24 through 24-G, and see if
10 you recognize those.
11 A. I recognize most of them. But it has been a while
12 since I printed these. So I don't have 100 percent
13 recollection of all of them.
14 Q. Okay. Was there a supplementary disclosure
15 memorandum that I wrote after I came over there and we looked
16 at these CDs?
17 A. Yes.
18 Q. Did you have a chance to review that?
19 A. Yes, I did.
20 Q. If you have it, does it summarize what was found on
21 JE3-NNN?
22 A. Yes, it does. Do you want me to read it?
23 Q. Well, look through that and see if that appears to
24 be consistent with the photographs that you see here today?
25 A. Yes, it is.

PIMA COUNTY SUPERIOR COURT

1   Q.   Okay.
2   MR. JENSVOLD: Your Honor, the State would move for
3   the admission of 23 through 23-C, as well as 24 through 24-G.
4   MR. EUCHNER: No objection, Your Honor.
5   THE COURT: State's 23 through 23-C are admitted,
6   and State's 24 through 24-G are admitted.
7   BY MR. JENSVOLD:
8   Q.   And, finally, did you get a chance to view another
9   CD labeled JE3-JJ?
10   A.   Yes.
11   Q.   Recently?
12   A.   Yes.
13   Q.   Okay. Will you please take a look at State's
14   Exhibits 33 through 33-J and see if you recognize those?
15   A.   Yes, I recognize those.
16   MR. JENSVOLD: Your Honor, the State would move for
17   the admission of 33 through 33-J as well.
18   MR. EUCHNER: No objection, Your Honor.
19   THE COURT: State's 33 through 33-J are admitted.
20   BY MR. JENSVOLD:
21   Q.   And, Detective, did you also secure some of these
22   CDs sometime during 2008 and send them to the Department Of
23   Public Safety in Phoenix for handwriting analysis?
24   A.   Yes, I did.
25   Q.   And did you get those back?

PIMA COUNTY SUPERIOR COURT

         A.   Yes, I did.
         Q.   And did you basically reseal all of these things in different packages when they came back from DPS?
         A.   Yes, I did.
         Q.   And again, I don't think there's any necessary comment for these photographs. I just wanted to show them.
              (Exhibits displayed for the jury.)
              The first series is 23 through 23-C. This is 23. This is 23-A. This is 23-B. 23-C.
              The next series is 24 through 24-G.
              THE COURT: That was 24?
              MR. JENSVOLD: That was 24. I'm sorry.
              24-A. 24-B. 24-C. 24-D.
              Do you want to stipulate as to who the persons are?
              MR. EUCHNER: These are just personal photos, Your Honor. And Your Honor just asked me to show a couple of the photos for representation. The jury already has them.
              THE COURT: I think he was asking about if you want to stipulate to the identities of one of the people in the photograph.
              MR. EUCHNER: We can do that.
              MR. JENSVOLD: The person in second from the left is Jacob Franks.
              24-E. 24-F. 24-G.
              Finally, this is the 33 series. This is 33. 33-A.

PIMA COUNTY SUPERIOR COURT

33-B. C. D. E. F. G. H. I. J.

I believe that's all I have.

Thank you.

THE COURT: Cross-Examination?

MR. EUCHNER: Yes, Your Honor.

Thank you.

CROSS-EXAMINATION

BY MR. EUCHNER:

Q. Hi, Detective.

A. Good afternoon.

Q. It's been a long time since we saw you, hasn't it been?

A. A couple of hours.

Q. About five days, hasn't it, to be exact?

A. Yes.

Q. So it was just Friday last week you and I met?

A. Yes.

Q. Mr. Skitzki was there?

A. Yes.

Q. We were in Mr. Jensvold's paralegal's office, Ty Summers?

A. That's correct.

Q. We had a short interview about your involvement in the case, what you have done the last few months?

PIMA COUNTY SUPERIOR COURT

A. That is correct.

Q. And we went over that you had only submitted one report in the case, that was a short report from August 15th, 2008, is that correct?

A. That is correct.

Q. And in that report, all that you say is that you reviewed some evidence with Mr. Jensvold, and some photos were taken of some snapshots?

A. That is correct.

Q. And that was the only report that you submitted in the case?

A. That is correct.

Q. And then on Friday, prior to going on tape, we showed you the supplementary disclosure memorandum that Mr. Jensvold authored to Mr. Skitzki and myself, is that correct?

A. That is correct.

Q. The memorandum was dated August 18th, 2008, is that correct?

A. Yes.

Q. And had you seen this memorandum prior to us showing you on Friday?

A. No, I had not.

Q. Prior to going on tape, though, we gave you a chance to review it and make sure that this was what happened, at

PIMA COUNTY SUPERIOR COURT

```
 1  least as far as your involvement is concerned.
 2      A.  That's correct.
 3      Q.  So we talked about some of the things that were in
 4  this memorandum, which is taking custody of CDs, correct?
 5      A.  That is correct.
 6      Q.  A lot of things that you just talked about on
 7  direct, that you sent the CDs up to DPS for handwriting
 8  analysis?
 9      A.  Yes.
10      Q.  And did we discuss at any point your working with
11  Detective Englander at the Sheriff's Department?
12      A.  I believe you asked if I had ever done that.
13      Q.  With Detective Englander?
14      A.  Correct. And the answer was no.
15      Q.  I just heard in the direct testimony, I heard you
16  were involved with Detective Englander?
17      A.  Yesterday.
18      Q.  Yesterday. And did you write a report about this?
19      A.  No, I did not.
20      Q.  Did you or Mr. Jensvold discuss contacting
21  Mr. Skitzki or myself to tell us what you did yesterday?
22      A.  Not that I'm aware of.
23      Q.  So, you didn't author a report on this, and
24  Mr. Jensvold didn't ask you to do that?
25      A.  No.
```

PIMA COUNTY SUPERIOR COURT

1 Q. Thank you. What did you do again? Can you repeat
2 this again. What did you do yesterday with Mr. Englander at
3 the Sheriff's station?
4 A. Mr. Englander was at the Sheriff's Department for
5 the purpose of reviewing evidence so that he could testify
6 tomorrow. My purpose was because he was using my lab, I
7 stayed and, basically, observed that he was there.
8 Q. I would like to get back to something that
9 Mr. Jensvold was asking you about a folder, that he asked you
10 to look at a hash value on the copy of the hard drive.
11 A. Yes.
12 Q. And my question is, did we discuss that on Friday?
13 A. We discussed MD-5 hashes, yes.
14 Q. Generally speaking, we discussed the hash values,
15 but did we discuss your looking for a hash value on any of the
16 hard drives?
17 A. I don't recollect if we had talked about that or
18 not. But if we hadn't -- no, we hadn't. I had not done a
19 MD-5 hash.
20 Q. And, in fact, the reason why we didn't talk about
21 this is because I specifically asked you, did you ever look at
22 the, do any hard drive analysis in this case whatsoever, and
23 you told me, no, you had not?
24 A. That's correct.
25 Q. And that was as of five days ago?

PIMA COUNTY SUPERIOR COURT

```
 1      A.   That's correct.
 2      Q.   When did you do this MD-5 hash analysis at
 3 Mr. Jensvold's request?
 4      A.   I haven't.
 5      Q.   What was the discussion about looking at the hard
 6 drive to see what was on the hard drive, what was the, the
 7 particular hash, the particular date created of this folder?
 8      A.   He was asking for a particular date, and there was a
 9 particular date on the file.  I have not done an MD-5 hash, or
10 a exam of the hard drives.
11      Q.   And I may be misspeaking because this is the first
12 I'm hearing about this, even though we met five days ago, but
13 you did look for a date created?
14      A.   Yes.
15      Q.   Within the last five days?
16      A.   No.
17      Q.   It was prior to five days ago?
18      A.   That is correct.
19      Q.   And you didn't submit a report on that in this case?
20      A.   That is correct.
21      Q.   And we asked you specifically, was there anything
22 else that you did in this case that was not contained in any
23 of the reports?
24      A.   Yes.
25      Q.   And you didn't volunteer that information.
```

PIMA COUNTY SUPERIOR COURT

1   A.   That is correct.
2   Q.   For example, this report that you -- of the work
3 that you did on August 15th, 2008, was, I believe, dictated on
4 August 18th, 2008, does that sound about right?
5   A.   Yes.
6   Q.   And it was done within a couple of days so that you
7 wouldn't forget what you did.
8   A.   Yes.
9   Q.   As we sit here now, do you remember when it was that
10 Mr. Jensvold had you look at the hard drive evidence to see
11 about a date created?
12   A.   No.
13   Q.   Was it in the last week?
14   A.   No.
15   Q.   Was it in the last month?
16   A.   I -- possibly. The purpose of my looking at the
17 date was in reference to a report that the County Attorney's
18 Office had received from your office indicating a date.
19   Q.   Please finish.
20   A.   That was the finish.
21   Q.   Okay. And while we're talking about reports, you
22 became aware that Mr. Skitzki and I discovered some
23 discrepancies in the hard drive in terms of last access dates,
24 is that correct?
25   A.   Yes.

PIMA COUNTY SUPERIOR COURT

Q. And did Mr. Jensvold make you aware of that?

A. Yes.

Q. And, specifically, what we're talking about is we discovered that 312 files had been last accessed on May 14th, 2003, is that correct?

A. I knew it was in May. I do not recollect the date.

Q. Okay. But it was May of 2003.

A. Yes.

Q. And given that you have access to all of the reports in this case, you know that all of the hard drives and all of the digital evidence in this case was seized on April 1st, 2003, is that correct?

A. Yes.

Q. So, you're aware that the property sheets show that the evidence was checked in in April of 2003?

A. Yes.

Q. And you're aware that the property sheets show that the evidence was checked out in November of 2004, is that correct?

A. Without looking at the property sheets, I would not be able to say November of 2004, no.

Q. You do recall that the property sheets never showed that the evidence had been checked out around May of 2003, is that correct?

A. No, I did find that they were checked out in May.

PIMA COUNTY SUPERIOR COURT

1	Q.	Do you have the original property sheets?
2	A.	No, I do not.
3	Q.	Did you find them?
4	A.	No.
5	Q.	Did you look for them?
6	A.	Yes.
7	Q.	Spent a lot of time looking for them, in fact, is that correct?
9	A.	No, I didn't, but the Property And Evidence Unit did.
11	Q.	And you looked into the computerized records. In fact, Mr. Skitzki and I were present in Ms. Summers' office when you were accessing the computerized records of the evidence checked out, is that correct?
15	A.	That is correct.
16	Q.	And the computerized records show that Jeff Englander had checked out the hard drives on May 22nd of 2003, is that correct?
19	A.	I believe that shows that he checked out the computer.
21	Q.	And the computer had the hard drives in it?
22	A.	At that time.
23	Q.	And that, when we look at these logs, it showed that it was returned on July 20th, 2003?
25	A.	I believe that was the date, yes.

PIMA COUNTY SUPERIOR COURT

Q. And in all of the property sheets that you had looked at in advance of our interview last week, you saw that those records never reflected any property sheets.

A. The issue I had with the property sheets is the back side -- the back side of the sheet that shows you the date of sign-out was missing.

Q. Did you do any other work with the hard drives other than what we've talked about today?

A. Not that I can recollect, no.

Q. And other than printing out the photos, that's basically what we're talking about here today, you just printed out these photos for Mr. Jensvold?

A. I also --

Q. Yes or no? Did you --

A. I printed that, yes. I printed the photos.

MR. EUCHNER: I have no further questions.

THE COURT: Redirect?

REDIRECT EXAMINATION
BY MR. JENSVOLD:

Q. Detective Mawhinney, the EO-1 files that you still have in your lab of the hard drives in this case, can you go back and verify the MD-5 hash values and compare them with the values that Detective Englander obtained in his initial report?

PIMA COUNTY SUPERIOR COURT

1   A.   Yes, I could.
2   Q.   Is that something that you can do tonight, or
3 tomorrow?
4   A.   Yes.
5   Q.   And do you recall, well, did I give you a copy or
6 relay to you information about Ms. Loehrs' report in this
7 case?
8   A.   You passed on information.
9   Q.   And was that the basis of me asking for you to check
10 the particular creation date of the folder?
11   A.   Yes.
12   Q.   Okay. And you didn't write that down after you
13 obtained that information?
14   A.   No, I did not.
15   Q.   Did you tell it to me over the phone?
16   A.   Yes, I did.
17   Q.   Okay. And I guess this will teach us not to write
18 things down. So, can you go back and do the same thing with
19 that creation date of that folder based on your EO-1 files and
20 come back to us with that information?
21   A.   Yes, I could.
22   Q.   By tomorrow?
23   A.   You're asking for the MD-5 hash, or just the created
24 date?
25   Q.   I guess for the second part, just the creation date.

1   A.   Yes, I can do that by tomorrow.
2   Q.   Are there MD-5 hash values that are associated with
3 folders as well as files?
4   A.   You can associate with a folder, because then it
5 would encompass everything inside that folder.
6   Q.   Okay. So can you do anything more specific with the
7 folder, if you had a hash value for a folder, and compare that
8 to what you have in your EO-1 files?
9   A.   Yes, I could. But I would have to have if Jeff
10 Englander had done a MD-5 hash on that specific folder.
11   Q.   Is that always done --
12   A.   No.
13   Q.   -- as part of that forensic analysis?
14   A.   If the MD-5 hash of the whole computer is done.
15   Q.   And sometimes it's done for particular files as
16 well?
17   A.   Yes.
18   MR. JENSVOLD: Your Honor, may we approach?
19   THE COURT: Yes, come on up.
20   (Whereupon the Court and counsel confer at the
21 bench, out of the hearing of the jurors, as follows:)
22   MR. JENSVOLD: Part of what Mr. Euchner related to
23 this jury about disclosure is not correct. Because, this is a
24 transcript of an interview that I had with Ms. Loehrs where I
25 specifically told Mr. Euchner and Mr. Skitzki and Ms. Loehrs

PIMA COUNTY SUPERIOR COURT

what Detective Mawhinney had told me. Now, it's not documented anywhere, and that's what I get for not asking him to write a report.

But I think somehow that needs to be corrected because it's not that I didn't disclose the information to him; he didn't write a report.

MR. EUCHNER: That's true.

I want to be clear, I don't recall that as we stand here right now. I would have to look at that again. But I don't have, I can read upside down and see that there's a reference to it. But, yeah, that's why we ask them to write reports.

THE COURT: Well, there's two separate issues. There's the issue about whether he wrote a report, which is fair game. But there's also an issue of an appearance in front of the jury that Mr. Jensvold didn't disclose something that he did.

MR. EUCHNER: And that's, if he repairs that then, if I accidently mislead the jury --

THE COURT: No.

Mr. EUCHNER: -- it's fair game.

THE COURT: I think sometimes we forget things are out in there, and he's going to do it in a way that doesn't impugn you at all.

MR. EUCHNER: I wouldn't even mind. I could do it

myself, too, if Shawn wants me to.

THE COURT: However you want to take it up.

(Whereupon proceedings continued in open court, on the record, as follows:)

MR. JENSVOLD: That's all the questions I have. Thank you.

THE COURT: Mr. Euchner, I believe you had one item you wanted to clear up.

MR. EUCHNER: Yes. And if I may have one question on re-cross, as well.

THE COURT: Yes.

RECROSS-EXAMINATION
BY MR. EUCHNER:
Q. Detective Mawhinney, you told Mr. Jensvold about that folder that you were looking at the, a date at, that had last access on?
A. Per his request, yes.
Q. And it was prior to Mr. Jensvold's interview with defense expert Ms. Loehrs?
A. Yes, it was after.
Q. Okay. And as we discussed at the bench, it appears that it was actually mentioned, but -- to the defense. The defense did have information of that. But, nonetheless, you didn't write a report about that?

PIMA COUNTY SUPERIOR COURT

1   A. That's correct.
2   Q. Okay. And one final question. Related to all of
3 the hard drive evidence, and all of the CDs in this case, that
4 were in EO-1 and EO-2 files, in EnCase format, all of the
5 information that was received from the defense was processed
6 by you, is that correct, or your staff?
7   A. What do you mean by processed?
8   Q. For example, a, anything that we have that's digital
9 evidence came from either you or somebody else in your office?
10   A. Copies were made, yes.
11   Q. And it's not the kind of evidence that lay people
12 would be able to look at themselves. It would require
13 somebody with EnCase software, is that correct?
14   A. Or forensic software. It doesn't have to be just
15 EnCase.
16   MR. EUCHNER: Thank you.
17   Nothing further.
18   THE COURT: Do any members of the jury have any
19 questions?
20   (Whereupon the Court and counsel confer at the
21 bench, out of the hearing of the jurors, as follows:)
22   (The Court and counsel review the jury question.)
23   MR. EUCHNER: Probably an answer tomorrow.
24   MR. JENSVOLD: Frankly depends on which CD they're
25 talking about. Somebody is going to have to look at the CDs

PIMA COUNTY SUPERIOR COURT

```
 1   to get the real answer.
 2           MR. EUCHNER: I think what they wanted to know is
 3   these 3 CDs. They'll get that tomorrow from Mr. Englander.
 4           I think he can answer the second one.
 5           Number 21, he can answer the second one, and the
 6   first one will be answered by Mr. Englander.
 7           MR. JENSVOLD: I think we can clarify, though, that
 8   none of these photos that were shown today were on any of the
 9   K-P CDs. Do you--
10           MR. EUCHNER: We can just offer that.
11           THE COURT: Okay.
12           (The Court and counsel review the jury question.)
13           MR. EUCHNER: On 22, he can answer the first and
14   second if he knows. And the third one he can't answer.
15           THE COURT: Okay. So just 1 and 2.
16           MR. EUCHNER: Yeah.
17           THE COURT: Okay.
18           MR. EUCHNER: I'm not sure I understand the question
19   but -- if he knows. Yeah, he can answer that.
20           MR. JENSVOLD: Yeah.
21           THE COURT: On 24, all good?
22           MR. EUCHNER: We're okay. On 23 --
23           (The Court and counsel review the jury question.)
24           THE COURT: This is 23.
25           MR. EUCHNER: Do you want me to clarify the first
```

```
 1   part?  We can do that.  We'll clarify -- which one was that?
 2             THE COURT:  21.
 3             MR. JENSVOLD:  I'll handle that part.
 4             MR. EUCHNER:  Right now.
 5             THE COURT:  Okay.
 6             (Whereupon proceedings continued in open court, on
 7   the record, as follows:)
 8             THE COURT:  Mr. Jensvold, I think there was a
 9   stipulation, at least to one of these questions.
10             MR. JENSVOLD:  Right.  The photos that you just saw,
11   the different series, what was it?  23, 24, 33, those
12   photographs were not found on any CD labeled K-P, they were
13   found on other CDs.
14             I think you'll get information later on about the
15   title of specific CDs and where they were found and that kind
16   of stuff.  Very technical answer.
17             THE COURT:  Do you have to go through an entire CD
18   to find photographs?
19             THE WITNESS:  Do I have to go through an entire CD
20   to find a particular photograph, or any photograph?
21             THE COURT:  Any photograph.
22             THE WITNESS:  No.
23             THE COURT:  Can a file creation date be altered by a
24   person who would be creating/burning that CD?
25             THE WITNESS:  Read the first part of it again.
```

PIMA COUNTY SUPERIOR COURT

1 THE COURT: Can a file creation date be altered by a
2 person who would be creating/burning that CD?
3 THE WITNESS: Yeah, that's how it's manufactured, is
4 when you create something onto the CD, that creates a date.
5 THE COURT: Where does the date and time come from?
6 THE WITNESS: From your computer.
7 THE COURT: Who made EO-1, you or Englander?
8 THE WITNESS: Englander.
9 THE COURT: Was your analysis exclusively on EO-1
10 files, or actual drives?
11 THE WITNESS: I did not do an analysis of the
12 computer. What I viewed was from an EO-1 file. The hard
13 drive was never touched.
14 THE COURT: By you.
15 THE WITNESS: By me.
16 THE COURT: Does EO-1 carry serial numbers to
17 correlate EO-1 to actual machine serial?
18 THE WITNESS: The file has a name that is EO-1. And
19 I do not recollect in this case, it was the case number, or
20 the hard drive letter JE1, an .EO-1, .EO-2, .EO-3.
21 THE COURT: In layman's terms, what does MD-5 hash
22 provide in terms of information or validation?
23 THE WITNESS: MD-5 is the ability for a single file
24 on your computer to be identified separately from any other
25 file in the world. That file would not have the same MD-5

1 hash as any other file on a computer, or on any other
2 computer. If you change one character of that file, it would
3 change the MD-5 hash.
4   THE COURT: Any additional questions from the jury?
5   (Whereupon the Court and counsel confer at the
6 bench, out of the hearing of the jurors, as follows:)
7   (The Court and counsel review the jury question.)
8   MR. EUCHNER: 24 is okay.
9   THE COURT: 24 is okay. Okay.
10   MR. EUCHNER: I think Mr. Skitzki wants this one.
11   THE COURT: With my help?
12   MR. JENSVOLD: It's not really a question.
13   MR. EUCHNER: Yeah, this is not a question. You
14 can't ask this.
15   MR. JENSVOLD: I think it will be tomorrow when I go
16 through with Englander.
17   THE COURT: I won't ask 25.
18   (Whereupon proceedings continued in open court, on
19 the record, as follows:)
20   THE COURT: Can't you change the date on your
21 computer to, therefore, reflect a different date other than
22 the true date you might burn a CD?
23   THE WITNESS: Yes.
24   THE COURT: Anymore questions?
25   (No response.)

PIMA COUNTY SUPERIOR COURT

```
 1            THE COURT:  Any follow-up questions by either
 2   counsel?
 3            MR. JENSVOLD:  No.
 4            THE COURT:  All right.
 5            MR. EUCHNER:  One question, Your Honor.
 6            Thank you.
 7            THE COURT:  You bet.
 8   BY MR. EUCHNER:
 9       Q.   Detective Mawhinney, you were talking about an MD-5
10   hash is the ability -- make sure I get this right, the ability
11   to identify a file on any computer, and it would distinguish
12   it from that same file on another computer?
13       A.   I lost you at the end there.
14       Q.   Suppose you have a file on your computer--
15       A.   Right.
16       Q.   --named, and you e-mail it to me as an e-mail
17   attachment.  Now I have that file to?
18       A.   As long as you don't alter it, I would be able to
19   find it via the MD-5 hash.
20            MR. EUCHNER:  No further questions.
21            THE COURT:  Any other questions from the jury?
22            (No response.)
23            THE COURT:  Can Detective Mawhinney be excused?
24            MR. JENSVOLD:  I guess until tomorrow.
25            THE COURT:  All right.  You're not excused.  You're
```

PIMA COUNTY SUPERIOR COURT

```
 1  still under subpoena.  So come back tomorrow, sir, when the
 2  counsel say they need you.  Okay.  Thanks for your time today.
 3          Mr. Jensvold.
 4          MR. JENSVOLD:  May I have just a moment?  I have to
 5  see if -- my last witness will be Sergeant Moretz.  I think
 6  he's out in the hall.
 7          THE COURT:  Sergeant Moretz, please step forward,
 8  sir.  We're going to have the clerk swear you in.
 9
10                          GERARD MORETZ,
11  having been first duly sworn, was examined and testified, as
12  follows:
13
14                        DIRECT EXAMINATION
15  BY MR. JENSVOLD:
16      Q.   Would you please introduce yourself to the jury.
17      A.   Gerard Moretz.  I'm a Sergeant with the Pima County
18  Sheriff's Department.
19      Q.   And what are your duties as a Sergeant currently?
20      A.   Right now I'm Supervisor of the School Resource
21  Officer Unit, in covering the south and the Vail area of Pima
22  County.
23      Q.   How long have you been a Sergeant?
24      A.   Since November of 2005.
25      Q.   And before that, what did you do with the Sheriff's
```

PIMA COUNTY SUPERIOR COURT

Department?

A. I was a Detective in the Crimes Against Children Unit.

Q. As part of that unit, you were not a computer forensic analyst?

A. No, I was not.

Q. But were you called to participate in the investigation in this case on April 1st of 2003?

A. Yes, sir, I was.

Q. And what did you do when you were called?

A. I was made aware of the case, and asked to interview Jacob Franks as a witness to the incident that had been reported.

Q. What information had been provided to you prior to your interviewing Mr. Franks?

A. I was briefed and told that, by my Sergeant, Sergeant Pesquira, that Jacob Franks had phoned in a report to the Sheriff's Department alleging that James Coghill was in possession of illegal items in an RV where Jacob had lived for a short period of time in Pima County, along with Mr. Coghill.

Q. So what was, can you characterize the purpose of your interview with Mr. Franks on April 1st?

A. Well, he was identified as the reportee, and obviously had some concern and some information about what he believed to be illegal items.

PIMA COUNTY SUPERIOR COURT

And so my purpose in interviewing him was to find out as much as I could about what it was that he was seeing, or what he had come into contact with that he believed to be illegal, and try to establish by what kind of experience would he be able to determine that something was of an illegal nature.

So essentially to find out as much as I could and to see if he was, if his allegation was credible.

Q. Was part of your interviewing Mr. Franks to evaluate his credibility to see if, you know, he was telling the truth?

A. Yes.

Q. Okay. Now, you're not going to make that determination, but your thinking, that is part of your investigation, does that lead your questions? Are you challenging Mr. Franks at all?

A. The purpose of any good interview, I think, is to find out what a person has to say. And if they are making an assertion of any kind, to try and find out what background they have, or what expertise, so to speak, they might have that would justify any claims that they make.

So, in terms of determining credibility, what I look for is consistency and detail over the course of an interview that would lead me to believe that a person is being truthful about the information.

Q. How long did the interview last with Mr. Franks, if

1 you remember?
2   A.   Just over an hour.
3   Q.   And what time of day was it when you did the
4 interview?
5   A.   It was in the morning hours on the 1st of April in
6 2003.
7   Q.   Let me show you what's been marked as State's
8 Exhibit 3. Do you recognize that?
9   A.   Yes. This is a copy of a report that I authored in
10 reference to the case.
11   Q.   Does that help to refresh your memory about exactly
12 when the interview took place?
13   A.   Yes, it does. It was from 9:39 until 10:25 in the
14 morning.
15   Q.   And who else was present besides you and Mr. Franks?
16   A.   Detective Bill Knuth. He was a member of the unit
17 at the time.
18   Q.   And did anybody else join in later?
19   A.   Later Detective Jeff Englander arrived and asked a
20 few more questions toward the end of the interview.
21   Q.   And have you had a chance today to go back and
22 listen to the tape of your interview with Mr. Franks?
23   A.   I did.
24   Q.   What was Mr. Franks' demeanor during the interview,
25 if you remember, and by listening to the tape?

PIMA COUNTY SUPERIOR COURT

1 A. He was calm, and clear in his answers, and
2 forthright.
3 Q. Did he tell you how long he'd been in Tucson?
4 A. Yes, he did.
5 Q. And how long did he tell you?
6 A. One week.
7 Q. At some point later in the interview, did Detective
8 Englander ask him a similar question?
9 A. Yes.
10 Q. And what was his response then?
11 A. He said between a week and 10 days, I believe.
12 Q. Did he ever, during that entire interview, tell you
13 that he had been in Tucson for a month?
14 A. No.
15 Q. When he first answered you regarding how long he had
16 been in Tucson, did he hesitate, did he have to think about
17 it?
18 A. No.
19 Q. Did he admit to things that were going on inside the
20 motor home regarding access to the computer?
21 A. Yes, he did.
22 Q. Did he admit that he was on the computer while he
23 was in Tucson?
24 A. Yes.
25 Q. Did he admit to touching some of the CDs that were

PIMA COUNTY SUPERIOR COURT

```
 1  labeled K-P?
 2       A.   Yes.
 3       Q.   Did he admit to downloading music from the Internet?
 4       A.   Yes, he did. I believe specifically music videos.
 5       Q.   Did he also admit that he'd been to prison on a
 6  number of occasions to you? Or at least one?
 7       A.   At least one. He mentioned DOC.
 8       Q.   And you knew what that meant?
 9       A.   I knew what that meant.
10       Q.   What does that mean?
11       A.   Department of Corrections.
12       Q.   Did he give you his e-mail address during the
13  interview?
14       A.   He did. As I recall there was a concern about
15  follow-up investigation, as these things usually take some
16  time to process. And so we try to get as many ways as
17  possible to get in touch with him in the future, because he
18  was going to Phoenix after that.
19       Q.   Did he express any reluctance to cooperate with you
20  later?
21       A.   No, he didn't.
22       Q.   And did he also admit to you that he had actually
23  seen some of these images that depicted child pornography in
24  his opinion while he was at least living with Mr. Coghill at
25  some point?
```

PIMA COUNTY SUPERIOR COURT

1   A.   Yes, he did.
2   MR. JENSVOLD: That's all I have.
3   Thank you.
4   THE COURT: Cross-Examination?
5
6   CROSS-EXAMINATION
7   BY MR. SKITZKI:
8   Q.   So, Sergeant Moretz, you're the prime officer
9   conducting the interview of Mr. Franks, correct?
10   A.   Yes.
11   Q.   Deputy Knuth, he's just sitting there just sort of
12   to be a witness?
13   A.   Yes. Oftentimes we interview with two people, and
14   one person is the primary and the other person is kind of
15   there to monitor the interview. And sometimes if we miss
16   something, there is a detail that needs to be cleared up, the
17   second interviewer will catch it. So we work in teams that
18   way.
19   Q.   But you were taking the lead and asking the majority
20   of the questions?
21   A.   Yes.
22   Q.   Then, I guess at some point in time in the context
23   of that interview, Detective Englander entered the room and he
24   began to participate?
25   A.   Yes, he did.

Q. And Detective Englander, when he came in and began to participate, basically let Mr. Franks know that he had spoken with Mr. Coghill.

A. I believe so.

Q. But in the course of you speaking with Mr. Franks, he admitted to you that he handled some of those disks that he was talking about.

A. Yes.

Q. And indicated that he might have touched those, but was clear that those did not belong to him?

A. That's right.

Q. But he did say to you in the course of that interview that he conceded that he did burn at least one disk that contained child pornography. He said he did it at the behest of Mr. Coghill, but he said that he burned a disk containing child pornography?

A. I don't remember if he was very specific about being certain as to the contents. I think he, it was lead on that that might be what was on it, and he did burn it.

Q. Mr. Franks admitted to you, in the course of that interview, that he was angry with Mr. Coghill?

A. Yes.

Q. Mr. Franks, in the course of that interview, he gave you some names of individuals that he claimed could corroborate what he was saying about Mr. Coghill and child pornography?

A. Yes.

Q. And, in fact, you included the names and some telephone numbers for these folks in your report?

A. Yes, I did.

Q. Did you ever contact those people to corroborate, to talk to them?

A. No, I didn't.

Q. Was that because Detective Englander is the case detective on this case?

A. It typically -- well, the answer is yes. But typically there is a primary Detective, and when a case comes out where people have to be called out, we get assigned specific tasks. And when those tasks are complete, we brief the Detective who's going to be taking the case and provide information to them and try to include everything in the case report with the date.

Q. So the purpose in putting that in your report is so that whoever the case Detective was in this case, would be aware that there was some contact information for individuals who could corroborate what Mr. Franks was claiming?

A. Yes.

Q. What was done with that, you don't know.

A. I don't know.

Q. Mr. Franks told you, when talking about some of this

1 child pornography, he indicated or gave you information about
2 something about R@ygold, is that correct?
3   A.   That's right.
4   Q.   From your work, are you familiar with that term,
5 R@ygold?
6   A.   I'm not. He was specific about the spelling, but it
7 was not familiar to me. But that was not my primary area to
8 work in the Internet-type cases.
9   Q.   So Mr. Franks was specific with you about the
10 spelling of this R@ygold, correct?
11   A.   Yes.
12   Q.   And it's not R-A-Y-G-O-L-D, I guess it's R-the at
13 sign-Y-G-O-L-D?
14   A.   Correct.
15   Q.   In the course of your interview with Mr. Franks, he
16 told that you he had lived in a variety of places since 1999?
17   A.   Yes, sir.
18   Q.   He told you that he had been kicked out of a number
19 of places in the course of that time period.
20   A.   Yes.
21   Q.   And in the course of that interview, he told you, in
22 response to a question, specifically what prompted him to make
23 the call to the Sheriff's Department?
24   A.   Yes.
25   Q.   And it was because Mr. Coghill was going to take him

PIMA COUNTY SUPERIOR COURT

```
 1  back to Phoenix, and wasn't going to take him to this job
 2  interview?
 3      A.  Yes.
 4      Q.  And that was going to prevent Mr. Franks from
 5  changing his life around for the better.
 6      A.  That's right.
 7      Q.  That Mr. Coghill was just going to drop him off on a
 8  street corner, and he was never going to speak to Mr. Coghill
 9  again anyway.  So he sort of lead on to you that he thought
10  his friendship with Mr. Coghill was done and finished.
11      A.  Yes.
12      Q.  He told you in the course of the interview that
13  people that he had been staying with, or he had been friends
14  with, were getting sick of him, they were getting tired of his
15  inability to get back on his own feet.
16      A.  I don't remember that specifically.  I do remember
17  that he'd lived several places.
18          MR. JENSVOLD:  It's State's 1, Paul.
19          MR. SKITZKI:  I've got it.  Thanks.
20          May I approach the witness?
21          THE COURT:  Yes.
22  BY MR. SKITZKI:
23      Q.  If I can show you what's been marked as State's
24  Exhibit 1, and ask you if you recognize what that is?
25      A.  I do.  It's a transcript of the interview I
```

PIMA COUNTY SUPERIOR COURT

1 conducted with Jacob Franks.
2   Q. If I could direct you to page 21 of that interview.
3 I think it's right about line 16, thereabouts. Do you see
4 that?
5   A. I do.
6   Q. It starts out:
7   Answer: I have no idea.
8   A. Yes.
9   Q. Okay. And, see, he's living with his girlfriend. I
10 have been put in this. I'm, everybody is getting sick of me.
11 Everyone is getting sick of me.
12   Now, does that refresh your recollection?
13   A. Yes, it does.
14   Q. Okay. When Detective Englander came in to
15 participate in the interview, Mr. Franks conceded to him that
16 he had plenty of access to the computer in Mr. Coghill's motor
17 home, correct?
18   A. Yes.
19   Q. Detective Englander then started pressing Mr. Franks
20 on basically how was he going, how is he going to be able to
21 prove that these disks, or these items belonged to Mr. Coghill
22 as opposed to Mr. Franks. Do you remember that?
23   A. Yes.
24   Q. And then Mr. Franks, in the course of that, seemed
25 to express some concern about the situation that he was in.

PIMA COUNTY SUPERIOR COURT

1   MR. JENSVOLD: Objection, argumentative.
2   THE COURT: He can answer "yes" or "no".
3   THE WITNESS: Can you point me to a specific? I
4 don't know how to characterize that.
5 BY MR. SKITZKI:
6   Q. On page 26, I guess starting about line three, going
7 to about line 13.
8   A. Yes, sir.
9   Q. So it was a situation where Detective Englander was
10 pointing out to Mr. Franks that, you know, there could be this
11 question as to who this stuff belonged to.
12   A. Yes.
13   Q. It was -- to your knowledge, was it made clear to
14 Mr. Franks that, you know, possession or control of child
15 pornography, that's some type of serious offense?
16   A. Yes.
17   Q. And at the bottom of page 26, I guess starting at
18 about maybe line 22, that's when he indicates that, he says
19 that Mr. Coghill had him burn a disk once, correct?
20   A. Yes.
21   Q. Then Mr. Franks tells you how he labeled that disk.
22   A. Yes.
23   Q. And then Mr. Franks says that he recalls on that
24 disk that there were files, R@ygold files?
25   A. Yes.

PIMA COUNTY SUPERIOR COURT

         MR. SKITZKI: I don't have any other questions.
         THE COURT: Any Redirect?
         MR. JENSVOLD: Yes, Your Honor.
         Thank you.

                    REDIRECT EXAMINATION
BY MR. JENSVOLD:
    Q.   Sergeant, did Jacob Franks tell you specifically
what he wrote on that CD?
    A.   Yes, he did.
    Q.   And what did he say he wrote?
    A.   Dirty.
    Q.   Did he also express to Detective Englander a way
that you all, as the investigators, might be able to tell
whether he or Mr. Coghill were responsible for the CDs?
    A.   Yes, he did.
    Q.   What did he say?
    A.   He mentioned handwriting samples.
    Q.   Did Mr. Franks ever indicate an interest in child
pornography to you?
    A.   No, he didn't.
    Q.   Did he give you any descriptions of how he felt
about child pornography?
    A.   Yes, he did.
    Q.   What did he say?

1   A.   That it was disgusting.

2   Q.   Did he actually use the world repulsive?

3   A.   I'm not a hundred percent sure if he said repulsive.

4   Q.   Take a look at page eight.

5   A.   I see that he said repulsive.

6   MR. JENSVOLD: That's all I have.

7   Thank you.

8   THE COURT: Do any members of the jury have any

9   questions for the Detective? I'm sorry, Sergeant Moretz.

10   No.

11   May he be excused?

12   MR. JENSVOLD: Yes.

13   THE COURT: Thank you, sir.

14   You're excused.

15   Please watch your step going down.

16   (Whereupon the witness was excused.)

17   All right, members of the jury, we're going to take

18   our evening recess at this time.

19   Remember the admonition. If you can be in the jury

20   room about 10:15 tomorrow morning, and we'll hopefully get

21   started as close to 10:30 as we can. We have a big calendar

22   tomorrow. I'll try to get through it as quickly as I can.

23   All right. We'll see you tomorrow.

24   Have a good evening, and remember the admonition.

25   (4:55 p.m. Whereupon the jury is excused and leaves

PIMA COUNTY SUPERIOR COURT

the courtroom, and proceedings continue in their absence, as follows:)

THE COURT: All right. The record will show the absence of the jury, the presence of all counsel and Mr. Coghill.

So, Mr. Jensvold, you'll finish with your case tomorrow?

MR. JENSVOLD: Yes.

THE COURT: You have Alan Kreitl, Englander, and recalling Mawhinney?

MR. JENSVOLD: That will be it, yes.

THE COURT: And do you have a witness that we can bring down tomorrow, perhaps, Mr. Hoppe?

MR. EUCHNER: No, Mr. Hoppe is coming from out of state for this. So he will be here first thing Friday morning. Well, I guess Friday afternoon. And our other witness is coming back from a trip to Europe. And they were both set for Friday.

THE COURT: I'll see what I can do to rearrange the appointment that I have on Friday, and I'll let y'all know that sometime tomorrow.

So, I mean, as long as you're not set in stone, if you could still get these folks in Friday morning, if I can reschedule my appointment, I don't know that I'll be able to, but I will try to do that. I just want to make sure you all have enough time to get everything taken care of by the end of the week.

MR. EUCHNER: And Shawn and Paul and I can talk as well, but I think, a 12:15 time, unless there is an extensive amount of rebuttal, which I doubt, but I think we might be able to finish even with the 12:15 start. Break --if we don't have a lunch break, the jury takes lunch, and we'll take the normal 15 minute breaks instead.

MR. JENSVOLD: I think we are pushing it for closings, but I guess we'll see.

THE COURT: All right. I'll let y'all know what I figure out tomorrow, and I will see you in the morning.

THE CLERK: 10:30?

THE COURT: 10:30.

(Whereupon proceedings were adjourned.)

PIMA COUNTY SUPERIOR COURT

C E R T I F I C A T E

STATE OF ARIZONA)
)
COUNTY OF PIMA)

I, BONITA ROBERTSON, Certified Court Reporter in and for the State of Arizona, do hereby certify that the foregoing transcript of the proceedings held on the 18th day of March, 2009, in Pima County Superior Court, is a true and accurate record of the proceedings had.

Bonita Robertson

BONITA ROBERTSON, RMR
CERTIFIED REPORTER, #50454

PIMA COUNTY SUPERIOR COURT

Day Two

Jake

March 18th, 2009

Page 11-22 Jake states he went to prison in 2001. This contradicts his prior testimony in in Trial 1 Vol. 1, Day 2, March 29th, 2006 Page 278-1 and 11.

Page 11-24 Jake went to prison in April 2001.

Page 12-1   Jake states he was imprisoned for three months. This contradicts his interviews and prior testimony in Trial 1 Vol. 1, Day 2, March 29, 2006 Page 278-1 and 11.

Page 11-24 Jake states he met defendant in 1999. Not true. It was 1998. Date is verifiable because after he met me he went to the Maricopa County Jail.

Page 13-23 Jake states he moved in with defendant in October 2001. Where was he living in September 2001 after being released from jail?

Page 21-5   Jake states he was living with defendant in August 2001 and Jensvold corrects him.

Page 22-4   Jake states I lived in Tucson a month before he came down.

Page 28-12 Jake states he observed defendant viewing contraband files while he was asleep on the couch. There is no evidence to support this statement. There is no evidence the files were ever viewed.

Page 34-25 Jake states he never gave defendant information about the police ticket. Not true.

Page 36-19   Jake's statement contradicts prior testimony in Trial 1 where he claimed the mental debate about whether or not to call the police took place during the 30 minutes he was in my motorhome after he returned. Not at the Circle K.

Page 37-16   Jake states he observed my meeting with the police through a fence.

Page 41-5   Is it a small spindle or a case? Can't be both.

Page 41-16   Jensvold calls Jake Mr. Coghill for the first time.

Page 43-22   Jake states he did not see who wrote the letters KP on the discs.

Page 58-15   Jake was led into my motorhome by police to get his possessions.

Page 60-2   Police did not inspect the possessions Jake took from my motorhome.

Page 60-17   Jake states the contraband discs were on the bottom of the stack. Contradicting what he told police on April 1st, 2003 and Trial 1 Vol. 1, Day 2 Page 310-25.

Page 71-14   Jensvold calls Jake Mr. Coghill a second time.

Page 74-7   Jake states there were discs in the collection containing contraband that were labeled differently or were not labeled at all. Statement not supported by evidence.

Page 76-12   Jake admits to downloading download accelerator and even states what the purpose of the program is.

Page 76-18   Jensvold reveals download accelerator was downloaded on March 4th, 2003. This is irrefutable proof that Jake was living in my motorhome the week of my birthday and that Jake has perjured himself.

Judd

Page 84-14   Jensvold calls Jake Mr. Coghill a third time.

Page 87-5   Jensvold calls Jake Mr. Coghill a fourth time.

Page 87-10   Judd states defendant told him that Jake had been his roommate for two months.

Page 90-18   Defense counsel Skitzki at the bench objects to the use of the word pornography during the questioning of Judd.

Page 91-5   The court violates its own ruling and allows questioning that will introduce the word pornography as defendants own statement.

Page 92-7   Skitzki objects. Court overrules.

Page 92-10   A juror verbally responds in open court to the question concerning pornography. Obviously this statement had some influence on the juror or they would not have responded.

Page 97-20   Judd states he may have handled the discs. This contradicts his earlier testimony on Trial 1 Vol. 1, Day 3, March 30, 2006, page 457-17.

Page 97-25   Judd doesn't remember wearing gloves.

Page 112-24 Defense Counsel moves for a mistrial. Court denies motion.

About The Author

My career began in the United States Coast Guard. My first unit was Coast Guard Station Saginaw River. There I was responsible for search and rescue in Saginaw Bay and Lake Huron, where I performed numerous rescues. Earned Coast Guard Good Conduct Award, Meritorious Unit Commendation with Operational Designator and Meritorious Unit Commendation I was also responsible for standing a radio watch, listening for distress calls on the VHF-FM marine radio. I was transferred to Coast Guard Cutter Bristol Bay WTGB 102 where I worked as a Fireman and Oiler I advanced to the rank of Machinery Technician Third Class at Yorktown, Virginia and spent my last two years of enlisted service at Search and Rescue Station Panama City Florida. Honorably Discharged after 4 years active duty service.

I obtained my FAA Airframe and Powerplant mechanics license in 1988 and began working as a mechanic for the Midway Commuter, which was a wholly owned subsidiary of Midway Airlines. From there I worked for Midway Aircraft Engineering in Miami, Florida working as a mechanic on DC-9 and B-737 aircraft. I advanced to the Position of Senior Aircraft Maintenance Planner where I was responsible for scheduling both routine overnight maintenance and heavy maintenance for one third of Midway's fleet. After Midway went out of business I moved to California and began working as a mechanic on B-747 aircraft which was something that I had always wanted to do. Later I began working in Phoenix, Arizona at Sky Harbor Airport and various repair stations throughout the region.

I obtained a Bachelor of Science Degree in Legal Study's from Kaplan University in 2011 while on the President's List. In 2013, I studied Computer Numeric Control at Glendale Community College and earned a position on the Dean's List and a Certificate of Completion in that program. I was released in 2017 after fighting my case for 14 years and obtained my Certificate of Absolute Discharge from the Arizona Department of Corrections in 2018. My only remaining requirement is to register for life and abide by all local SO laws as well.

www.ingramcontent.com/pod-product-compliance
Lightning Source LLC
Chambersburg PA
CBHW082103220526
45472CB00009B/2028